How to study law

AUSTRALIA
The Law Book Company
Sydney

CANADA
The Carswell Company
Ottawa : Toronto : Calgary : Montreal : Vancouver

INDIA
N. M. Tripathi (Private) Ltd.
Bombay
and
Eastern Law House (Private) Ltd.
Calcutta

M.P.P. House
Bangalore
and
Universal Book Traders
Delhi

ISRAEL
Steimatzky's Agency Ltd.
Tel Aviv

PAKISTAN
Pakistan Law House
Karachi

How to study law

Second Edition

ANTHONY BRADNEY, LL.B., B.A.
The Late VICTORIA FISHER LL.B., M.A.
Lecturers in Law in the University of Leicester
JUDITH MASSON, M.A., Ph.D.
Professor Elect, University of Warwick
ALAN C. NEAL, LL.B., LL.M., D.G.L.S., Barrister
Professor of Law in the University of Leicester
DAVID NEWELL, L.L.B., M. Phil., *Solicitor*
Head of Government and Legal Affairs, The Newspaper Society

LONDON
SWEET & MAXWELL
1991

Published in 1991 by
Sweet & Maxwell Ltd., of
South Quay Plaza, 183 Marsh Wall, London, E14 9FT
Computerset by
Promenade Graphics Ltd., Cheltenham
Printed in England by Clays Ltd, St Ives plc

Reprinted 1993

British Library Cataloguing-in-Publication Data

How to Study law. — 2nd ed.
 I. Bradney, A.
 340.07

ISBN 0–421–43990–4

PREFACE TO THE SECOND EDITION

We have made several changes to the second edition of "How to Study Law". Some of these are minor. We have up-dated materials where necessary (for example, to take account of the expanding number of newspapers producing law reports). We have also introduced two new short sections on the use of encyclopaedias as the use of materials from the legal system of the European Economic Community. One major change we have made is to the format of the exercises. Whilst we have retained a section of questions with answers at the back of the book for those students using this book for self-study purposes we have added a separate section of questions without answers to each of the first 5 exercises. This is to enable the book to be used more easily as part of a course preparing students for the study of law.

One of the original authors of this book, Victoria Fisher, died after publication of the first edition. Had Vicky lived, and had she been able to contribute to this second edition, it would be a much better book than it is.

A Memorial Prize in memory of Vicky has been set up by her friends and colleagues. This awards an annual prize (currently amounting to £150) for the best essay on a topic relating to Women and Law. For details of this competition write to:

The Secretary,
The Victoria Fisher Memorial Prize Committee,
Faculty of Law,
University of Leicester,
University Road,
Leicester,
LE1 7RH.

AGDB, JMM, ACN, DRN

PREFACE TO THE FIRST EDITION

This book is intended to show the reader how to use legal materials.

We have assumed that the reader is completely unfamiliar with law and the legal system. Part I of the book begins with a brief description of the legal system, the sources of law and the different classifications of law. Part II of the book explains the various ways in which legal materials can be found, up-dated and used. By legal materials we mean both the case reports and statutes familiar to those who practise in law and also the research reports and surveys used by academics to analyse the workings of the legal system. We have included as one of the skills we attempt to explain, the general skill of how to study. Since we have found that students rarely profit from simply being told how to do something, in Part III of the book we have set out some exercises testing each of the skills explained in Part II. Some of the techniques this book attempts to explain involve the use of law libraries. However, so that all readers will be able to attempt the exercises in Part III, whatever the state of the library resources available to them, the book incorporates the cases, statutes and articles upon which the exercises are based. Examples of statutes and cases are also found in the chapter explaining how to use them. Where the questions need access to a library we have graded them according to the extent of library resources needed. Outline answers to the exercises are to be found at the back of the book. Finally, in Part IV of the book, we have given some indication of the kind of careers open to those interested in law and also discussed the kinds reading law at University or Polytechnic.

This book has developed out of our joint experience of teaching law to students at both degree and other levels. In particular we have benefited from collaborating with a number of other colleagues on a course designed to introduce students to the LL.B. degree at Leicester University. However, whilst we hope that the book is suitable for use as a basis for a short course teaching legal skills, we are conscious that many students never have the opportunity to participate in such a course. We have thus written the book as a self-study manual. Equally, although the book is suitable for use at degree level, it is also suitable for those students who intend to combine law with some other subject at degree level, who are pursuing a course leading to a professional qualification in law or with some law content or who are studying law at sub-degree level.

We hope the order of the contents of the book is clear and logical. Students who are just beginning a law degree course should begin at Chapter 1 and work their way through to the end unless directed otherwise by their tutor. However, not every student will derive the greatest benefit from reading the book in this way. If, for example, you are thinking about reading law at University or Polytechnic, you should read Chapter 8 first of all, so that you know what such law courses involve, before reading the main body of the book. If you are in doubt, look carefully at both the Contents pages and the Index before deciding the order in which you should read the book. Some students may find that they can omit reading one or more chapters, either because they are already familiar with the contents or because the content is irrelevant to their needs. It is, however, best to be very careful when omitting chapters. How do you know you are already familiar with <u>all</u> of a chapter's contents if you have not read it? How can you be sure its contents are irrelevant to your course before you have finished the course?

This book is only an introduction. For some readers the information contained within it will be enough in itself. Others will need, or want, to go on to read more specialised literature. Appendix III is a list of further reading, together with comments on the nature of the material recommended, for different sections of the book.

We gratefully acknowledge the help of our colleagues in developing the ideas that are contained in this book. In particular, David Bonner and John Woodliffe both collaborated on the course which stimulated us to write this book. Roger Benedictus helped us with his detailed knowledge of careers open to those interested in law. The Law Society offered valuable comments on the sections about solicitors. Errors are, of course, our own responsibility.

ACKNOWLEDGMENTS

The authors and publishers wish to thank the following for permission to reprint material from publications in which they have copyright.

Rod Morgan and Sweet & Maxwell Ltd. for the article "Remands in Custody: Problems and Prospects" from the 1989 *Criminal Law Review* 481

Butterworth & Co. (Publishers) Ltd. for extracts from the *All England Reports*

Crown Copyright ©—Coal Industry Act 1983, Human Organs Transplants Act 1989, Mobile Homes Act 1983

CONTENTS

PART 3

Part 1

CHAPTER 1

Sources of the law

DISCOVERING THE LAW

We could begin by asking "what is law?". Ordinary people regularly make law for their own circumstances. Freely-negotiated commercial contracts may bind them to behave in particular ways. By becoming members of a sports club or a trade union they agree to comply with a set of rules. Sometimes these forms of law will use the courts to enforce their arrangements. In other cases privately-instituted adjudication bodies are established; a third party being appointed to decide whether an agreement or rule has been broken or not. These kinds of arrangements may seem very different from the normal idea of law, especially if law is thought of mainly in terms of the criminal law. However it is possible to see law simply as a way of regulating behaviour, of deciding what can be done and what cannot be done.

Most laws are not about something dramatic like murder but, rather, about the everyday details of ordinary life. Every time a purchase is made, a contract is made. Both parties make promises about what they will do; one to hand over the goods, one to pay the price. In this and other ways, everybody is involved in law every day of their lives. In some cases the state steps in to say what people can do, perhaps by saying how they can contract or, more dramatically, by saying when they can kill each other. This is the kind of law, that which comes from the state, we most frequently think about. Most courses involving law are interested only in this one kind of law and that is what this book is about.

There are many generally acknowledged sources of English law. Some are more obvious than others. Thus, "the Queen in Parliament" (the House of Commons, the House of Lords and the monarch) is a vital source of modern English law. Here proposals for legislation (*Bills*) are presented to, debated by, and voted upon by the House of Commons and the House of Lords, finally receiving the assent of the monarch and thus becoming legislation (*Statutes* or *Acts*). It is also indisputable that judges are significant sources of law, since the English legal system places great emphasis upon judgments in previous legal cases as guidance for future judicial decision-making. There are, however, less obvious sources of English law. Some are direct: for example, in some circumstances the European Economic Community may make law for England. Others are more indirect: thus customs of a particular trade may be incorporated into the law by the judges or Parliament or international law (the law between states) may be a basis for national law.

All of the above are sources of *legal rules*. What precisely it is that is meant by the term legal rules, is a subject much debated by philosophers of law. Generally speaking, when the term is used it indicates that a particular course of action should, or should not, be followed. Legal rules are said to be *binding*. This means if they are not followed some action in the courts may result. Some of the questions about the nature of law are discussed in Chapter 5, "Law in Action/Law in Books."

It will suffice for present purposes if we consider just two of these sources of law: Parliament and the judiciary. In so doing, we will discover the central positions occupied within the English legal system by "statute law" and "judge-made law." There is a further explanation of international law and the European Economic Community in Chapter 2.

PARLIAMENT

Parliament creates law but not all the law that is created through Parliament is of the same kind. There is a need, in particular, to distinguish between various levels of legislation.

The legislation with which most people are familiar is statute law. Bills proposed in Parliament become Acts. These Acts may either be *General* or *Personal and Local*. Both of these are sometimes known as *primary legislation*. General Acts apply to everybody, everywhere within the legal system. In this context it is important to remember that there are several different legal systems within the United Kingdom; one for England and Wales, one for Scotland and one for Northern Ireland. A legal rule in a statute can only be changed by another statute. Any statute, no matter how important it seems, can be changed in the same way as any other.

Some Acts apply to all the legal systems; many apply only to one or two of them. Personal and local Acts apply either to particular individuals or (more usually) to particular areas. Thus, before divorce was part of the general law, it was possible to get a divorce by Act of Parliament. The most common example of local legislation is that which applies to individual cities. The law in Leicester is sometimes not the same as the law in London. General legislation is much more common than personal and local legislation.

Most legislation consists of a direct statement about how people should behave or indicates the consequences of certain behaviour. For example, a statute may define a crime and say what the punishment will be for that crime. Sometimes Parliament cannot decide exactly what the law should be on a particular point. It may not have the necessary expertise or it may be that the area is one where frequent changes are needed. In such cases Parliament may pass an Act giving somebody else the power to make law in the appropriate area. Such power is often given to government ministers or local authorities. This is the most common example of what is known as *delegated or secondary legislation*. A person or body to whom legislative power is delegated cannot, as can Parliament, make law about anything. The Act (sometimes called *the parent Act*) will determine the area in which law can be made, it may say something about the content of the law, but the details of that law will be left to the person or body to whom legislative power is delegated. They may also have the power to change that law from time to time. Most delegated legislation is published as *a statutory instrument*. Although people are frequently unaware of this type of legislation it is very important, affecting most people's lives. For example, much of the social security system is based on delegated legislation.

The final type of legislation that we have to consider is the range of directives, circulars, and guidance notes produced by various State agencies and bodies such as the Inland Revenue, the DSS and the Department of Employment. Some of these documents bind the people to whom they are addressed to behave in particular ways. Many are not legally binding. They do not compel people in the way that statutes or statutory instruments do. Even so, such documents are often very influential. In practice officials receiving them may always act in the way they indicate. Thus we might consider them all as a form of legislation.

In Chapter 4 you will find an explanation of how to find statutes and statutory instruments and in Chapter 5 an explanation of how you use them to find out where the law stands about something.

LEGISLATION IN PRACTICE

Even if we can find a statute the question still remains, "What will be its effect?". What will happen when somebody acts in a way which is contrary to the statute?

At this stage it is important to appreciate the relationship between the judges and statute law. The judiciary are bound by and, legally, must apply legislation, whether it is primary legislation or secondary legislation. However, an Act or piece of delegated legislation may be unclear or ambiguous. In some cases the difficulty will be resolved by applying one of the general Interpretation Acts. These are Acts which give a definition of words commonly found in legislation. Thus, for example, one Interpretation Act says that where a piece of legislation uses the word "he" this should be taken to mean "he or she" unless it is plain from the context that this should not be so. Some Acts have their own interpretation section, in which certain important words or phrases used in the Act are defined. However, if a difficulty cannot be resolved by such an Act or section; if the ambiguity or lack of clarity remains, it is for the judiciary to decide what the legislation means.

In order to discover the way in which legislation should be applied, the judges have developed a complex network of principles for statutory interpretation, which are designed to assist in the proper application of the law. These principles of statutory interpretation seek, it is said, to combine an interpretation of the natural meaning of the English language used to frame the particular statutory provisions with common-sense meaning and an avoidance of inconsistency. In particular, where primary legislation is involved, it is said that it is not the task of the judges to make law but merely to apply it. Nevertheless, there have been numerous occasions when the judges have been accused of "perverting the true intention" of Parliament. It must be evident that the very process of statutory interpretation always carries with it the risk of divergence between Parliament and the courts in the eventual conclusion reached.

Some of the principles which the judiciary use are very narrow. For example, they might apply only to the meaning of one phrase in a particular type of statute. Others are much broader. Books are written analysing the judicial approach to the interpretation of difficult legislation. At this point it is sufficient for you to know three broad principles. First, judges normally apply the actual words in the legislation not the words the legislator might have intended to use. Secondly, faced with ambiguity, the judges choose the least absurd meaning. Thirdly, when a statute is designed to remedy a problem, the statute will be interpreted in the light of that intent. Plainly these principles will leave many problems unresolved, including that of when to apply one rather than another principle. Leaving aside the difficulties caused in deciding what these principles of interpretation might mean, it is a matter of controversy whether they act as rules deciding what the judges do or provide rationalisations for what the judiciary have already decided.

JUDGE-MADE LAW

Not all legal rules are laid down in an Act of Parliament or some other piece of legislation. A number of fundamental rules are found in the statements of judges made in the course of deciding cases brought before them. A rule made in the course of deciding cases, rather than legislation, is called a rule of *common law*. A common law rule has as much force as a rule derived from statute.

Many important areas of English law, such as contract, tort, crime, land law and constitutional law, have their origins in common law. Some of the earliest common law rules still survive, though many have been supplemented or supplanted by statute. Common law rules are still being made today, though as a source of new legal rules common law is less important than statute. Strictly speaking, the term common law is confined to rules which have been developed entirely by judicial decisions. It excludes new rules made by judges when they interpret statutes. The term *case law* covers both kinds of new rules.

The application of case law is easiest to understand when the issue presently before the court has been raised in some previous analogous case. In such a situation the court will look to see if there is a potentially applicable rule in the reports of previously decided cases. Then they will decide whether they have to, or should, apply that rule. It is therefore vital that accurate and comprehensive records be kept of past court decisions and judicial pronouncements. Thus the importance of the numerous and varied series of Law Reports can be appreciated. Anybody entering a law library in England can hardly help being impressed at the volume of materials falling within this category of Law Reports. Row upon row of bound volumes, containing the judgments in thousands of past cases, dominate the holdings of any major English law library.

More information about the various kinds of Law Reports and how to use them can be found in Chapter 4. An explanation of how cases should be read is found in Chapter 5.

Cases are decided in court. Different kinds of legal disputes are decided in different kinds of courts. Sometimes it is possible to bring a legal dispute before two or more different kinds of court. In some situations, once a court has given judgment, it is possible to appeal against that judgment to another court. Some courts only hear appeals.

Not every judgment in every case is of equal importance. The weight which is to be given to them as guidelines for future judicial activity will depend upon two things. One is the level of the court in which that case was decided. In English law there is a principle of *a hierarchy of precedents*. Judgments given by superior courts in the hierarchy are binding on inferior courts.

A brief overview of the court structure seen from this hierarchical view appears below on page 9.

The highest, and thus most important court is the House of Lords. The results of cases heard in the House of Lords and in the Court of Appeal will normally be fully reported in the series of Law Reports as a matter of course. Other courts' judgments will either be reported only when they are considered important by those compiling the reports or, in the case of very lowly courts, will not be reported at all.

Even if a previous case is said to be binding, only some parts of the judgment are important. Lawyers distinguish two parts of a judgment: (a) the *ratio decidendi* and (b) the *obiter dicta*. Put most simply, the *ratio decidendi* is that part of reasoning in the judgment which is necessary in order to determine the law on the issue in the particular case before the judge. It is this which is binding on other courts in the hierarchy. The *obiter dicta*, on the other hand, is a term used to describe the remainder of the judgment. This is not binding but may be *persuasive*. In the absence of a binding *ratio decidendi* the court may be influenced by *obiter dicta*. These two terms are commonly shortened to *ratio* and *obiter*. There is a further discussion of this and other topics at this point in Chapter 5 at pages 64–67.

Thus, in asking whether a particular judgment is "important" from the point of view of influencing future decisions, and so representing the "state of the law" on any particular matter, we need to consider both its importance in terms of the court which delivered the judgment and whether the *ratio decidendi* of the case is sufficiently clear and relevant to future issues of law arising in later cases. The identification of the *ratio decidendi* is not always an easy matter. There is also great debate amongst academics as to what importance the *obiter dicta* in a previous case may or should have. Some

Importance in Precedence

| HOUSE OF LORDS (deals only with appeals) | Binds courts below but not itself |

| COURT OF APPEAL (deals only with appeals) | Binds courts below and normally binds itself |

HIGH COURT
different divisions deal with different
kinds of legal dispute (deals with both
appeals and new cases)

| FAMILY DIVISION | CHANCERY DIVISION | QUEEN'S BENCH DIVISION |

Binds courts below but not itself

COUNTY COURT (deals with civil law disputes)

CROWN COURT (deals mainly with criminal law disputes)

Binds no-one

MAGISTRATES' COURT (main business—criminal, matrimonial and licensing matters)

Binds no-one

academics, whilst accepting that terms like *ratio* and *obiter* are used in judgments, and whilst accepting that at least some judges think they construct their judgments on the basis of *ratio* and *obiter* in previous judgments, believe that important influences on decisions made by judges are to be found in the nature of matters such as the social background of judges, the economic circumstances of the time or even the very nature of language itself.

In some instances there will be no binding precedent applicable to a problem before the court. No court may have been faced with the same issue or the courts which were faced with the issue may have been at the same point or lower in the hierarchy of courts. Even if a court is not bound by a previous judgment it may still consider that judgment to see whether or not it provides a good answer to the problem. The judgment may be persuasive. The importance of the previous case will then depend not simply on its position within the court hierarchy but upon factors such as the identity and experience of the individual judge or the composition of the bench of judges sitting to hear the case, the detail of the legal arguments put before the court, and whether the line laid down in the case has since been adopted by courts deciding subsequent cases.

When looking for the law created and developed by the judges, it will clearly be important to look at reports of cases decided in the higher levels of courts. Nevertheless, it should not be assumed that these are the only important courts. Only a very small proportion of all cases handled in the court system find their way to the Court of Appeal, let alone the House of Lords. The magistrates' courts are very much more important than the House of Lords in terms of the number of cases with which they deal. Nor would it be correct to assume that it is always the "important" cases which work their way through the appeal system, since much of the motivation for bringing an appeal will depend upon financial considerations which are often totally independent of the merits of the dispute in relation to which the case has been brought, or the importance or complexity of the law to be applied to that dispute.

The legislature plainly makes new legal rules. Whether or not, in an effort to meet new developments, problems, and shifts in society's values, genuine departures from established rules of common law actually occur, is a matter of debate. The traditional notion is that common law rules do not alter to meet the requirements of society (or "public opinion"); it is the role of the legislator to remedy this through statutory intervention with specific legislation, and not for the judges to create new rules. The legislature makes law, the judiciary merely apply it. However, many academics and some judges would now argue that the judiciary sometimes do more than simply apply existing law; that in looking for rules of law in previous cases the judiciary subtly change the rules, consciously or otherwise, so that they produce the conclusions which they seek. If this is correct the judiciary are, in this sense, just as much legislators as Parliament.

COMMON LAW AND EQUITY

In the section above the term "common law" is used as a synonym for rules of law derived from judicial decisions rather than statute. This is a proper and common usage of the phrase. However another equally frequent sense of the word is as an antonym to "equity." English law has deep historical roots. The opposition of common law and equity refers to the system of rules which originally developed in different courts within the legal system. Common law rules arose first. Later, these rules were seen as being over-formal and concerned too much with the way a case was presented rather than with the justice in the issues at stake. Thus a less strict system of equitable rules was developed. In time, the rules of equity also became formalised. Eventually, the different courts were merged and now all courts can apply both the rules of common law and equity.

CHAPTER 2

Divisions of law

INTRODUCTION

Legal rules can be divided up in many different ways. This chapter introduces some common ways of classifying law. Not all legal rules are of the same type. They show differences in purpose, in origin and form, in the consequences when the rules are breached, and in matters of procedure, remedies and enforcement. The divisions described below are of the broadest kind, chosen to highlight these kinds of differences in legal rules. One kind of division of legal rules has already been introduced, that between statute and case or common law. This division and the others now described overlap. For example, the legal rule defining murder originates in common law, not statute. It is a rule of criminal law rather than civil law; of public law rather than private law and of national law rather than international law.

There are ways other than those discussed here of dividing up the law. One way is to take the legal rules relating to a given topic, grouping them under a title such as "housing law" or "accountancy law." Categorising rules in this way can be very useful: for example, it is not necessary for a personnel manager to know the whole of the general law of contracts before becoming proficient in essential employment law. However, such subject groupings can also be confusing without some understanding of the basic differences between the rules.

CRIMINAL AND CIVIL LAW

One of the most fundamental divisions in law is the division between criminal and civil law. Newcomers to the study of law tend to assume that criminal law occupies the bulk of a lawyer's caseload and of a law student's studies. This is an interesting by-product of the portrayal of the legal system by the media. Criminal law weighs very lightly in terms of volume when measured against non-criminal (civil) law. There are more rules of civil law than there are of criminal law; more court cases involve breach of the civil law than involve breach of the criminal law. Law degree students will find that criminal law is generally only one course out of 12 to 15 subjects in a three-year law degree, although some criminal offences may be referred to in other courses.

Criminal law means the law relating to crime only. Civil law can be taken to mean all the rest. The distinction relies not so much on the nature of the conduct which is the object of a legal rule but in the nature of the proceedings and the sanctions which may follow. Some kinds of conduct give rise to criminal liability, some to civil liability and some to both civil and criminal liability. The seriousness of the conduct does not necessarily determine the type of liability to which it gives rise; conduct which is contrary to the criminal law is not always "worse" than conduct which is against the civil law. Few people would consider every criminal offence a moral wrong (except, perhaps, in the sense that every breach of the law might be thought to be a moral wrong). Equally, some actions which are purely breaches of the civil law might be considered breaches of morality. Nor is harm, in the sense of damage done to individuals, something which is found to a greater degree in the criminal law as against the civil law. The person who parks on a "double-yellow line" breaches the criminal law. The company which fails to pay for the goods that it has bought, thereby bank-rupting another company, commits only a breach of the civil law. Who has done the greater harm? Concepts of morality have had some influence on the development of English law but historical accident, political policy and pragmatic considerations have played just as important a part in developing our law.

Some conduct which might be considered "criminal" gives rise only to civil liability or to no liability at all and some conduct which you may consider "harmless" may give rise to both criminal and civil liability. It will be easier to see that "harm," "morality" and the division between criminal and civil law do not follow any clear pattern if you consider some fictitious examples. In considering them, ask yourself whether or not the conduct described should give rise to any legal liability; if it should, what form should that liability take and what should the legal consequences be which flow from the conduct described? Should any of the people be compensated for the harm done to them and, if so, by whom and for what? Should any of the characters be punished and, if so, for what reason and how? Who should decide whether or not legal proceedings of any variety should be instigated against any of the individuals? The probable legal consequences that follow from each example are found at the end of the chapter. Do not look at these until you have thought about the examples yourself.

Examples

1. Norman drinks 10 pints of beer. He drives his car into a queue at the bus station injuring a young woman and her child.

2. Sue, who is pregnant, lives with Chris. She smokes 50 cigarettes a day. Sue is also carrying on an occasional affair with Richard.

3. Robert agrees to pay Joan, a professional decorator, £500 if she paints his house. She completes the work to a very high standard. Robert, who is a millionaire, refuses to pay her.

Even when a person's actions clearly infringe either the criminal law or civil law, it does not necessarily mean that any actual legal consequences will follow. In criminal and civil cases persons with the legal right to take any legal action have a discretion as to whether or not they initiate legal proceedings. There is a difference between *liability* and *proceedings*. Conduct gives rise to liability. It is for someone else to decide whether or not to take the matter to court by starting proceedings.

In criminal proceedings *a prosecutor* prosecutes *the defendant*. The case is heard in the magistrates' court or the Crown Court, depending on the seriousness of the offence. The prosecutor will have to prove to the court, *beyond all reasonable doubt*, that the defendant committed the offence charged. The court will have to determine whether or not the defendant is guilty. In the magistrates' court it will be for the magistrates to determine this question, in the Crown Court it will be for the jury to decide questions of fact and for the judge to decide questions of law. A finding of "not guilty" will lead to the defendant's acquittal. A finding of "guilty" will lead to a conviction and may lead to a sentence of imprisonment or some other form of punishment such as a fine or probation.

One of the major objectives of the criminal law is to punish the wrongdoer for action which is deemed to be contrary to the interests of the state and its citizens. Criminal proceedings do not have as a major objective the provision of compensation or support for the victim of crime. It is significant that the exercise of the discretion to prosecute is seldom carried out by the victim of the crime. Criminal proceedings are normally initiated by the state or its agents and brought in the name of the Queen or the prosecuting official.

In civil proceedings it is generally *the plaintiff* (the party harmed) who sues *the defendant*, although in some areas of the civil law other terms are used. For example, in the case of a divorce *the petitioner* sues *the respondent*. The case will usually be heard in either the county court or the High Court, depending on the nature of the case and the size of the loss involved. The plaintiff usually has to prove, *on the balance of probabilities*, that the events took place in the manner claimed. This is a lower standard of proof than in criminal cases. If the plaintiff proves their case, the court will make some kind of order. What this will be, will depend upon the kind of case and what the plaintiff has asked for. The basic choice before the court is whether to order the defendant to compensate the plaintiff for their loss by awarding damages, or to order the defendant to act, or refrain from acting, in some specific way in the future, or to make both kinds of orders.

The function of civil law is to provide individuals with remedies which are enforceable in the courts where they have suffered a wrong which is recognised by a statute or decided cases. The civil law creates a framework which delineates the rights and obligations of individuals in their dealings with one another. It is primarily founded on the law of contract and tort, which are mainly areas of common law. The law of contract determines which forms of agreement entered into between individuals are legally binding and on whom they will be binding. The law of tort covers categories of civil wrong, other than breach of contract, which may give rise to legal causes of action. It includes the law of negligence, trespass and libel and slander. Just as a set of facts can give rise to conduct which may result in both civil and criminal proceedings, so a set of facts can give rise to actions in contract and in tort. Most plaintiffs' primary motivation for bringing civil proceedings will be to obtain an effective remedy for the civil wrong which has been perpetrated. The fact that there is liability will not necessarily mean that they will take action. For example, there may be no point in suing a person for damages if you know they have no money.

The emphasis of the civil law has changed over the last hundred years with an increase in the role of the state and the importance of legislation as opposed to case law as the major source of law. Civil law does not just regulate relations between individuals covering such matters as their property transactions, but also deals with relations between the state and individuals. It covers unemployment and social security benefit entitlement, tax and planning questions, and council tenants' relationships with their local authorities. All of these areas are covered by statute law which has created new rights and obligations. These are often enforced in tribunals as opposed to courts.

Statutory provisions have also been enacted in order to minimise the common law rights which have resulted from the judicial development of contract law and the notion of freedom of contract. For example, employment protection and landlord and tenant legislation give employees and tenants statutory rights which will often modify or override terms in their contracts which give their employers or landlords specific rights to dismiss or evict them.

NATIONAL, INTERNATIONAL AND EEC LAW

The term "national" or "municipal" law is used to mean the internal legal rules of a particular country, in contrast to international law which deals with the external relationships of a state with other states. In the United Kingdom, national law is normally unaffected by international legal obligations unless these obligations have been transferred into national law by an Act of Parliament. EEC law, however, cuts across this conventional notion that national and international law operate at different and distinct levels. It is a form of international law in that it is in part concerned with legal relations between Member States, but EEC law may also directly affect the national law of Member States. It will therefore be considered separately from both national and international law.

National law

The system of national law has already been considered in Chapter 1.

International law

Public international law regulates the external relations of states with one another. It is a form of law very different from national law. There is no world government or legislature issuing and enforcing laws to which all nations are subject. The international legal order is essentially decentralised and operates by agreement between states. This means that the creation, interpretation and enforcement of international law lies primarily in the hands of states themselves. Its scope and effectiveness depends on the capacity of states to agree and the sense of mutual benefit and obligation involved in adhering to the rules.

International law is created in two main ways: by treaty and by custom. Treaties are agreements between two or more states, and are binding on the states involved if they have given their consent to be so bound. Customary law is established by showing that states have adopted broadly consistent practices towards a particular matter and that they have acted in this way out of a sense of legal obligation. International law is neither comprehensive nor systematic. Few treaties or customary rules involve the majority of world states. Most are bilateral understandings or involve only a handful of parties to a multilateral agreement.

Disputes about the scope and interpretation of international law are rarely resolved by the use of international courts or binding arbitration procedures of an international organisation. This is because submission to an international court or similar process is entirely voluntary and few states are likely to agree to this if there is a serious risk of losing their case or where important political or national interests are at stake. Negotiation is far more common. International courts are used occasionally, for example where settlement is urgent, or protracted negotiations have failed, where the dispute is minor or is affecting other international relations; in other words, in cases where failure to settle is more damaging than an unfavourable outcome. Where international law has been breached, an injured state must rely primarily on self-help for enforcement. There is no effective international institutional machinery to ensure compliance when the law is challenged. This means that in practice powerful states are better able to protect their rights and assert new claims.

Breaching established rules is one, rather clumsy, way of changing international law. In a decentralised system, change can only be effected by common consent or by the assertion of a new claim being met by inaction or acquiescence by others. The lack of powerful enforcement machinery does not mean that international law is widely disregarded. On the contrary, legal rules are regularly followed, not least because states require security and predictability in the conduct of normal everyday inter-state relations.

International law also plays an important role in the promotion of common interests such as controlling pollution, restricting over-fishing, or establishing satellite and telecommunication link-ups.

A large number of global or regional international organisations have been established for the regulation and review of current inter-state activity. The best-known example, though perhaps not the most effective, is the United Nations, whose primary function is the maintenance of international peace and security.

In the United Kingdom, international law has no direct effect on national law and, on a given matter, national law may in fact be inconsistent with the United Kingdom's international obligations. The Government has authority to enter into treaties which may bind the United Kingdom *vis-à-vis* other states. However a treaty will not alter the law to be applied within the United Kingdom unless the provisions are adopted by means of an Act of Parliament. Customary international law may have been incorporated into national law but will enjoy no higher status than any other provision of national law and is, therefore, liable to be superseded by statute. However, it is a principle of judicial interpretation that, unless there is clear legal authority to the contrary, Parliament does not intend to act in breach of international law. In some other countries, international law is accorded a different status. In Holland and West Germany, for example, international law takes effect in municipal law and where these conflict international law prevails.

The lack of direct application should not be taken to mean that international law is of no importance in United Kingdom courts or for United Kingdom citizens. National courts regularly decide domestic cases having presumed the existence and application of international law. For example, under the Vienna Convention of 1961, diplomats enjoy immunity from criminal prosecution. If a defendant claims diplomatic immunity, a court must decide whether the defendant falls within the terms of the treaty before proceeding further. Secondly, individuals may have rights under international law, enforceable not through national courts but through international institutions. The European Convention on Human Rights gives individuals the right to complain of breaches of the Convention to the European Commission on Human Rights which may then refer the case to the European Court of Human Rights. (These institutions should not be confused with EEC bodies: they are quite separate.) Although the United Kingdom ratified the Convention in 1951, it was only in 1966 that the United Kingdom agreed to the articles of the treaty which recognised the right of individual petition and the compulsory jurisdiction of the Court.

EEC law

In joining the European Communities in 1973, the United Kingdom agreed to apply and be bound by Community law, accepting that Community law would override any conflicting provisions of national law. Unlike other forms of international law, EEC law is capable of passing directly into national law; it is applicable in the United Kingdom without being adopted by an Act of Parliament. These principles were given legal effect by the passage of the European Communities Act 1972. The European Communities are made up of three organisations: the European Economic Community (EEC), the European Coal and Steel Community (ECSC) and the European Community for Atomic Energy (Euratom). This section will concentrate on the implications of membership of the EEC for United Kingdom law.

The EEC is an international organisation established and developed by treaty between Member States. The basic framework is set out in the EEC Treaty of 1957 ("Treaty of Rome"), which defines the objectives of the Community, the powers and duties of Community institutions, and the rights and obligations of Member States. This treaty goes much further than just creating law which binds both Member States and Community institutions. It contains many detailed substantive provisions, some of which create rights for individuals which are enforceable directly in national courts. The EEC Treaty, and certain others which have followed it, are thus primary sources of Community law.

The EEC has four major institutions: the Council of Ministers, the Commission, the Assembly (or European Parliament) and the Court of Justice. The terms of the various treaties give the EEC a powerful legislative, administrative and judicial machinery. The Treaty provides that further legislation may be made by the Council of Ministers and the Commission. This is called secondary legislation and takes three forms.

Regulations, once made, pass into the law of a Member State automatically. Regulations are "directly applicable," which means that Member States do not have to take any action (such as passing an Act of Parliament) to implement them or to incorporate them into national law. Regulations are intended to be applied uniformly throughout the Community, and override any conflicting provisions in national law.

Directives are binding on Member States as to the result to be achieved, but leave each Member State with a choice about the method used to achieve that result. Member States are given a transitional period in which to implement the directive. This may involve passing a new law, making new administrative arrangements, or, where national law already conforms with the directive, taking no action. The Commission can initiate proceedings against a Member State if it believes the steps taken do not achieve the desired result. Although directives are addressed to Member States, in some circumstances an individual may be able to rely directly on certain parts, whether or not the Member State has taken implementing action. This is when the relevant part lays down an unconditional obligation and grants enforceable individual rights.

Decisions can be addressed to Member States, individuals or companies. They are binding only on the person to whom they are addressed and take effect on notification.

Community law is applied in Member States by their ordinary system of national courts and tribunals. When a point of Community law is crucial to a court's decision, the court may refer the case to the Court of Justice for a preliminary ruling on the interpretation of the point in question. Courts against whose decision there is no appeal, (*e.g.* the House of Lords) must make a reference to the Court of Justice when the case hinges on EEC law unless the Court has already ruled on that particular issue. Once the Court of Justice has given a preliminary ruling, the case is referred back to the national court from which it originated, which must then decide the case. The Court of Justice will only answer questions put to it about the interpretation of EEC law; it will not rule on national law or on conflict between national and EEC law or apply its interpretation to the facts of the case. These are all matters for national courts. The Commission may bring an action in the Court of Justice against a Member State for breach of a Community obligation, such as the non-implementation of a directive. Proceedings may be taken against the Commission or the Council for failing to act where the EEC Treaty imposes a duty to act. There are also provisions for annulling legislation adopted by the Commission or Council, for example, where the action has exceeded the powers laid down by treaty.

PUBLIC AND PRIVATE LAW

Another distinction that may be drawn between different types of law is the division between "public" law and "private" law. Public law is concerned with the distribution and exercise of power by the state and the legal relations between the state and the individual. For example, the rules governing the powers and duties of local authorities, the operation of the National Health Service, the regulation of building standards, the issuing of passports and the compulsory purchase of land to build a motorway all fall within the ambit of public law. In contrast, private law is concerned with the legal relationships between individuals, such as the liability of employers towards their employees for injuries sustained at work, consumers' rights against shopkeepers and manufacturers over faulty goods, or owners' rights to prevent others walking across their land. The division of law into public and private law and civil and criminal law are two clear examples of categories which overlap. Thus, for example, some public law is civil and some is criminal.

The significance of the public/private law distinction operates at two levels. First, it is a very useful general classification through which we can highlight some broad differences, such as those in the purposes of law, in sources and forms of legal rules, and in remedies and enforcement. This is the way the idea of public/private law will be discussed here. However, the distinction is also used in a second, narrower sense; as a way of defining the procedure by which claims can be raised in court. The problem of a precise demarcation of public law cases from private law cases for the purposes of establishing which cases must go through this special procedure is currently vexing the judges and cannot be explored in this brief introduction.

One way of thinking about a legal rule is to consider its purpose. The primary purpose underlying most private law rules is the protection of individual interests, whereas the aim of most public law provisions is the promotion of social objectives and the protection of collective rather than individual interests. The methods used to achieve these purposes also differ. A characteristic feature of public law is the creation of a public body with special powers of investigation, decision-making and/or enforcement in relation to a particular problem, whereas private law achieves its ends by giving individuals the right to take action in defence of their interests.

Many problems are addressed by both public and private law. Sometimes a single statute may include both private rights and liabilities alongside public law provisions. This can be seen both by looking at statutes characteristic of public law and by looking at an example in practice.

The Equal Pay Act and the Sex Discrimination Act both came into force in 1975. These Acts made it unlawful to discriminate on the grounds of sex in many important areas such as employment, education and housing. For the individual who had suffered discrimination, the Acts created new private rights to take complaints to industrial tribunals or county courts and claim compensation or other appropriate remedies. At the same time, the Equal Opportunities Commission was set up, with public powers and duties to investigate matters of sex discrimination and promote equal opportunities.

Example

Ann lives next door to an industrial workshop run by Brenda. The machinery is very noisy and the process discharges fumes which make Ann feel ill. This sort of problem is tackled by both public and private law in a number of different ways.

(i) As a neighbour, Ann may bring a private law action in nuisance, which is a claim that Brenda's activities unreasonably interfere with the use of Ann's land. Ann could claim compensation for the harm she has suffered and could seek an injunction to stop the harmful process continuing.

(ii) There are also public law rules which may be invoked whether or not an individual has or may be harmed, aimed at preventing the problem arising in the first place or controlling the situation for the public benefit. For example, when Brenda first started her workshop she would have needed to get planning permission from the local authority if her activities constituted a change in the use of the land. Planning legislation thus gives the local authority an opportunity to prevent industrial development in residential areas by refusing planning permission, or control it by laying down conditions. Other legislation gives the local authority powers to monitor and control various kinds of pollution and nuisances in their area, including noise and dangerous fumes. A further complex set of private rights and public regulations govern the working conditions of the workshop employees, who would also be affected by the noise and smells.

Public and private law also show differences in their origins and form. Some of the most important principles of private law are of ancient origin and were developed through the common law as individuals took their private disputes to court and demanded a remedy. The rules of private rights in contract, over land and inheritance, to compensation for physical injury or damage to property or reputation, were all first fashioned by judges in the course of deciding cases brought before them.

In contrast, most public law rules are of comparatively recent origin first originating in statute, not judicial decisions. There are obvious exceptions. Criminal law and the criminal justice system itself are prime examples where standards of behaviour are set by the state and enforced by a network of public officials with powers of arrest, prosecution, trial and punishment. Much of the early development of this field of public law lies in common law.

An important function of public law has its roots in constitutional theory. The actions of public bodies are only lawful if there is a legal rule granting the body authority to act in a given situation. A private individual needs no legal authority merely to act. It is assumed that a person acts lawfully unless there is a legal rule prohibiting or curtailing that behaviour. Public law therefore has a facilitative function, for which there is no equivalent in private law, permitting a public body to take action that would otherwise be unlawful. A feature of much recent public law is a shift towards the grant of broad discretionary powers to public bodies. This means that the same legislative framework can be used more flexibly, accommodating changes in public policy as to the purposes to which the powers should be put or the criteria for the exercise of these powers. This characteristic form of modern public law contrasts quite sharply with the relatively specific rights and duties to be found in private law, and in turn affects the way public and private law can be enforced.

All private law is enforced by granting individuals the right to take action in defence of a recognised personal interest. For example, a householder may make a contract with a builder over the repair of a roof, and may sue the builder if the work or materials are of a lower standard than was specified in the contract. Not all public law can be enforced by way of individual action. The enforcement of public law can be viewed from two perspectives.

First, public law can be enforced as when an official ensures that individuals or companies comply with standards set in statutes or delegated legislation, *e.g.* public health officials making orders in relation to or prosecuting restaurants. Secondly, the enforcement of public law can also be seen as the matter of ensuring public authorities themselves carry out their duties and do not exceed their legal powers. Here, the form of public law statutes, mentioned above, rarely ties a public body to supplying a particular standard of service, as a contract may tie a builder, but gives a wide choice of lawful behaviour.

Even where legislation lays a duty on a public authority, there may be no corresponding right of individual action. For example, under the Education Act 1944, local education authorities are under a duty to ensure that there are sufficient schools, in numbers, character and equipment, for providing educational opportunities for all pupils in their area. However, nobody can sue the authority if the schools are overcrowded or badly equipped. The only remedy is to complain to the Secretary of State, who can make orders if satisfied that the authority is in default of their duties. The mechanism for controlling standards of public bodies is generally by way of political accountability to the electorate or ministers rather than the legal process.

Some parts of public law do create individual rights and permit individual enforcement. In social security legislation, for example, qualified claimants have a right to certain benefits and may appeal against decisions of benefit officers to a tribunal. There is a procedure, special to public law, called "judicial review of administrative action" (often referred to simply as *judicial review*), whereby an individual may go to the High Court alleging unlawful behaviour on the part of a public body. However, in order to go to court, the individual must show "sufficient interest" in the issue in question (this being legally defined) and the court has a discretion whether to hear the case or grant a remedy. This is quite different from proceedings in private law, where a plaintiff does not need the court's permission for the case to be heard but has a right to a hearing if a recognised cause of action is asserted and also a right to a remedy of some kind if successful.

CRIMINAL LAW AND CIVIL LAW

Legal consequences in questions 1–3:

1. Norman's actions may give rise to both criminal and civil proceedings. He may be prosecuted for drunk driving and related road traffic offences and, if convicted, will have a criminal record. All road traffic offences, including parking offences, are just as much part of the criminal law as murder is. He may also be sued by the woman or child who would wish to recover damages for the personal injuries they have suffered. Such an action would

be a civil action. The same set of facts may give rise to both criminal and civil liability.

2. Sue has committed no criminal offence. Neither the unborn child nor Richard have any right of civil action for any harm they may consider Sue has done to them.

3. Robert has not committed any criminal offence. He is in no different a position in law to the person who has no money. Joan will be able to commence civil proceedings against him. She will be able to sue him for breach of contract. Robert's wealth makes it more likely that Joan will consider it worth suing him as she is more likely to be able to recover any damages. However she will also have to remember that Robert will, if he wishes be able to hire the best lawyers so as to delay Joan's inevitable court victory.

CHAPTER 3

Law in action/Law in books

INTRODUCTION

This chapter is about the different kinds of questions that arise when studying law and the different techniques you need when studying them. You might think that studying law is purely a matter of learning a large number of legal rules. If this were the case only one kind of question would ever arise—what is the content of any particular legal rule? However, simply learning a large number of legal rules is not always a very useful way of learning about law. Learning the rules is like memorising the answers to a set of sums. It is of no help when the sums change. If all you do is learn a set of legal rules, when the rules change, when the law is altered, you are back where you started. At the very least, to use your legal knowledge, you also need to know how to find legal rules and how to find out if they have been changed. Thus, to the question "what is the content of the legal rule?" are added questions about how to find them.

Not everyone interested in law is interested in questions about the content of legal rules. For example, we might ask whether it is ever right to disobey the law. This is a question of ethics which might in part relate to the content of a legal rule but is much more about the nature of moral judgement. Equally questions about how the legal system works in practice are only partially concerned with the content of legal rules. Legal rules are about what should happen. Questions about practice are concerned with what does happen.

The various questions above are not merely different questions, they are different kinds of questions. Because they are questions about different things and because the different questions demand different techniques to answer them they are often put into separate categories. The terms for these categories vary. Some terms are more precise than others. We have taken one commonly drawn distinction, that between the law in action and the law in books, as the title for this chapter. This is because the distinction is a very basic one that can be applied to most areas of law. The law in action is that which actually happens in the legal system and is concerned with people's behaviour. The law in books is the system of legal rules which can be deduced from reading cases and statutes. A question about how defendants are treated in court is a question about the law in action. A question about the definition of theft in English law is a question about the law in books.

Although the distinction between the law in action and the law in books is both easy to see and useful to use it is also limited. Some questions about law seem to fit into neither category. For example, is our earlier question about disobedience to law a question about the law in action or the law in books? Information about what actually happens in the legal system will only tell us what people do, not whether their action is morally correct. Equally, being told what the legal rule says is of little help in helping us assess whether we are correct to obey it or not. The question does not appear to fall into either category.

The distinction between the law in action and the law in books is broad but crude. More sophisticated categories provide narrower, more precise distinctions. Thus questions about the nature of law, which can include whether or not one has a duty to obey it, can be grouped together under the title the philosophy of law. Such categories are not firmly fixed and may be defined by different people in different ways. Thus some people would use the term the sociology of law to refer to all questions about the operation of the legal system in practice. Others would distinguish between questions about the relationship between law and other social forces and questions about how effective a legal rule is. They would see the first kind of question as falling within the sociology of law and the second as coming under the heading socio-legal studies. It is more important to be able to identify the different kinds of questions than give them the labels.

DIFFERENT QUESTIONS MEAN DIFFERENT ANSWERS

Knowing that there are different kinds of questions asked when studying law is of intellectual interest but does it have any further significance? What happens if you fail properly to identify the kind of question that you are asking? We can answer these questions by looking at one way in which different kinds of questions are commonly confused.

For many years it was assumed that legal rules which laid down what should happen were an accurate guide to what actually happened. The law in action was thought to be a reflection of the law in books. It was accepted that there were divergencies but these were thought to be on a small scale and of no importance. More recently academics have begun to realise that there is often a very great difference between legal rules and the practice in the legal system. One example of this can be seen in the area of criminal law when people are being prosecuted.

In the United States it is common practice for a prosecutor to agree to drop some criminal charges in return for a guilty plea from the defendant in respect of others. The defendant benefits because those charges are lesser ones, attracting a lower sentence. The prosecution benefits because the trial takes less time and money is saved. This is the practice known as plea-bargaining. In Great Britain the Court of Appeal has said that the defendant should not be subject to any pressure to plead guilty to a charge by being offered a lower sentence in return for that plea. In particular, the Court of Appeal has said, a judge should never indicate a willingness to give a lesser kind of sentence (for example a fine instead of a prison sentence) in return for a guilty plea. The existence of these rules, which were intended to prevent plea-bargaining, led many people to assume either that plea-bargaining did not exist in Great Britain or that it was very rare. However, when researchers enquired into this area, questioning defendants and looking at court records, they produced evidence which they thought showed that various forms of plea-bargaining were common in the court they studied.

The difference between the law in action and the law in books in this area is important for several reasons. First, confusing the different kinds of questions resulted in an inaccurate description. People accepted the wrong kind of material as evidence for their answers. Secondly, because of that misdescription, those involved in advising others on the law may have given misleading advice. Finally, those involved in considering whether or not the law and legal system are effective and just looked not at the real legal system but at a shadowy reflection of it.

WHICH KIND OF QUESTION AM I ASKING?

Somebody has been divorced and you are asked how their financial affairs will be settled by the courts. Are you being asked what the relevant rules are, or what will actually happen in court, or both?

Outside your course of study it may be very difficult to sort out what kind of question you are being asked. For study purposes the task will generally be simpler. The kind of question that you are being asked is likely to be indicated by the nature of your course as a whole. The title of your course may give you a clue. A course on "the sociology of law" is unlikely to be much concerned with questions about the content of legal rules. Some kinds of courses are more usually taught with one kind of question in mind than another. For example, courses on "land law" or the "law of contract" are more often concerned with the law in books than the law in action. These kinds of courses are sometimes termed *black-letter law* courses.

Even when it is clear what kind of question your course is generally concerned with problems may still arise. It is not only important to know the kind of question that you are interested in. You must also be able to identify the kind of question that the author of a book or article which you are using is interested in. If you know the type of answer they are trying to give you will be in a better position to judge the quality of their argument and, thus, the value of their work. Even when you have identified the kind of question an author is most interested in you will also have to be careful to see that other kinds of question are not introduced. For example, it is not uncommon to find a book largely devoted to discussion of the content of legal rules also including a few remarks on the value or justice of those rules. There is nothing wrong with this if the author realises that a different kind of question is being addressed and uses the appropriate material to answer it. Unfortunately this is not always so.

ARE THERE REALLY DIFFERENT QUESTIONS?

There are some people who would argue that it is misleading to distinguish between different questions in the way we have done above. Some would argue that all the distinctions drawn are wrong. Others would argue that only some of them are invalid.

One argument that might be advanced is about the distinction between the law in action and the law in books. In our earlier example we saw that there was a difference between the legal rule laid down in the Court of Appeal and the actual practice studied. If we assume that the practice of all courts was the same as the court studied, and if this practice continued for many years, what would it mean to say that the legal rule was that which was laid down by the Court of Appeal? People would only be affected by what happened in practice which would always be different from that which the legal rule said should happen. Could we really say that the legal rule had any significance? If the legal rule has no significance, then surely all we ought to study is what happens in practice, ignoring questions about the law in books?

Other more complicated forms of the above argument exist. Some people would argue that when a judge makes a decision that decision is influenced by the judge's social background, political views and education. The result of any case is therefore not solely determined by the neutral application of legal rules but by factors personal to the particular judge in the case. If this is so, then what kinds of questions will discussion about the content of legal rules answer? If we are to advise people how to act so as to win cases in court what we need to discuss is not, or not only, the content of legal rules but, rather, who are the judges and what their background is. If we want to find out what the law is we have to ask a whole series of questions other than those about ratios or statutes.

In a similiar fashion not everyone accepts that questions about the morality of law and questions about the content of law are different. For these people, the very idea of an immoral law, which is a law that, because it is immoral, should not be obeyed, is a contradiction in terms. They think that all law must have an irreducible minimum moral content. Without that content the "law," in their view, is merely a collection of words that make a command which may be backed by the physical power of the state but do not have the authority of law.

The authors of this book would accept that the distinctions drawn in previous sections are open to question. The relationship between the different questions, if there are different questions, may be more complicated than the simple divisions above. However most books and most courses in law draw the kinds of distinction outlined. At this early stage in your study of law it will be enough if you understand them. Even if later you come to reject all or some of them, you will still find yourself reading material which is based upon them.

ANSWERING QUESTIONS

This chapter has drawn a distinction between three types of question; those concerned with the nature of law, those concerned with the content of legal rules and those which address the operation of law and legal system in practice. Each type of question has a technique appropriate for answering it.

Questions about the nature of law are those which are most difficult to answer. The questions are basic ones, appearing to be very simple. For example, how is law different from other types of command? What is the difference between a gunman telling me to do something and the state, through law, telling me to do something? Are both simply applications of power or is there something fundamentally different between them? Neither the content of particular legal rules nor the operation of the law in practice provide any answer. Arguments in this area are abstract. In advancing and judging such arguments it is necessary to see that all the terms are explained and that the argument is coherent. They must also match the world they purport to explain. In practice these simple conditions are very difficult to meet.

The ultimate source for answers to questions about the law in books is the law reports and statutes which have already been discussed in Chapter 1. Only these sources will give you a definitive answer to any question you are asked. You are told how to find these materials in Chapter 4 and how to use them in Chapter 5. In some cases you may not have either the time or the resources to consult original materials. In such instance you can look at some of the various commentaries on the law. These vary in size, depth of coverage and price. Different commentaries serve different purposes. Some are student texts. Others are written for specific professions or occupations. Most cover only a limited area of law. However there are some general guides to the law and some encyclopedias of law. The best encyclopedia of general English law is Halsbury's Laws of England. This has a section on almost every area of law. Most good reference libraries will have a copy of this. All commentaries try to explain legal rules. You should select one suitable to your interests. Always remember that a commentary is one person's opinion about the law. It may be wrong. You can only be sure what the rule is if you consult the orginal cases and statutes.

Finding out how the law works in practice is frequently much more difficult than deciding what a legal rule means. It is easy to find opinions about how things work. Almost everybody who has contact with the law, even if only through reading about it in the newspapers, has an opinion on such questions. However, such opinions have little value. At best they are the experience of one person. That experience may be unusual or misinterpreted by that person. What we are trying to understand is how the legal system works, not the anecdotes of one person. Thus, to answer this kind of question, we need to turn to the materials and techniques of the social scientist.

SEEING THE LAW IN ACTION

One obvious source of detailed information about the legal system is statistical analyses. "You can prove anything with statistics" is a hostile comment suggesting that nothing at all can be proved with statistics. However, is this so? What use are statistics to anyone studying law?

Information about the number of cases handled by a court shows in specific terms what the court's workload is. Changes from year to year may indicate some effects of changes in the law and practice. Statistics here can be used descriptively to provide a clearer picture than general phrases such as "some," "many" or "a few." Statistical tests can establish that there is a relationship, a correlation, between different things. For example, the length of a sentence for theft may correlate with the value of the items stolen or the experience of the judge who heard the case. This means that the sentence will be longer if, for example, more items are stolen or the judge is more experienced. Statisticians have produced tests to show whether, given the number of examples you have, there is a strong correlation or not. Where this correlation fits with a theory (sometimes termed a hypothesis) it provides evidence tending to confirm the theory. Such confirmation is important; without it we have little to establish the effect the law has, being forced to rely on personal knowledge of individual instances of its application and having to assume that these have general truth. Empirical study of the operation of law may reveal areas for improvement. It can also confirm that measured by particular standards, the courts are working well.

If we want to use statistics where will we get them from? Government departments collect and print a large number of statistics relating to their operations. A comprehensive index to these, the *Guide to Official Statistics*, is published by the Central Statistical Office. Some of these official statistics provide background information for the study of the operation of law. Thus the Office of Population Censuses and Surveys (OPCS) publishes details of the size, composition and distribution of the United Kingdom population. This information is essential if one is to be sure that other changes do not merely reflect population changes. The Department of Social Security provides figures for the number of social security claimants and also the number of children in the care of local authorities. Details of use and expenditure on the Legal Aid scheme come from the Legal Aid Advisory Committee reports. The Home Office produces the annual criminal statistics as well as information about the police forces and immigration. The Lord Chancellor's Department produces the civil judicial statistics which contain figures for the work of the civil and all appellate courts. Most official statistics are collected from returns filed by local offices of the relevant departments. The content of these is determined by what the department needs to know about its activities and also by what Parliament has asked it to report on. Even minor changes in the collection of official statistics mean that it is often impossible to make comparisons over a period of years. The information collected in one year is about something slightly different from that in other years. Moreover, because of the way in which information is collected and the purpose of collecting it, these statistics can only answer a few of the questions asked about the way the law operates. For example, the judicial statistics list the number of cases brought each year in the County Court, broken down according to the type of claim. They provide little or no information about the applicants, the specific point of law relied on or whether the judgment was successfully enforced.

Official statistics, as a source of information, are limited. They provide information about things of importance to those who collected them. These are not necessarily the things which are important to the researcher. Government departments, the research councils and some private bodies sponsor research into specific areas of law. Small-scale research is often undertaken without sponsorship. Although this research may be based upon official statistics it may involve first collecting the necessary statistics and then deciding what they mean. The researchers must collect the data they need for each project. They have to design the study, that is to select the methods they will use and choose the sample to ensure that they have all the information relevant to their chosen topic. There is a more detailed discussion of some of these issues in Chapter 6, "Reading Research Materials."

Researchers will not necessarily be concerned solely with statistics. This is only one way of describing law and the legal system. Statistics are useful for describing things like the number of events but are poor for describing things like motivations. Thus researchers will also have to decide whether they want to interview people or even directly observe what is happening in the area in which they are interested. In each case they must decide how they can do this so as to ensure that the material they collect is an accurate reflection of the world as a whole.

Whatever kind of question you are dealing with it is important that you decide what the answer is. Merely being able to repeat a passage from a book on legal philosophy, a paragraph from a judgement or the conclusion to a survey is not the same as knowing the answer. If you do not understand the answer you will neither be able to remember it nor apply it.

Part 2

CHAPTER 4

Finding cases and statutes

In Chapter 1 the importance of cases and statutes as sources of
law was explained. This chapter explains how you find reports
of cases and copies of statutes and how you make sure they are
up-to-date. As has been explained these materials are sources of
law. From them it is possible to derive the legal rules in which
you are interested in. Chapter 5 will explain in more detail how
this is done.

FINDING CASES

In the following, the task of discovering case reports will be considered for three different sets of circumstances:

(a) Where a well-stocked and supported law library is available.
(b) Where some research or library facilities are available,
but without access to a fully-equipped law library.
(c) With the aid of on-line computerised retrieval facilities.

Most readers will have different facilities available at different
times. For example, a reader who has access to a fully-equipped
law library can only use it during opening hours. Equally, even if
computer facilities are available it may not always be appropriate
to use them. It is important that you are aware of the different
ways in which to find cases so that you can decide which is the best
method to use at any particular time.

USING FULL LAW LIBRARY NON-ELECTRONIC
RESEARCH FACILITIES

The traditional, and still the most comprehensive, form of
research in relation to law reports is performed in law libraries

containing a wide selection of materials and a variety of support systems, indexes, catalogues, etc., designed to assist the researcher in the task of locating and using particular items. Such libraries are found in academic institutions such as Universities and Polytechnics as well as in professional institutions such as the Bar. In many cases it is possible to use such libraries even if you are not a member of the institution.

What follows in this chapter is an attempt to introduce the reader to the major series of law reports, and to indicate basic methods of locating and checking up-to-date material and of up-dating earlier materials. A helpful guide for those interested in more sophisticated use of the whole range of facilities made available in major law libraries is to be found in *How to Use a Law Library*, by J. Dane and P. Thomas. In particular, that work contains detailed explanations of how to use the various indexes and catalogues available in such libraries, and thus provides a more comprehensive guide on the "mechanics" of locating and using legal materials than is offered here.

Law reports go back over 700 years although most of the case reports you will find in a normal law library have been decided during the last 150 years. Reports are divided into different series. These series do not necessarily reflect any systematic attempt to present the reports of decided cases, (*e.g.* by subject-matter covered), but tend instead to indicate the commercial means by which such reports have been made available. Thus, older cases can be found in series which bear the title of the name (or names) of the law reporter(s). Such a series is the nineteenth century series of Barnewall and Alderson (Bar & Ald). (All law reports have abbreviations which are customarily used when discussing them. Whenever a series is first mentioned here its usual abbreviation will be given, in brackets, as above. Appendix II to this book is a list of useful abbreviations, including those to the main law reports.) The only necessary coherence these cases have is that the reporter thought it was worthwhile to print them. The range and variety of these older cases is enormous, although some help has now been provided to modern legal researchers with some of the old series reprinted in a new series under the title of The English Reports (E.R.).

In 1865 the Incorporated Council of Law Reporting introduced "The Law Reports," a series which was divided according to the different courts of the day. The Council has continued to produce these reports to the present day although the current court divisions and, thus, the current divisions of the reports, are different. Today one can find the following divisions:

(a) Appeal Cases (A.C.)—reports of cases in the Court of Appeal, the House of Lords and the Privy Council.

(b) Chancery Division (Ch.)—reports of cases in the Chancery Division of the High Court and cases appealed from there to the Court of Appeal.

(c) Queen's Bench (Q.B.)—reports of cases in the Queen's Bench Division of the High Court and cases appealed from there to the Court of Appeal.

(d) Family Division (Fam.)—reports of cases in the Family Division of the High Court and cases appealed from there to the Court of Appeal. (Until 1972 the Family Division was the Probate, Divorce and Admiralty Division (P.).)

This series is the closest to an "official" series of case reports. If a case is reported in several different series and there is a discrepancy between the different reports it is The Law Reports that should normally be followed.

There is, nowadays, a wide range of privately-published law reports series. Most of these series concentrate upon a particular area of legal developments, (*e.g.* the law relating to industrial relations, or the law concerning road traffic). However, there are two series which publish cases dealing with decisions affecting a wide range of legal issues. These general series, with which most students of law will quickly become familiar, are the Weekly Law Reports (W.L.R.) and the All England Law Reports (All E.R.).

Each of the series above reports fully any case contained in its volumes. There are, in addition, some sources which provide a short summary of, or extracts from, judgments given. In addition to these general series, it is possible to find short reports of case developments in a variety of sources. The most up-to-date of these sources are those newspapers which print law reports. Most of the quality daily newspapers contain law reports as well as news items on matters of legal interest. *The Times* has contained such reports for the longest time and is regarded as being the most authoritative source of such reports. Case-note sections published in legal periodicals such as the *New Law Journal* (N.L.J.) or the *Solicitors' Journal* (S.J. or Sol.Jo.), are also a good source of such summaries.

There have always been specialist series of reports concerned either with one area of law or one type of occupation. In recent years the number of such series has increased. If your interest is not in law as a whole but in particular areas of law, one of these series of reports may be a valuable tool. Indeed sometimes such series are the only source for a report of a particular case. However, such series should be used with caution. First, these reports may not be as accurate as the series discussed above. Secondly, they represent not reports of the law but reports of such law as the publishers of the series think important. Their greater selectivity may be useful in giving you a guide as to what is important, but dangerous if you think cases not reported in the series must be irrelevant. Helpful lists of such reports can be found in law dictionaries.

USING LAW REPORTS

Every case which is reported in a series of law reports can be referred to by way of the names of the parties concerned in the action. Thus, where a court action is brought by somebody called Harriman in dispute with somebody called Martin, the case can be referred to as *Harriman* v. *Martin*. However referring to a case in this way is of limited usefulness. The reference does not tell the reader the date of the case nor does it indicate the series of reports in which it is found. It does not even tell us to which case involving a Harriman and a Martin the reader is being referred. There may be several. Thus, in addition to its name, each reported case possesses a unique reference indicator. This normally includes (although not always in the same order):

(1) A reference to the title of the series of law reports in which the report is to be found.
(2) A date (year) reference. Some series have a volume number for each year. Where the date reference tells you the year in which the case was decided the date is normally enclosed in square brackets.
(3) A reference to the volume number (if there is more than one volume of the particular law reports series in the year concerned).
(4) A reference to the page or paragraph number at which the report of the case may be located.

If the case of *Harriman* v. *Martin* is reported in the first volume of the Weekly Law Reports for 1962, at page 739, the reference would be [1962] 1 W.L.R. 739. This is sometimes called the *citation* for the case. Knowing this reference or citation, it is possible to go directly to the shelves of the law library which house the volumes containing that reference and to turn directly to the report of the case.

If you know only the names of the parties in the case, you will need first to ascertain the specific reference. Although it would be possible to search the indexes for each individual series of law reports for the name of a case, this would be an inefficient and time-consuming approach. Normally, therefore, recourse is had to a general reference manual, which is known as a *case citator*. Such a case citator is provided with the commercial reference service known as *Current Law*. Other means are also available for locating the references of specific cases but Current Law is that which is most readily available. What follows is a brief description of the *Current Law* case citator.

The Current Law system of citations for cases works through a combination of three separate reference items:

(1) Two hard-bound citators covering the periods 1947–1976 and 1977–1988.
(2) A laminated volume covering the period from 1989 (a new, up-dated version of this volume is issued every year).
(3) "Monthly Parts," which are issued regularly in pamphlet form, for the current year. These are subsequently replaced by a bound volume for the year.

The importance of using all three items to complement one another will appear when we consider the problem of locating up-to-date references (see below).

Entries in the *Current Law* case citator are listed by title of case, arranged alphabetically. Thus, to find the law reports reference to the case of *Harriman* v. *Martin* you need to turn to the alphabetical heading under "Harriman." This indicates:

> *Harriman* v. *Martin* [1962] 1 W.L.R. 739; 106 S.J. 507; [1962] 1 All E.R. 225, C.A. . . . . Digested 62/1249: Referred to, 72/2355.

From this information, we discover not only the law reports reference to the first volume of the Weekly Law Reports for 1962, at page 739 but also that there are reports of the same case in:

106 S.J. 507   *i.e.* the 106th volume of the Solicitors' Journal at page 507.

and:

[1962] 1 All E.R. 225   *i.e.* the first volume of the All
                                     England Reports for 1962 at
                                     page 225.

We are also informed that the court which delivered the decision
reported at those locations was:

C.A.   *i.e.* the Court of Appeal.

Next, we are told that a "digest" (a brief summary) of the case has
been included in a companion volume to the Current Law citator
at:

62/1249   *i.e.* in the companion year
                                     volume of Current Law for
                                     1962 at paragraph 1249.

Finally, we are told that the case was "referred to" (in another
case) and that that case is to be found at:

72/2355   *i.e.* in the companion year
                                     volume of Current Law for
                                     1972 at paragraph 2355.

It now only remains to locate one of these volumes in the law
library, and to turn to the appropriate page for a report of the case
of *Harriman* v. *Martin*.

The above is not only a method for finding the reference to a case.
If you already have a reference to a case, but you find that volume
already in use in the library, you can use the method above to find
an alternative citation for the case.

UP-DATING CASES

It is not enough to know merely what was said in a particular case
in order to know the importance which should be attached to that
case. It is also necessary to know whether such an earlier case has
been used or referred to subsequently by the judges, or, indeed,
whether it has been expressly approved or disapproved of by a
later court.

If a case is approved by a court which is further up the hierarchy of
courts than the court orginally giving judgment (and that approval
is part of the ratio of that later case) then the case will take on the
status of the later decision. Thus a decision of the High Court
approved by the Court of Appeal will take on the status of the
Court of Appeal. Even if the approval forms part of the *obiter*

within the later judgment this will be significant, indicating the way in which the court is likely to give judgment once the matter becomes central in a decision at that level. Disapproval of a case will be important in a similiar fashion. Such information can be discovered by using the *Current Law* case citator.

We can regard a case as reliable (or, at least, not unreliable) where we are informed that it has been "referred to," "considered," "explained," "followed," "approved" or "applied." On the other hand, considerable care must be taken with a case which has been "distinguished," while cases which have been "disapproved" or "overruled" are unlikely to prove reliable for future purposes.

Example

If, for example, at some time during April 1990, we had looked for information on the case of *Roberts* v. *Roberts* (which was decided in 1962), we would have found the following:

1. From the Current Law citator volume 1947–1976:

Roberts v. *Roberts* [1962] P. 212; [1962] 3 W.L.R. 448; 126 J.P. 438; 106 S.J. 513; [1962] 2 All E.R. 967; [26 M.L.R. 92], D.C. . . . Digested, 62/996: Considered, 62/995; 69/1124: Followed, 71/3362.

This tells us the various locations of reports of the case, as explained above. When there is a reference enclosed in square brackets it also tells us that there has been a note or article written explaining what the decision means:

[26 M.L.R. 92]   *i.e.* in volume 26 of the
                                  Modern Law Review at page
                                  92.

The court which decided the case is indicated (as explained previously) as D.C., (*i.e.* the Divisional Court or the High Court exercising its appelate function), and we are told that a digest of the case is to be found in the *Current Law Year Book* for 1962 at paragraph 996.

We are, however, additionally informed that the case has been "considered" by a court on two subsequent occasions, and that we can discover information about the cases in which that happened by turning to the paragraphs indicated in the *Current Law Year Book* series:

| 62/995 | *i.e.* a digest entry for the case of *Smith* v. *Smith and Brown* [1962] 1 W.L.R. 1218, in the Court of Appeal. |
| 69/1124 | *i.e.* a digest for the case of *P* v. *P* [1969] 1 W.L.R. 898. |

We are also informed that the case has been "followed" on one occasion in a case digested at paragraph 3362 of the *Current Law Year Book* for 1971. However, if we turn to that reference, we find that even the compilers of citator volumes are human! There is no reference to our case of *Roberts* v. *Roberts*, although, if we look above at paragraph 3361, we will find a digest for the case of *Snow* v. *Snow* (1971) 115 S.J. 566, in the Court of Appeal, which does "follow" the case of *Roberts* v. *Roberts*.

2. From the supplementary volume 1977–1988:

Roberts v. *Roberts* [1962] . . . Considered 84/190; 85/168

As in the case of the 1947–1976 volume we are referred to digest entries where *Roberts* v. *Roberts* has been "considered."

| 84/190 | *i.e.* a digest entry for the case of *W* v. *W* which is reported in *The Times* for November 3rd, 1984. |
| 85/168 | *i.e.* a digest entry for the case of *Willets* v. *Wells* [1985] 1 WLR 237. |

The next thing we would normally do is consult the year volume for 1989 but, at the date of writing, this had not yet been issued. Therefore we must look at the Monthly Parts for 1989. These are cumulative, *i.e.* information in the later Parts refers back to information in the earlier Parts for the same year. Thus, initially, we need only look at the Part for December. Cases are listed alphabetically. Cases which have been previously listed, such as *Roberts* v. *Roberts*, are noted in italic script. There is no reference to our case therefore we know that the case was not mentioned in Current Law in 1989. Finally we need to look at the February Monthly Part for 1990, the most recent Monthly Part at the date of writing. Again there is no mention of our case. We therefore know that there was no mention of our case in Current Law up to that date.

USING LIMITED LIBRARY FACILITIES

The problems of finding and using cases and law reports where limited resources are available are significant. Clearly, it will not be possible to find reports of all the case which you may need, since the available reports may only be found in series which are not at your disposal. By the same token, you may not have access to sufficiently comprehensive reference manuals, such as a case law citator or similar.

You may have access to one of the general series of law reports. This will often be a set of All England Law Reports. Many public reference libraries possess a set of these law reports. If this is the case, some searching for cases can be done using the indexes contained in those volumes; though this will, of course, be time consuming. Alternatively, if you are concerned only with a limited specialist area you may have access to a specialised series of law reports.

Whatever your source of available material, however, it is of paramount importance that you familiarise yourself with the specific indexing and cross-referencing system adopted by that source. If you do this, you will be able to use the material at your disposal, limited though it may be by comparison with the resources of a fully-equipped and supported law library, in the most efficient manner.

It will also be important to discover whether you can obtain access to some means for up-dating the material contained in your available sources. The use of a citator, as explained above, is clearly of major benefit, for the consolidation of information within one reference item avoids the necessity of searching through a range of separate volumes and series. Amongst possible sources of up-dated information might be the general legal periodicals, such as the *New Law Journal* or the *Solicitors' Journal* (both of which have been referred to above). Many public libraries subscribe to one of these, or to other relevant periodicals. Where your needs relate to a specific area, the periodicals available in relation to that area may be of assistance in obtaining up-to-date information. Thus, for example, many personnel management journals contain information about cases decided by the courts in relation to employment law. All of these will probably refer you to sources of information which you do not have but they will also enable you to make the most efficient use of those sources which are available.

A further common source of information will be text-books on the subject about which you are seeking information. The important rule here is to check that you have access to the latest possible edition of the book, and to bear in mind the possibility that case-law developments may have overtaken the legal position as it was stated at the time of writing of the book. Most books dealing with the law will contain a statement in the "Foreword" stating the date on which the information given in the book is said to be current.

In some instances you may have access to a *case-book*. This term is something of a misnomer since case books frequently contain not just cases but also statutes and comments on the law. Such books are generally concerned with a specific topic, for example "contract law," and contain edited material relevant to the area. These books can be a very useful source where you have access only to limited library facilities. However, they suffer from several deficiencies. First, the reader relies on the editor of the volume to select the most appropriate material. There is no way in which the quality of the work can be checked. Secondly, the material presented may only be given in part. Again, the reader must trust that the editor has not given misleading excerpts. Finally, the reader has no means of up-dating the material. In some areas of law encyclopedias are produced. These are similiar to case-books, although they are generally more detailed. Publishers of this kind of work often supply an up-dating service. Increasingly encyclopedias are produced in a loose-leaf form and the reader will substitute new pages as supplements are issued. (The use of encyclopedias is considered at the end of this chapter.)

USING ELECTRONIC RETRIEVAL FACILITIES

To complete this section on finding and using reports of cases, mention must be made of the important and fast-developing range of computerised information retrieval systems.

The major system, relevant to English case-law, is the service known as LEXIS. It should also be noted that a range of similar services are available through various organisations which enable users to gain access to legal materials and case-law from many foreign systems and in a range of foreign languages.

As regards LEXIS, access is made through a terminal located in the office or library of the researcher. This terminal is connected to a large computer, operated by the providers of the service, either by direct telephone-line or by direct communication through a "network" system such as the British Telecom PSS system. The large computer contains an electronic "data base" in which are housed the reports of thousands of cases. In general, these reports are in exactly the same form as they are to be found in traditional series of law reports. Not all law reports found in traditional series are available by electronic means, while, on the other hand, a variety of "unreported" cases are available on different electronic retrieval services.

Searching for a case using an electronic retrieval system is done on the basis of selecting "key words". Thus, the user may ask the large computer to indicate where a specific term or "string" of letters and/or numbers occurs in its data base. The system will respond by telling the user how often that term or "string" has been found and will indicate the number of cases in which that word is to be found. In response to this, the user may attempt to narrow down the number of "responses," by further limiting the selected "key word." This is done by requesting the system to indicate where the original "key word" or "string" is to be found in conjunction with another "string."

Eventually, the number of occasions on which the requested string or strings is to be found on the data base will be small enough for the user to take a look at those instances which the computer has discovered. At this stage, it is possible for the user to ask for the text of the reports containing the requested string(s) to be displayed on the terminal. The full text of a law report may be requested, or there may just be a call for a selected portion of the report, such as the title, the decision, or the names of the lawyers acting in the case.

Any information displayed on the user's terminal can be printed simultaneously, and used as a record of the "search."

Since the computer which houses the case-law data base works on the basis of matching "strings" of text within that data base with the "key words" selected by the user, it is possible to search on the basis of names, (*e.g.* asking for the occasions on which "Harriman" appears, with a view to locating the case of *Harriman* v. *Martin*) dates, court, or subject-matter. The sophistication of any search undertaken using this method depends in large measure upon the ability of the user to ask for matching of sufficiently specific and relevant "key words."

Access to systems for on-line electronic retrieval of legal information offers the experienced user the possibility of making detailed and exhaustive searches in relation to known cases or around particular subject areas. It also makes possible speedy searches of law reports series, as well as offering access to the facilities of a large, well-equipped and constantly up-dated law library in the comfort of the user's office.

FINDING AND UP-DATING STATUTES

Finding and updating statutory material is approached in very much the same manner as that described for case-law. With statutes there are three main problems. Is the statute in force? Has the statute been repealed by Parliament, (*i.e.* replaced by some other statute)? Has the statute been amended by Parliament, (*i.e.* had part of its contents altered by Parliament)?

Having started out with a provision in an Act of Parliament (either in the form in which it was originally passed, or in a form amended subsequently and stated to be effective at a given date), it is necessary to use one of the "citator" systems in order to discover the most up-to-date changes (if any) which have affected that provision. There are several different ways of performing this updating task, all of which are explained in detail in *How to Use a Law Library*. To assist you in the task, the following example shows how to update a relatively recent statutory provision using the *Current Law Statute Citator*.

Example

Let us take the provisions of section 13 of the Trade Union and Labour Relations Act 1974. In its original form, this provision was set out as follows:

Restrictions on legal liability and legal proceedings

Acts in contemplation or furtherance of trade disputes.

13.—(1) An act done by a person in contemplation or furtherance of a trade dispute shall not be actionable in tort on the ground only—

    (*a*) that it induces another person to break a contract of employment; or

    (*b*) that it consists in his threatening that a contract of employment (whether one to which he is a party or not) will be broken or that he will induce another person to break a contract of employment to which that other person is a party.

(2) For the avoidance of doubt it is hereby declared that an act done by a person in contemplation or furtherance of a trade dispute is not actionable in tort on the ground only that it is an interference with the trade, business or employment of another person, or with the right of another person to dispose of his capital or his labour as he wills.

(3) For the avoidance of doubt it is hereby declared that—

- (*a*) an act which by reason of subsection (1) or (2) above is itself not actionable;
- (*b*) a breach of contract in contemplation or furtherance of a trade dispute;

shall not be regarded as the doing of an unlawful act or as the use of unlawful means for the purpose of establishing liability in tort.

(4) An agreement or combination by two or more persons to do or procure the doing of any act in contemplation or furtherance of a trade dispute shall not be actionable in tort if the act is one which, if done without any such agreement or combination, would not be actionable in tort.

Let us now assume that, in April 1990, we wish to discover what has happened subsequently in relation to this section. In order to do this, it is necessary to turn to the most recent available version of the *Current Law Statute Citator*. In April 1990, this was the Citator for 1972–88.

The Statute Citator is arranged in chronological order, by year and then by Chapter number for each Act. Chapter numbers are fully explained at page 73 but, briefly, they are a unique way of identifying the statute. Each statute in a year has its own Chapter number. For the Trade Union and Labour Relations Act 1974 this is Chapter 52. To find our section, we turn to 1974, and eventually reach Chapter 52. Having come this far, we now only have to continue until we reach the required section number (s.13). The entry at this point tells us the following:

s.13, amended: 1976, c. 7, s.3; repealed in pt.: 1980, c. 42, s.17, Sched. 2; 1982, c. 46, s.19, Sched. 4.

From the information contained in this entry, we can now tell that:

- (1) The section was amended in 1976, by section 3 of the statute whose reference is 1976 Chapter 7;
- (2) Part of that amended section was repealed in 1980, by section 17 and Schedule 2 of the statute whose reference is 1980 Chapter 42; and
- (3) A further part of the remainder of the amended section was repealed in 1982, by section 19 and Schedule 4 of the statute whose reference is 1982 Chapter 46.

It is now up to us to find the relevant provisions indicated in the above information. This we can do either by looking up the relevant references on the shelves of statute series in a Law Library, or by turning to the chronological list of entries in the *Current Law Statute Citator* in order to discover the titles of the Acts whose references we now possess.

Our search will lead us to discover that:

(1) the 1976 amendment was brought about by the Trade Union and Labour Relations (Amendment) Act 1976;
(2) the 1980 partial repeal was effected by the Employment Act 1980; and
(3) the further partial repeal in 1982 was produced by the Employment Act 1982.

We can now turn to the relevant provisions in the statutes which we have discovered and, by applying the amending or repealing provisions to the original version of the section with which we started, we can ascertain what s.13 of the Trade Union and Labour Relations Act 1974 (as amended) now currently provides. By comparison with the original version, that section, in April 1990, had the following content:

Restrictions on legal liability and legal proceedings

Acts in contemplation or furtherance of trade disputes.

13.—[(1) An act done by a person in contemplation or furtherance of a trade dispute shall not be actionable in tort on the ground only—

(*a*) that is induces another person to break a contract or interferes or induces any other person to interfere with its performance; or
(*b*) that is consists in his threatening that a contract (whether one to which he is a party or not) will be broken or its performance interfered with, or that he will induce another person to break a contract or to interfere with its performance.]¹

(2) [*Repealed by Employment Act* 1982 (*c.* 46), *s.* 19, *Sched.* 4]

(3) [*Repealed by Employment Act* 1980 (*c.* 42), *s.* 17, *Sched.* 2]

(4) An agreement or combination by two or more persons to

¹ s.13(1) Substituted by Trade Union and Labour Relations (Amendment) Act 1976 (c. 7), s.3(2).

do or procure the doing of any act in contemplation or furtherance of a trade dispute shall not be actionable in tort if the act is one which, if done without any such agreement or combination, would not be actionable in tort.

This method will not only allow us to see whether a statute has been amended. It will also enable us to find out if a statute has come into force by, commencement order, a statutory instrument, by using the method above to see if any such order has been made. Finally, using the method above will also give us the citation of any case interpreting the section in the statute.

HOW TO USE ENCYCLOPAEDIAS

Encyclopaedias are not, in the strictest sense, a source of law (although they may contain sources of law). Cases and statutes are sources of law. They are what will be used when judges are deciding what the outcome of a case is to be. However, for some people encyclopaedias will be the only material they have available. Thus it is important to consider how they can be used most effectively.

Different examples of encyclopaedias vary in form and content. They do not all contain the same kind of material nor are they ordered in the same way. Therefore it is not possible to give a series of rules saying how encyclopaedias should be used. What follows are points that a reader should consider when first using any encyclopaedia.

The first thing to look at is the kind of material that the encyclopaedia contains. One advantage of an encyclopaedia can be that it brings together a wide variety of material about particular subject-matter. Thus, you may find the encyclopaedia that you are reading contains all the statutes in a particular area, all the statutory instruments, government circulars and other non-statutory material, references to relevant cases (with some description of their contents) together with some discussion of the application of legal rules in the area. On the other hand the encyclopaedia may contain only some of the material or may excerpt some of it. Thus, for example, instead of having all of a statute you may find you have only parts of it.

Even if the encyclopaedia claims to be fully comprehensive, remember that it is no more than a claim. The editors of the encyclopaedia may feel that they have included all relevant statutes; others may disagree with them. It is always as important to be aware of what you do not know as what you do know. Relying on an encyclopaedia means that there may be gaps in your knowledge of the particular area of law. However, you may feel it worth relying on the encyclopaedia because it is the only source avaliable. Equally you may find it quicker to use an encyclopaedia and judge that more important than any element of doubt in your knowledge of the area.

Most encyclopaedias excerpt at least some of the material that they cover. That is to say they contain extracts of a statute, stautory instrument or whatever rather than the whole. Here the problem is that in excerpting material the editor of the encyclopaedia limits your knowledge of the law. You rely on them to excerpt that which is relevant and cannot check the matter for yourself.

As a source of law, the less comprehensive an encyclopaedia is the less useful it is. However, the more comprehensive an encyclopaedia is the slower it may be to use. Before using the encyclopaedia you need to consider the kind of question that you are trying to answer. If the question is a very broad and general one about the framework of some area of law you may find an encyclopaedia with less detail easier to use. However, if you are trying to answer a very detailed point, perhaps applying the law to a very precise factual situation, you need the most comprehensive encyclopaedia that you can find.

Most encyclopaedias, and increasingly many other books about law, are now issued in loose-leaf form. This means that the publisher issues supplements to the encyclopaedia on a regular basis. These supplements, which contain descriptions of changes in the law, are then substituted for the pages which discuss the out-of-date law. The advantage of the loose-leaf form over ordinary books is that it means the encyclopaedia is more likely to be accurate. When using loose-leaf encyclopaedias before looking up the point of law that interests you always see when it was last updated. You will usually find a page at the front of the first volume of the encyclopaedia which tells you when it was last up-dated.

The technique for finding out about points of law in an encyclopaedia will vary depending upon the encyclopaedia being used. Some are organised according to different areas of law within the subject of the encyclopaedia. Others have different volumes for different kinds of material; one volume for statutes, one for discussion of the law and so forth. Most will have both indexes and detailed contents pages. Most encyclopaedias have a discussion of how they should be used at the beginning of their first volume. Always consult this when first using an encyclopaedia.

FINDING AND USING MATERIAL ON THE LAW OF THE EUROPEAN COMMUNITY

All basic material in this area is published in English. However, some material is not made available in all of the official languages of the Community immediately. What is said here refers specifically to English language versions of community material.

The *Official Journal of the European Communities* is the authoritative voice of the European Communities, and is used to publish daily information. The Official Journal (the O.J.) is divided into two major parts (the L and the C series). There are also separately published notices of recruitment, notices and public contracts and the like, which are published in a Supplement and in Annexes. Twice a year the O.J. issues a *Directory of Community legislation in force and other acts of the Community institutions.*

LEGISLATION

The L series (Legislation) contains the text of Community legislation. The series is arranged by Volume, starting in 1958, and by issue number sequentially throughout the issue year. Thus, the text of *Commission Regulation (EEC) No. 1049/90 of April 27, 1990 fixing the conversion rates for the calculation of monetary compensation amounts and to be applied for certain amounts in the agricultural sector* is to be found in the Official Journal of 30th April 1990.

The Volume number for 1990 is	Volume 33
The issue number of the OJ L series for 30th April 1990 is	L110
The text of the Regulation is set out on page 1 and thus the page reference is	1

Thus, the official reference for the Regulation will be

OJ No L 110, 30.4.1990, p.1

INFORMATION AND NOTICES

The C series (Information and Notices) contains, amongst a host of other items, key extracts ("the operative part") from judgments of the Court of Justice of the European Communities (the ECJ) and the Court of First Instance (*i.e.* one of the national courts of a Member State). Where the language of the particular court being reported is not English, the C series will include a "provisional translation": the definitive translation being found in the separately published *Reports of Cases before the Court*. There is also brief coverage of actions brought before the ECJ by Member States against the Council of the European Communities, as well as questions referred to the ECJ by national courts of member states.

Also, to be found in the C series will be *Preparatory Acts* in the course of being made into legislation by the European Communities. Thus, for example, the Official Journal for May 3, 1990 contains the text of a Proposal for a Council Decision concerning the conclusion of an agreement between the European Economic Community and the Prinicipality of Liechtenstein establishing cooperation in the field of training in the context of the implementation of Commett II (1990–94). The text for this had been submitted by the Commission of the European Communities on March 26, 1990.

The Volume Number for 1990 is	Volume 33
The issue of the OJ C series for 3rd May 1990 is	C 109
The page number at which the proposed Decision is found is 14 and thus the reference is	14
The text of the proposed Decision is item 20 in issue C 109	20

Thus the full reference for the Decision is

OJ 90/C 109/20

Whilst the Official Journal is the best Official source of information about Community law it should be noted that a wide range of documentation does not find its way into the Official Journal and other sources may have to be considered for those wanting a comprehensive list of European materials.

Judgments of the European court of Justice are reported in two series of law reports. One series is that published by the European Community itself, the European Court Reports (E.C.R.). The other series is the privately produced Common Market Law Reports (C.M.L.R.). Both can be found in the normal manner.

Finally, it is worth noting that the European Community has its own legal database, C.E.L.E.X., which is updated on a weekly basis.

CHAPTER 5

Reading cases and statutes

This chapter will explain how you should use the primary sources for legal rules, cases and statutes. You will find a specimen case report and a specimen statute in each section. Skill in the use of the techniques described here can only be acquired with practice. For this reason there are a series of exercises in Part III of the book.

READING A CASE

The contents of law reports are explained here so that you can start to read cases, understand the law which they contain, and make useful notes about them. You will find the court structure, and how cases are decided, explained in Chapter 1. You will find a copy of a case, *R. v. Terry*, on pp. 58–63. All specific references in this section will be to that case. The copy is taken from the All England Law Reports, which are the most commonly available law reports. However, if you have access to other kinds of law reports you will find that they look very much the same as the All England Law Reports. The techniques discussed here will be just as useful in reading other series of law reports. The different series of law reports and their use has been explained in Chapter 4.

The case is *R. v. Terry*. Lawyers pronounce this Regina (or the Queen, or King, or the Crown) *against* Terry. Most criminal cases are written like this. In civil cases, the names of the parties are usually given, as in *Donoghue* v. *Stevenson*, the case being pronounced Donoghue *and* Stevenson.

Underneath the name of the case at (**a**) you will see three pieces of information. First, you are told the court in which the case was heard. In this case it was the House of Lords. It is important to know which court heard a case because of the doctrine of precedent (see pages 8–10 for an explanation of the doctrine of precedent). The report then gives the names of the judges who took part in the case. This information is used to help evaluate the decision. Some judges are known to be very experienced in particular areas of law. Their decisions may be given extra weight. Finally, you are told when the case was heard and when the court gave its decision. In the House of Lords this process is called "delivering opinions," but in other courts it is known as "giving judgment."

a

R v Terry

HOUSE OF LORDS
LORD FRASER OF TULLYBELTON, LORD SCARMAN, LORD BRIDGE OF HARWICH, LORD BRANDON OF
OAKBROOK AND LORD BRIGHTMAN
28 NOVEMBER, 15 DECEMBER 1983

b
Road traffic – Excise licence – Fraudulent use of licence – Intention to defraud – Intent – What
intent must be proved – Whether necessary to prove intent to avoid paying proper licence fee –
Whether sufficient merely to prove intent to deceive person performing public duty – Vehicles
(Excise) Act 1971, s 26(1).

c
It is not necessary, on a charge of fraudulently using an excise licence contrary to s 26(1)[a]
of the Vehicles (Excise) Act 1971, for the Crown to establish an intent to avoid paying
the proper licence fee; it is sufficient merely for the Crown to prove an intent by deceit
to cause a person responsible for a public duty to act, or refrain from acting, in a way in
which he otherwise would not have done (see p 66 j, p 67 b c and p 68 b to p 69 a, post).

Welham v DPP [1960] 1 All ER 805 and dicta of Viscount Dilhorne and of Lord Diplock
d in *Scott v Comr of Police for the Metropolis* [1974] 3 All ER at 1037, 1040 applied.

R v Manners-Astley [1967] 3 All ER 899 overruled.

Notes
For fraudulent use of vehicle licences, see 40 Halsbury's Laws (4th edn) para 179.
For the Vehicles (Excise) Act 1971, s 26, see 41 Halsbury's Statutes (3rd edn) 456.

e **Cases referred to in opinions**
R v Manners-Astley [1967] 3 All ER 899, [1967] 1 WLR 1505, CA.
Scott v Comr of Police for the Metropolis [1974] 3 All ER 1032, [1975] AC 819, [1974] 2
WLR 379, HL.
Welham v DPP [1960] 1 All ER 805, [1961] AC 103, [1960] 2 WLR 669, HL.

f **Appeal**
The Crown appealed with leave of the Court of Appeal, Criminal Division against the
decision of that court (Dunn LJ, Balcombe and Leonard JJ) on 5 May 1983 allowing an
appeal by the respondent, Neil William Terry, against his conviction on 25 February
1982 in the Crown Court at Warrington before Mr Recorder R E Snape and a jury of
fraudulently using an excise licence contrary to s 26(1) of the Vehicles (Excise) Act 1971.
g The Court of Appeal certified, under s 33(2) of the Criminal Appeal Act 1968, that the
following point of law of general public importance was involved in the decision:
whether, on a charge of fraudulently using an excise licence contrary to s 26(1) of the
1971 Act, the Crown was required to establish an intent to avoid paying the proper
licence fee or whether it was sufficient to prove an intent by deceit to cause a person
responsible for a public duty to act, or refrain from acting, in a way in which he otherwise
h would not have done. The facts are set out in the opinion of Lord Fraser.

John M T Rogers QC and *Thomas Teague* for the appellant.
Rhys Davies QC and *Paul O'Brien* for the respondent.

Their Lordships took time for consideration.

j 15 December. The following opinions were delivered.

LORD FRASER OF TULLYBELTON. My Lords, on 25 February 1982 the
respondent was convicted in the Crown Court at Warrington on two counts, viz (1) theft

---
a Section 26(1), so far as material, is set out at p 65 *c*, post

of a vehicle excise licence and (2) fraudulently using an excise licence contrary to s 26(1)
of the Vehicles (Excise) Act 1971. He appealed against his conviction on the second **a**
count. On 5 May 1983 his appeal was allowed by the Court of Appeal, Criminal Division
(Dunn LJ, Balcombe and Leonard JJ) on the ground that a person does not 'fraudulently'
use an excise licence within the meaning of that section unless he uses it in an attempt to
evade paying the proper licence fee, and that the respondent had not been shown to have
used it for that purpose. In reaching that decision the Court of Appeal was, as it
recognised, bound by its own decision in *R v Manners-Astley* [1967] 3 All ER 899, [1967] **b**
1 WLR 1505. Accordingly, the present appeal is in substance against the decision in *R v
Manners-Astley*.

Section 26(1) of the 1971 Act, so far as relevant, provides:

> 'If any persons forges or fraudulently alters or uses . . . (a) any mark to be fixed or
> sign to be exhibited on a mechanically propelled vehicle in accordance with section
> 19 or 21 of this Act; or . . . (c) any licence or registration document under this Act, **c**
> he shall be liable on summary conviction to a fine . . . or on conviction on indictment
> to imprisonment . . .'

The relevant provisions of that section are substantially the same as the provisions of
s 17(1) of the Vehicles (Excise) Act 1962, which was the section under consideration in *R
v Manners-Astley*. **d**

The facts in this case were as follows. On 18 May 1981 the respondent hired a Ford
Escort car from a car-hire firm. When he returned it on 22 May 1981 its excise licence
disc was missing. On 1 June 1981 he was driving his own car, a Ford Cortina, which had
no licence disc displayed on the windscreen. He was stopped by a police officer, who
asked him where his excise licence was. The police officer had been riding a motor cycle
and at the time he asked the question he had not seen the licence disc. When he looked **e**
into the car he saw an excise licence disc lying on the dashboard of the car. The respondent
reached into the car, picked up the licence and handed it to the police officer saying, 'I
don't think this is the right one'. The police officer at once noticed that the licence did
not relate to the respondent's Cortina car. In fact it related to the Escort car which he had
hired some days previously. The Crown case is that the respondent stole the excise licence
relating to the Escort and that he fraudulently used it on his own Cortina with the **f**
intention that a police officer who saw it would wrongly think that the Cortina was
properly licensed. The respondent's case was that the licence had fallen off the Escort
while on hire to him, and that he had taken it into his house unintentionally and was
about to return it to the hire company. Further, he said that by 1 June he had already
applied for a new licence for his own Cortina and that he was not using the licence from
the Escort in an attempt to avoid paying the licence fee on the Cortina. The recorder **g**
directed the jury that they had only to consider two questions on this count: first,
whether the licence relating to the Escort had been exhibited on the dashboard of the
Cortina, and, if so, second, whether it had been placed there by the respondent with the
intention that it would be accepted as a genuine document applicable to the Cortina. The
respondent contends that this was a misdirection because it left it open to the jury to
convict him even if they accepted his statement that he had already applied for a licence **h**
for the Cortina and was therefore not trying to avoid paying the proper licence fee for
that car but was merely trying to avoid being charged with using the car without a
licence being exhibited in breach of s 12(4) of the 1971 Act. The issue therefore is
whether an attempt to avoid paying the licence fee is an essential element of the offence
of using a licence fraudulently.

My Lords, the meaning of the words 'with intent to defraud' was considered by this **j**
House in *Welham v DPP* [1960] 1 All ER 805, [1961] AC 103. For the purposes of this
appeal there is in my opinion no relevant difference of meaning between 'with intent to
defraud' and 'fraudulently'. In *Welham v DPP* the appellant was convicted under s 6 of
the Forgery Act 1913 on a charge of having 'within intent to defraud' uttered a forged
hire-purchase proposal and a forged hire-purchase agreement. His defence was that he

a had no intention of defrauding the finance companies which advanced money and that the reason for bringing the forged documents into existence was to evade credit restrictions by misleading the relevant authorities into thinking that the finance companies were advancing money not as straight loans (which would have been illegal) but under hire-purchase agreements (which would have been legal). His appeal against conviction was dismissed by the Court of Criminal Appeal, whose decision was affirmed by this House. The grounds of decision by this House were that 'with intent to defraud'
b was not confined to the idea of depriving a person by deceit of some economic advantage or inflicting on him some economic loss, but that they applied where a document was brought into existence for no other purpose than of deceiving a person responsible for a public duty into doing something that he would not have done but for the deceit, or not doing something that but for it he would have done. I shall cite two passages from the speech of Lord Radcliffe (see [1960] 1 All ER 805 at 808, [1961] AC 103 at 123–124),
c with whose speech Lord Tucker, Lord Keith and Lord Morris agreed. The first is as follows:

> 'Now I think that there are one or two things that can be said with confidence about the meaning of this word "defraud". It requires a person as its object; that is, defrauding involves doing something to someone. Although in the nature of things it is almost invariably associated with the obtaining of an advantage for the person
d who commits the fraud, it is the effect on the person who is the object of the fraud that ultimately determines its meaning . . . Secondly, popular speech does not give, and I do not think ever has given, any sure guide as to the limits of what is meant by "to defraud". It may mean to cheat someone. It may mean to practise a fraud on someone. It may mean to deprive someone by deceit of something which is regarded
e as belonging to him or, though not belonging to him, as due to him or his right.'

In the second passage, after referring to a dictionary definition and to the writings of Rudyard Kipling, Lord Radcliffe went on:

> 'There is nothing in any of this that suggests that to defraud is, in ordinary speech, confined to the idea of depriving a man by deceit of some economic advantage or inflicting on him some economic loss. Has the law ever so confined it? In my
f opinion, there is no warrant for saying that it has. What it has looked for in considering the effect of cheating on another person and so in defining the criminal intent is the prejudice of that person . . . Of course, as I have said, in ninety-nine cases out of a hundred the intent to deceive one person to his prejudice merely connotes the deceiver's intention of obtaining an advantage for himself by inflicting
g a corresponding loss on the person deceived. In all such cases, the economic explanation is sufficient. But in that special line of cases where the person deceived is a public authority or a person holding a public office, deceit may secure an advantage for the deceiver without causing anything that can fairly be called either a pecuniary or an economic injury to the person deceived. If there could be no intent to defraud in the eyes of the law without an intent to inflict a pecuniary or
h economic injury, such cases as these could not have been punished as forgeries at common law, in which an intent to defraud is an essential element of the offence, yet I am satisfied that they were regularly so treated.'

Lord Denning, with whose speech Lord Radcliffe expressed his agreement, said ([1960] 1 All ER 805 at 816, [1961] AC 103 at 134):

j > '. . . it appears that the appellant on his own evidence had an intent to defraud; because he uttered the hire-purchase documents for the purpose of fraud and deceit. He intended to practise a fraud on whomsoever might be called on to investigate the loans made by the finance companies to the motor dealers. Such a person might be prejudiced in his investigation by the fraud. That is enough to show an intent to defraud.'

Welham v DPP was considered by the Court of Appeal in *R v Manners-Astley*, where the appellant had been convicted of fraudulently using an excise licence contrary to s 17(1) *a* of the 1962 Act by displaying a vehicle licence issued for one vehicle on another vehicle. The Court of Appeal quashed the conviction on two grounds, one of which was that the jury had not been directed to consider whether the appellant had intended to defraud the Excise by avoiding payment of the licence fee. The Court of Appeal distinguished the decision in *Welham* as being one limited to cases under the Forgery Act 1913. In taking that limited view of the decision the court was, in my respectful opinion, wrong. The *b* speeches in *Welham* were directed to the meaning of 'intent to defraud' in general and were not limited to its meaning in the Forgery Act 1913. I agree with the view expressed by Viscount Dilhorne in *Scott v Comr of Police for the Metropolis* [1974] 3 All ER 1032 at 1037, [1975] AC 819 at 838, where he said:

> 'While the meaning to be given to words may be affected by their context and *c*
> Lord Radcliffe [in *Welham*] was only considering the meaning of intent to defraud
> in s 4 of the Forgery Act 1913, the passages which I have cited from his speech are, I
> think, of general application . . .'

(The passages cited by Viscount Dilhorne were those in the first quotation that I have made above.)

Lord Diplock, who also took part in the decision of *Scott v Comr of Police for the* *d* *Metropolis*, summarised the law in three propositions, of which the third was as follows ([1974] 3 All ER 1032 at 1040, [1975] AC 819 at 841):

> 'Where the intended victim of a "conspiracy to defraud" is a person performing
> public duties as distinct from a private individual it is sufficient if the purpose is to
> cause him to act contrary to his public duty, and the intended means of achieving *e*
> this purpose are dishonest. The purpose need not involve causing economic loss to
> anyone.'

In the present case I see nothing in s 26(1) of the Vehicles (Excise) Act 1971 which leads me to think that the word 'fraudulently' ought to be given a more limited meaning than that attributed to the words 'intent to defraud' in *Welham v DPP*. On the contrary the context indicates that they should bear a wide meaning. One of the offences created *f* by s 26(1)(a) is fraudulently using any mark (ie a number plate) which is required to be fixed to a vehicle: see s 19(1). It is easy to imagine cases where false number plates might be used by dishonest persons for the purpose of deceiving police officers and causing them to act in the way that they would not otherwise have acted, without any intention of evading payment of the licence fee, and I have no doubt that s 26(1) is applicable to such cases. There is nothing in the section to exclude the application of the general rule *g* stated in *Welham*.

I am accordingly of opinion that the decision in *R v Manners-Astley* was erroneous and should now be overruled. It follows that the decision of the Court of Appeal, Criminal Division in the present appeal was wrong.

For these reasons I would allow the appeal and restore the conviction of the respondent. The first alternative in the certified question should be answered in the negative, and the *h* second alternative in the affirmative.

LORD SCARMAN. My Lords, I agree with the speech of my noble and learned friend Lord Fraser. I would allow the appeal and answer the certified question as he proposes.

LORD BRIDGE OF HARWICH. My Lords, for the reasons given in the speech of *j* my noble and learned friend Lord Fraser, I agree that this appeal should be allowed and the certified question answered in the manner he indicates.

LORD BRANDON OF OAKBROOK. My Lords, I have had the advantage of reading in draft the speech prepared by my noble and learned friend Lord Fraser. I agree *a*   with it, and for the reasons which he gives I would allow the appeal, restore the respondent's conviction, and answer the certified question in the manner proposed.

LORD BRIGHTMAN. My Lords, I agree.

b

Appeal allowed. Conviction restored. First alternative in certified question answered in the negative, second alternative in the affirmative.

Solicitors: *Sharpe Pritchard & Co,* agents for *E C Woodcock,* Chester (for the Crown); *Manches & Co,* agents for *Ashalls,* Warrington (for the respondent).

Mary Rose Plummer   Barrister.

c

The material in italics, at **b** on the first page of the report, is written by the editor of the report. It indicates the subject-matter of the case and the issue which it concerned. The subject index at the front of each volume of law reports includes a similiar entry under the first words; in this instance "Road Traffic."

The next section, at **c**, is called the *headnote*. It is not part of the case proper, and is prepared by the law reporter, not by the judges. The headnote should summarise the case accurately giving references to important parts of the court's opinion or judgment and any cases cited. Because it is written when the case is reported, the headnote may stress or omit elements of the case which are later thought to be important. Therefore, care should be taken when using the headnote.

The notes, just below **d**, direct the reader to appropriate volumes of *Halsbury's Laws of England* and *Halsbury's Statutes of England*. *Halsbury's Laws* provides a concise statement of the relevant law, subject by subject, including references to the main cases and statutes. *Halsbury's Statutes* gives the complete text of all statutes together with annotations which explain them. Although law students and others may need to research the law using *Halsbury* it is not necessary to turn to reference works when reading every case. In most instances, the background law will be sufficiently explained by the judge.

At **e** there is a list of all the cases referred to by the judges. In each case, a list of different places where the cases may be found is given. Where counsel have cited additional cases to which the judges did not refer, to this is given in a separate list under the heading "cases also cited."

At **f** to **g** you will find a full history of the proceedings of the case. This indicates all the courts which have previously considered the case before the present one. The final sentence of this section indicates where a full account of the facts of the case may be found.

Below **h** you will find the names of the counsel (the barristers) who appeared in the case. Senior counsel are called Q.C.'s (Queen's Counsel), or K.C.'s (King's Counsel) when the monarch is a King. The appellant, named first in the title of the report, was the Crown (in other words the state), while Terry was the respondent. The names of the solicitors who represented the two parties and instructed the counsel appear at the very end of the report. Academics may use this information to obtain further information about the case. Solicitors may use it in order to find out which are the best counsel to instruct.

Not all series of law reports have marginal letters as this one does. When they do, these letters can be used to give a precise reference to any part of the case. Thus, the beginning of Lord Fraser's opinion is [1984] 1 All E.R. 65j.

Whilst the matters above provide an introduction to the case, the substance is to be found in the judgments. Every law case raises a question or series of questions to be answered by the judge(s). In civil cases, some of these will be questions of fact (in criminal cases these will be answered by the jury). For example, it may be necessary to know at what speed a car was travelling when an accident occurred. In practice, the answers to these factual questions are very important. Once they have been settled, the legal issues in the case may be simple. However, when it comes to the study of law, it is only the legal questions which matter.

Lawyers and students of law are concerned primarily not with the outcome of a case but with the reasoning which the judge gave for the conclusion. The reasoning is important because within it will be found the *ratio decidendi*. The ratio is that part of the the legal reasoning which is essential for the decision in the case. It is the ratio which is binding under the doctrine of precedent and which is thus part of the law. The ratio and the reasons for the decision are not necessarily the same thing. Not all the reasons given for the decision will be essential. In courts where there is more than one judge, each may give a separate judgment. If they do, each judgment will have its own reasons, and thus its own ratio. The judges must agree a conclusion to the case (although they may do so only by majority). However, they do not have to have the same reasons for their decision. If they have different reasons the judgments have different ratios and, thus, the case itself may have no ratio. Lawyers will rarely agree that a case has no ratio at all.

Finding the ratio in a case is crucial. It is also the most difficult part of reading cases, particularly when the case involves several judgments. The ratio is the essence of the case and, thus, may not be found simply by quoting from a judgment. Discovering the ratio involves skills of interpretation—understanding and explaining what judges meant, how they reached their conclusions—in order to see the common ground. Although the ratio is the law, it cannot be divorced entirely from the facts. Facts which are essential for a decision provide the conditions for the operation of the rule and are, thus, part of the rule itself. Deciding which are essential, as opposed to subsidiary, facts takes skill and practice. Lawyers frequently disagree on exactly what the ratio to a decision is. Some may view it broadly, seeing the decision as having few conditions but laying down a general rule. Others may take a narrower approach, suggesting that only in very limited circumstances would a decision bind a future court. Subsequent cases often help to clarify what the ratio of a previous case is accepted as being.

The editors of a law report write what they consider the ratio to be in the headnote. They may be wrong. Even if their interpretation is plausible when they write it, a later case may take a different view. For these reasons, statements of law in the headnote cannot be relied on.

If we look at *R.* v. *Terry* we can see that some some of the things that we are told in the judgment are irrelevant for the purposes of constructing the ratio. Thus, for example, the fact that the accused was driving a Ford Cortina rather than a Rolls Royce is of no account. On the other hand, the fact that he was driving a motor car rather than a horse and cart is significant. The Vehicle (Excise) Act 1971 is only concerned, we are told, with something which is "a mechanically propelled vehicle." Particulars of the individuals in a case and details of the time or place where the events relevant to the case took place are rarely important for the ratio.

After giving the facts of the case Lord Fraser, in his judgment, goes on to consider what the word "fraudulently" means. This is the central issue in deciding what the relevant statutory provision requires. Lord Fraser does this by analysing previous judgments which had considered the phrase "with intent to defraud." This phrase, he asserts, is synonomous with the word "fraudulently." He shows that these previous judgments have argued that "with intent to defraud" does not necessarily imply that one is trying to gain an economic advantage (avoiding to pay a bill or whatever) but merely that some species of deceit is involved. However, one previous Court of Appeal decision had held that this line of analysis did not apply to the Vechiles (Excise) Act; it applied only to the statute which the analysis had directly been concerned with, the Forgery Act 1913. Lord Fraser, in his judgment, says that this Court of Appeal decision is wrong. The analysis of "with intent to defraud" was a general one applying to other statutes using this or similiar phrases. Since Lord Fraser is sitting in the House of Lords, a court superior to the Court of Appeal, he can overrule a previous Court of Appeal decision providing the majority of his fellow judges in the case agree with him (which they do in this case).

From the above it would seem that it is relatively simple to construct the ratio of *R.* v. *Terry*. "Fraudulently" in the Vehicle (Excise) Act 1971 implies some deceit on the part of the accused but that deceit need not necessarily be an attempt to gain economic advantage. However, two questions remain. First, is it just in the context of the facts of the present case that "fraudulently" will take on this meaning? Secondly, and much more importantly, will fraudulently (or similiar phrases) always have this meaning? Lord Fraser, in his judgment, says "[i]n the present case I see nothing [to suggest that 'fraudulently' does not imply, broadly, some general form of deceit]." "In the present case" could reasonably be taken to imply that in other cases the analysis would be different.

R. v. *Terry* contains only a single judgment. That judgment is a short one. If one had a longer judgment (and most judgments are longer) or multiple judgments in the same case the task of constructing a ratio would be much more difficult. When one has to consider one judgment and its obscurities in the light of other judgments the process of analysing the law becomes even more uncertain.

A court must follow the ratio of any relevant case which is binding on it under the doctrine of precedent. Thus, the question arises, when is a case relevant? A case in the same area must be followed unless it can be distinguished on the basis of its facts. If the facts of the case cannot be distinguished, if the case is "on all fours," then it must be followed. The process of distinguishing cases is really just another way of deciding what the ratio of the case is. If the material facts necessary for the operation of the legal rule in the first case are not found in the second, or are different, there is no precedent. Just as lawyers differ about what the ratio to a case is, so they differ about whether a case is binding in a particular situation or not. Judges sometime distinguish cases on flimsy grounds simply to avoid having to follow precedents which they find unwelcome.

That which is not part of the ratio of the case is said to be the *obiter dictum*. This is usually refered to as the *obiter*. Obiter is said to have persuasive authority. That which was said obiter in a court such as the House of Lords may be very persuasive indeed for a relatively inferior court such as a County Court. Moreover, remarks made obiter may indicate which way the law is developing or which kinds of arguments judges find particularly persuasive. Equally, judges are not always very careful about differentiating between ratio and obiter.

The remainder of this section provides some guidance on how to study cases. The first question a student should ask about a case is "Why has this case been set?" The purpose of studying cases is to obtain an understanding of the relevance of the case to the area of law being studied. Some cases will be more important than others. A leading House of Lords decision will require more time and closer examination than a decision which is merely illustrative of a point mentioned in a lecture or included in a problem. Where a case has developed or defined an area of law it is usually helpful to start by reading what the textbook writers say about it. Where more than one case has to be read on the same point of law, they should, if possible, be read in chronological order and each one digested before moving on to the next. If the subject under consideration is not an area of substantive law, such as tort or contract, but procedure or precedent, different aspects of the case will be important. In reading the case it is essential that the relevance of the case is borne in mind.

A second question to ask when reading cases is, "How much time is available?" Try to spend more time on important decisions and important judgments, even if you have to rely on a headnote or a textbook when it comes to the others. Do not spend the greater proportion of your time reading cases which have been overruled or which have novel or interesting facts but no new point of law. The headnote is helpful when allocating time. Treat judgments in the same way you treat cases. Do not waste your time reading judgments which merely repeat something you have already read. Spend more time on the leading judgments than the others. Again the headnote will be helpful for this. Some judgments are more clearly written than others. Some judgments are shorter than others. Neither clarity not brevity necessarily mean that the judgment is more important. Choose what you read because it is the best for your purposes, not because it is the easiest.

Notes on any case should start with the case name and any references. They should then include:

(1) a brief statement of the facts of the case.
(2) the history of the case.
(3) the point of law under consideration.
(4) the decision with the reasons for it, together with any names of cases relied on.

One side of A4 paper should provide enough space for this basic information leaving the reverse side free for individual notes from judgments and, where necessary, any comments. Some students prefer to keep notes of cases on file cards. These are easier to refer to quickly but less can be put on them.

When reading judgments in order to make notes look for agreement and disgreement on each of the points relevant to your study.

It is often useful to make separate notes on each of the points raised by the case and then see what different judges said about them. Do not forget to make it clear in your notes whether a judge was dissenting or not.

HOW TO READ A STATUTE

This section will explain how you should read statutes. The way in which statutes are created is explained on pages 4–6. Looking for a particular legal rule in a statute can be confusing. Some statutes are over 100 pages long, although most are shorter. The language they use often appears complicated and obscure. If you understand the structure of a statute and follow a few simple rules in reading them statutes will become much clearer.

A copy of a statute, the Coal Industry Act 1983, is reproduced below. All subsequent references here are to this statute.

ELIZABETH II   c. 60   1

[Royal Seal]

Coal Industry Act 1983

1983 CHAPTER 60

An Act to increase the limit on the borrowing powers of the
National Coal Board; and to make further provision
with respect to grants and payments by the Secretary
of State in connection with the coal industry.
                                    [21st December 1983]

BE IT ENACTED by the Queen's most Excellent Majesty, by and
with the advice and consent of the Lords Spiritual and
Temporal, and Commons, in this present Parliament
assembled, and by the authority of the same, as follows:—

1. In section 1(3) of the 1965 Act (which, as amended by
section 1 of the 1982 Act, provides for a limit of £4,500 million
on the borrowing of the Board and their wholly owned subsidiaries but enables that limit to be increased by order up to
£5,000 million) for "£4,500 million" and "£5,000 million"
there shall be substituted "£5,500 million" and "£6,000 million" respectively.

Borrowing
powers of
National Coal
Board.

2.—(1) In subsection (1) of section 3 of the 1980 Act (which,
as amended by section 2(1) of the 1982 Act, provides for the
payment of grants in respect of group deficits for financial years
of the Board ending in or before March 1984) for the words
from "for a financial year of the Board" onwards there shall
be substituted "for the financial years of the Board ending in
March 1984, 1985 and 1986".

Deficit and
operating
grants.

(2) For subsection (4) of that section there shall be substituted—

"(4) The aggregate of the grants made under this section during the financial years of the Board referred to in subsection (1) above shall not exceed £1,200 million, but the Secretary of State may with the approval of the Treasury, on one or more occasions, by order made by statutory instrument increase or further increase that limit up to £2,000 million.

(5) An order shall not be made under subsection (4) above unless a draft of the order has been laid before and approved by a resolution of the House of Commons."

(3) The following enactments shall cease to have effect, namely—

section 8 of the 1973 Act (grants as respects coking coal supplied during the financial years of the Board ending in March 1980, 1981, 1982 and 1983);

section 2 of the 1977 Act (grants for or by reference to those financial years for promoting the sale of coal to Electricity Boards);

section 3 of the 1977 Act (grants towards costs incurred in those financial years in connection with stocks of coal or coke); and

sections 4 and 5(2) of the 1980 Act (limit on aggregate amount of grants under the above enactments and under section 3 of the 1980 Act).

Grants in connection with pit closures.

3.—(1) Section 6 of the 1977 Act (grants in connection with pit closures) shall be amended as follows.

(2) In subsection (3) (which, as amended by section 6(1)(a) of the 1980 Act, provides for such grants to be made towards expenditure of the Board for financial years of the Board ending in or before March 1984) for "and 1984" there shall be substituted "1984, 1985 and 1986."

(3) In subsection (5) (which, as amended by section 4(1) of the 1982 Act, provides for a limit of £200 million on the aggregate amount of grants under section 6), for "£200 million" there shall be substituted "£400 million".

Payments to or in respect of redundant workers.

4.—(1) Section 7 of the 1977 Act (payments to or in respect of redundant workers) shall be amended as follows.

(2) In subsection (1) (which, as amended by section 7(2) of the 1980 Act, provides that the qualifying period for payments under

a scheme under section 7 ends with March 1984) for " 1st April 1984 " there shall be substituted " 30th March 1986 ".

(3) In subsection (5) (which, as amended by section 4(2) of the 1982 Act, provides for a limit of £300 million on the aggregate amount of such payments during the financial years of the Board ending in or before March 1984) for the words from "and 1984 " onwards there shall be substituted " 1984, 1985 and 1986 shall not exceed £1,200 million."

5. In this Act—	Interpretation.
" the 1965 Act " means the Coal Industry Act 1965 ;	1965 c. 82.
" the 1973 Act " means the Coal Industry Act 1973 ;	1973 c. 8.
" the 1977 Act " means the Coal Industry Act 1977 ;	1977 c. 39.
" the 1980 Act " means the Coal Industry Act 1980 ;	1980 c. 50.
" the 1982 Act " means the Coal Industry Act 1982 ;	1982 c. 15.
" the Board " means the National Coal Board.	

6.—(1) This Act may be cited as the Coal Industry Act 1983. Citation, repeals and
(2) This Act and the Coal Industry Acts 1946 to 1982 may be extent.
cited together as the Coal Industry Acts 1946 to 1983.

(3) The enactments mentioned in the Schedule to this Act (which include certain spent provisions) are hereby repealed to the extent specified in the third column of that Schedule.

(4) This Act does not extend to Northern Ireland.

4   c. 60   *Coal Industry Act 1983*

Section 6(3).   S C H E D U L E
                                    REPEALS

Chapter	Short title	Extent of repeal
1973 c. 8.	The Coal Industry Act 1973.	Section 8.
1977 c. 39.	The Coal Industry Act 1977.	Sections 2 and 3.
1980 c. 50.	The Coal Industry Act 1980.	Sections 4 and 5. Section 7(2).
1982 c. 15.	The Coal Industry Act 1982.	Sections 1 and 2. Section 4. In section 5, the definitions of " the Act of 1965 " and " the Act of 1980 ".

You can find statutes in a number of different ways. Not all of the statutes which you find will look the same as the one which we have reproduced for you. One way to find a statute is to buy it from Her Majesty's Stationery Office, the official stockist for Government publications, or one of its agents. These copies look much the same as the one which we have reproduced but they have, in addition, a contents list at the beginning. Statutes are also printed in a number of different series with different volumes for each year. The copy of the Coal Industry Act 1983 which you are referring to is taken from such a series published by the Incorporated Council of Law Reporting. Some series of statutes are printed in an annotated form. This means that the statute is printed with an accompanying explanatory text, telling you what the statute does. If you use an annotated statute, remember that only the words of the statute are definitive. The explanatory text, although often helpful, is only the opinion of the author.

The different parts

1. This is the *short title* of the Act, together with its year of publication. When you are writing about a statute, it is normal to use the short title and year of publication to describe the statute. Sometimes, when a statute is referred to constantly, the short title is abbreviated. Thus, the Matrimonial Causes Act 1973 is often referred to as the M.C.A. 1973. If you work in a particular area of law, you will quickly learn the standard abbreviations for that area.

2. This is the official *citation* for the statute. Each Act passed in any one year is given its own number. This is known as its *chapter number*. Thus you can decribe a statute by its chapter number and year. The citation, 1983 Chapter 60, could only mean the Coal Industry Act 1983. Chapter in the official citation may be abbreviated to c. as in the top right hand corner of your copy of the statute. This form of official citation began in 1963. Before that stautes were identified by the regnal year in which they occurred in, followed by their chapter number. A regnal year is a year of a monarch's reign. Thus, "30 Geo 3 Chapter 3" refers to the Treason Act 1790 which was passed in the 30th year of George III's reign. It is much easier to remember and use the short title of an Act rather than its official citation.

3. This is the *long title* of the Act. The long title gives some indication of the purpose behind the Act. It may be of some use in deciding what the Act is all about. However the long title may be misleading. For example the long title of the Parliament Act 1911

indicates that the Act is part of a process of abolishing the House of Lords. The House of Lords is still there. Long titles are sometimes vague and may conflict with the main body of the Act. In the event of such a conflict the legal rule is that expressed in the main body of the Act.

4. This indicates when the *royal assent* was given and the Coal Industry Bill 1983 became an Act. Statutes become law on the date when they receive the royal assent *unless the Act says otherwise*. The statute itself may say that it becomes law on a fixed date after the royal assent or it may give a Government Minister the power to decide when it becomes law. When a Minister brings a statute into effect after the date on which it has been passed a commencement order must be made. This is a form of delegated legislation. Statutes do not have a retrospective effect unless the Act expressly says so.

5. This is known as the *enacting formula*. It is the standard form of words used to indicate that a Bill has been properly passed by all the different parts of the legislature.

6. By each section you will find a short explanation of the content of that section. These *marginal notes* may help you understand the content of the section if it is otherwise unclear.

The main body of the statute which follows is broken up into numbered *sections*. Each section contains a different rule of law. When you refer to a rule of law contained in a statute, you should say where that rule of law is to be found. This enables others to check your source and to see whether or not they agree with your interpretation of the law. Instead of writing "section," it is usual to abbreviate it to "s." Thus, section 1 becomes s.1. Sections are often further subdivided. These sub-divisions are known as subsections. When you wish to refer to a subsection you should add it in brackets after the main section.

Example

Does the Coal Industry Act 1983 apply to Northern Ireland? No. See s.6(4) Coal Industry Act 1983.

In larger statutes, sections may be grouped together into different *Parts*. Each Part will deal with a separate area of law. Looking for the correct Part will help you to find the particular legal rule that you want.

Some statutes have one or more *Schedules* at the end. The content of these varies. Some contain detailed provisions which are not found in the main body of the Act. Others are merely convenient reminders and summaries of legal rules, and changes to legal rules, found elsewhere in the Act. In the Coal Industry Act 1983, for example, there is one Schedule to say which sections of previous statutes have been repealed by the 1983 Act. However this Schedule is just there as a reminder. The actual repeals have already been detailed in the main body of the Act. References to Schedules are often abbreviated as "Sched." Where a Schedule is divided up, the divisions are known as *paragraphs* and can be abbreviated as "para.".

USING A STATUTE

Your use of statutory material will vary. Sometimes you will be referred to a particular section or sections of a statute in a case, article, or book that you are reading. In other instances, a new statute will be passed which you need to assess as a whole in order to see how it affects those areas of law that you are interested in. In either case, when first reading statutory material, you may be able to gain some help in deciding what it means from commentaries. Commentaries are explanations of the law written by legal academics or practitioners. Annotated statutes, which were discussed earlier, are one useful source of such commentaries. You may also find such commentaries in books and articles on the area of law in which the statute falls. Always remember that a commentary represents only one author's opinion of what the statute says. In the case of a very new statute there will probably be no commentary. Therefore, you will need to be able to read a statute yourself, so that you can assess the value of other's opinions and form your own view when there is no other help available.

When reading a statute, do not begin at the beginning and then work your way through to the end, section by section. Statutes do not necessarily use words to mean the same thing that they do in ordinary conversation. Before you can decide what a statute is about you need to know if there are any special meanings attached to words in it. These special meanings can be found in the Act, often in sections called *definition* or *interpretation sections*. These are frequently found towards the end of the Act. For example, in the Coal Industry Act 1983, definitions of some of the phrases used in the Act are found in section 5. An Act may have more than one definition section. Sometimes Parliament, when laying down a particular meaning for a word will say that that meaning will apply in all statutes in which that word appears. Unless a statute specifically says this, you should assume that a definition in a statute applies only to the use of the word in that statute.

You are now in a position to decide what new legal rules the statute creates. Some people begin this task by reading the long title of
the Act to give themselves some idea of the general aim of the statute. Although this can be helpful, as we saw above in the section
on the different parts of the Act, it can also be misleading.

Statutes should be read carefully and slowly. The general rule is
that a statute means precisely what it says. Each word is important. Because of this, some words which we use loosely in ordinary
conversation take on special significance when found in a statute.
For example, it is important to distinguish between words like
"may" and "shall," one saying you can do something and the
other saying you must do something. Conjunctives, such as "and,"
joining things together, must be distinguished from disjunctives,
such as "or," dividing things apart.

Example

> Part of one process of getting a divorce involves showing that
> a husband and wife have been separated for 2 years *and* that
> they both consent to the divorce. (Section 1(2)(*d*) Matri-
> monial Causes Act 1973) This would be a very different pro-
> vision if it said that it was necessary for there to be proof that
> the couple had been separated for 2 years *or* that they had
> both consented to the divorce. As the law stands the couple
> must show that both requirements are fulfilled. If a disjunc-
> tive were substituted, in the law, a couple would need to
> prove only one or other of the conditions existed.

So far, the emphasis has been upon closely reading the particular
statute. You should also remember that the statute should be read
in the context of the general Acts, rules and principles of statutory
interpretation discussed in Chapter 1.

One further thing to remember when reading a statute is that the
fact that it has been printed does not mean that it is part of the law
of the land. It may have been repealed. It may not yet be in force.
Re-read pages 48–51 if you cannot remember how to find out if a
statute has been repealed. Go back and read about the royal
assent on page 74 if you cannot remember how to find out if a statute is in force.

STATUTORY INSTRUMENTS

What statutory instruments are, the way in which they are created,
and the purposes which they have, are discussed on page 5.

Statutory instruments should be read in the same way as statutes. However, whilst statutes make relatively little reference to other sources, statutory instruments because of their purpose, make very frequent reference either to other statutory instruments or to their parent statute. The legislative power has been given only for a limited purpose, the statutory instrument is a small part of a larger whole. For this reason, you will find it much more difficult to understand a statutory instrument if you do not have access to the surrounding legislation. Before reading a statutory instrument it is vital that you understand the legislative framework into which it fits.

CHAPTER 6

Reading research materials

Chapter 4 explained that one of the ways of answering questions about law was the use of the research methods of the social scientist. Because this kind of research is the only way in which some questions about law can be answered, it is important that those interested in law can understand it.

In order to understand research into law you have to understand how and why it is written in the particular way that it is. Once you can understand the structure of the material, you will be able to see whether or not it helps to answer the questions in which you are interested.

Haphazard approaches to research are likely to be unsuccessful, the information gathered being too unrepresentative of the world at large and, therefore, too inaccurate for any conclusions to be drawn safely. Good research is done systematically. Research methods are highly developed.

There are three sources of information about how and why the law operates: records, people and activities. There are also three principle methods used in socio-legal research. The researcher may read records, interview people (or send questionnaires), or observe activities.

RECORD READING

The researcher reads the records and collects the required information, which is then either written down or noted on a prepared recording sheet. The researcher must ensure that the information collected from each record is as accurate and as complete as possible. This may involve searching through disordered files of letters and notes or simply copying the details from a form, such as a divorce petition.

INTERVIEWS AND QUESTIONNAIRES

Interviews are conducted in person; questionnaires are given, or sent, to the respondents to complete. It is important, in so far as is possible, to ask the same questions in the same way each time so as to get comparable information. Questions may be "open-ended," allowing the respondent to reply in his or her own words, or be "closed," requiring selection of the answer from a choice given by the interviewer. The style and wording of the question is selected to fit the data sought. Whatever the questions, the interview must be recorded. This may be done by using a tape recorder or by the interviewer noting the replies. Interviews are most useful for finding out what reasons people have for what they have done and for exploring their feelings. If questions are asked about the future, the answers can only indicate what respondents currently think they would do. It has also been established that recollection of past events may be inaccurate, particularly about dates, times and the exact sequence of events. Interview and questionnaire design requires considerable skill, as does interviewing itself, if it is to reflect the respondent's views rather than those of the researcher.

OBSERVATION

The observer attends the event and records what occurs there. The observer may be an outsider, for example, a person watching court proceedings from the public gallery. Alternatively, the observer may be a person actually taking part in the events being described, for example, a police officer researching into the police force. Observation needs to be done systematically and accurately in order to avoid bias. Observers cannot record everything that they see. They must be careful that they do not record only what they want to see and neglect that which is unexpected and, perhaps, thereby unwelcome. One great difficulty in noting observations lies in deciding what to note down and what to omit. What seems unimportant at the time the notes were taken may take on a greater significance when a later analysis is made. It is important that the observer's record is contemporaneous, otherwise the data is weakened by what has been forgotten.

For any particular piece of research, one method may be more suitable than another, because of the nature of the data sources or the approach which the researcher wishes to take. If, for example, you want to research into the reasons magistrates have for their decisions, there is little point in reading records of what those decisions were. Here, the best place to start would be to interview magistrates. No single method can be said to provide the truth about every situation; some would argue that no method can provide *the* truth about any situation, for no one truth exists. Each method provides information based on the perceptions of the people who provide it, the record keepers, the interviewers or the observers.

Choice of research method depends not only on what information is sought but also on practicalities. The researcher may not be given access to records or permitted to carry out interviews. Professional bodies and employers are not always willing to let their members or staff participate in research. This may be because they consider the research unethical (perhaps requiring them to divulge information given in confidence), because they are too busy, because they do not see the value of the research or because they wish to conceal the very information in which the researcher is interested. Thus, for example, it is unusual for researchers to be able to interview judges about cases, although there is nothing to prevent them sitting in the public gallery and watching cases from there.

For many research studies more than one method is used to obtain a complete picture. However, practical matters, including budget and time limits, may mean that not every avenue of enquiry is pursued. What is important is that the methods chosen are appropriate to the subject of study, the approach of the researcher and the conclusions drawn.

SAMPLING

Looking at every case is not normally practical in detailed social research. Instead, the researcher takes a *sample* of cases. Thus, one may interview some lawyers or some defendants or observe, or read records at some courts. If a completely random sample is taken, then it should have the characteristics of the population as a whole. A sample of judges should, for example, include judges of the different ages, backgrounds and experience to be found amongst the judiciary. However, if a characteristic is very rare, a sample may not contain any example having that characteristic. Thus, a 10 per cent. sample of judges, (*i.e.* contacting every tenth judge) might well fail to include any women judges since there are very few of them. The size of sample and method of sampling must be chosen to fit with the study. In a study of attitudes of clients to lawyers there is clearly no point in interviewing only successful clients. The number of people refusing to take part in a study is also important. Researchers will try to obtain a high *response rate* (over 75 per cent.) and also attempt to find out if those who refuse are likely to be different in any material way from those who agree to participate in the study.

RESEARCH FINDINGS

The account of any research will usually include some background information about the subject, the purpose of the study (the questions to be answered) and the methods used. Findings presented in words should cause no difficulty to the reader, but numbers may be quite confusing. Where comparisons are made, it is usually thought better to use either *proportions* or *percentages* rather than actual numbers. It is then important to be clear what the percentage represents: for example, was it 20 per cent. of all plaintiffs or 20 per cent. of successful plaintiffs. Some researchers do not give the actual figures, but prefer to use words such as "some," "most" or "the majority." This is not very helpful, since a word like "majority" can mean anything from 51 per cent. to 99 per cent. There is a variety of ways of presenting figures so as to make them clearer. *Tables* (lists of figures) are commonly used because they make it easier to compare two or more categories or questions. *Graphic presentation*, using bar charts (histograms), pie charts or graphs, can create a clear overall impression of a complex set of figures.

Figure 1 below is a *bar chart*. It shows clearly the different numbers of the three offences where guns were used. It also shows for each the relative proportion in which particular types of gun were used. As can be seen from this example, the greatest advantage of a bar chart is the way in which it makes a quick visual comparison of information easy.

Figure 2 is a *pie chart*. The whole circle represents 100 per cent. of the particular group. The segments represent different percentages. In this example, the exact percentages represented in the different segments have been printed on to the chart. This is not always done. Different circles represent both different types of original sentence and different courts in which that sentence was imposed. The segments themselves indicate what happened to people who breached their orginal sentence: for example, by committing a further crime whilst on probation.

Figure 3 is a *graph*. This is probably the best way of showing a trend over time. The graph is designed to show the rise in the

Figure 1 Notifiable offences in which firearms were reported to have been used, by type of offence and type of weapon

England and Wales 1982

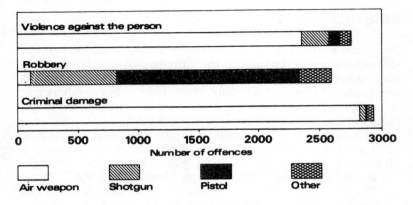

Figures 1, 2 and 3 on pp. 77–78 are from *Criminal Statistics 1982*, HMSO.

Figure 2 Persons breaching their original sentence or order by type of sentence or order imposed for the breach

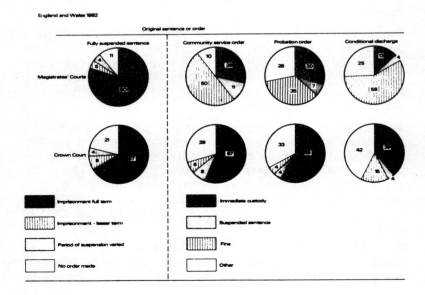

Figure 3 Females found guilty of, or cautioned for, indictable offences[1] per 100,000 population in the age group by age

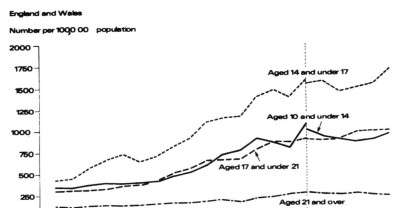

England and Wales

Number per 100,000 population

[1] 1962–76 not adjusted for Criminal Law Act 1977 nor the change in the counting of proceedings.

number of females found guilty of indictable (basically, serious offences). There are two major problems in doing this. One is that an increase in numbers caused by an increase in the size of the population as a whole is not very interesting. Thus, rather than counting the absolute number of offenders, the graph shows the number of offenders per 100,000 in the population. Secondly, the law relating to who is guilty of an indictable offence was changed in the course of the period which the graph records. Thus, some of the increase in the number of offenders may be due to the fact that the categories of indictable crime have become different. The graph indicates this by showing a dotted vertical line through 1977 (the year in which the change took effect).

As well as graphs and tables, most researchers will state the conclusions that they have drawn from the material and summarise the main findings of the study. It is crucial that the data should establish no more and no less than is stated in the conclusions. Some researchers make great claims for their data, whilst others do not draw out all the answers which it could provide. To avoid being persuaded by poor reasoning, look at the data and see what conclusions seem appropriate, then read the explanation given, and compare it with what you originally thought.

A critical approach to any empirical research should always consider the following three questions. First, are the methods chosen appropriate? This includes both, "have the right questions been asked" and "have the right people (people who should know about the topic) been asked?" There may have been better sources of information available to the researcher, but were the ones used good enough for this study? Secondly, is the sample big enough and has it been properly drawn? Thirdly, does the data justify the conclusions which have been drawn? If it does not, can you see any other conclusions which it would justify?

Research often leaves as many questions raised as answers provided. Further studies may be indicated, interesting new areas which need to be explored. Studying this type of material will, hopefully, increase your interest and insight into the operation of law. It will not provide you with all the answers.

CHAPTER 7

Study skills

INTRODUCTION

The purpose of this chapter is to help you to think about study techniques. Probably the most important thing to aim for is to take an active approach to your studying and the techniques you use. This means working out for yourself what methods work for you. It also means thinking about new strategies when you run into difficulties, such as when you have problems in understanding, or in maintaining interest or concentration. A passive attitude to learning means relying too much on lecturers, teachers and others to tell you what to do or what is good or bad about your work. These external sources should be helpful, but are additional to, and not a substitute for, self-monitoring and personal adaptation. *There is no single set of "good" study methods which works for everyone.* Successful students use a wide range of techniques. Some of these are suggested below. Be prepared to try out some of them: be critical. The test of your study technique is not whether it resembles that of a (non-existent) "ideal" student, but whether it suits your personality and is appropriate for the level of understanding which you require.

UNDERSTANDING YOUR COURSE

Many students do not know very much about the courses they start. You are likely to get more out of your course if you understand what is required and how the course is organised. For each subject, check:

> * *syllabus*: what topics are covered? Is there a recommended textbook(s)? Make sure you get hold of all lecture handouts and reading lists.

* *assessment*: by exam/exam and course work/course work only? Make sure you know exam dates and coursework deadlines.

* *assignments*: how many essays, projects or other written assignments have to be submitted, and when?

* *tutorials/seminars/discussion groups*: how many? When? What preparation is expected?

* *lectures*: how many, where and when? Compulsory or optional?

ORGANISING YOUR TIME

Make a list of the things which you have to do. Make both a weekly and a daily time-table. Put in lectures, tutorials, seminars, sessions for private study, social life and routine things. Be realistic about the time you spend on recreation, coffee breaks, shopping, cleaning, eating and so on. Keep an element of flexibility in planning your timetable. Remember when and where you work best and what puts you off.

Try to avoid long periods of time under a vague heading of "studying." Instead, try and break down your work as much as possible into smaller units, for example, a series of tasks each taking 45–55 minutes. Have a specific target in mind, such as reading certain cases or a chapter of your textbook, and concentrate on completing one task at a time. Sandwich the more difficult or less enjoyable tasks between the others. Make use of the spare time which crops up between timetabled classes. Time-limits and targets help both concentration and motivation.

READING AND NOTE-TAKING

Many students spend a lot of time reading, yet have difficulty in concentrating and feel that they have taken nothing in when they have finished. These problems usually arise because the student is reading everything in the same way and is not used to adapting the reading to suit different purposes. Common mistakes are:

* *unnecessary reading, e.g.* reading the whole of a chapter or case when all you want is a specific piece of information in one paragraph.

* *wrong type of reading, e.g.* reading generally when you should be reading critically, or trying to get a detailed understanding of each page when you only need an overview.

REMEMBER: *Books, articles, cases and statutes are read at different rates, and in different ways, for different purposes.*

1. Before you start reading, identify your purpose. For example, is it:

* background reading for an essay?

* checking a detail mentioned in a lecture?

* setting out a line of argument for a seminar?

* criticising the logic of a judgment?

* understanding the basic principles of an area of law?

2. Select the type of reading suitable for your purpose. There are five main types of reading, in increasing order of intensity:

(a) reading for *enjoyment*: light reading.

(b) reading for *overview*: getting a general idea of the gist of a topic.

(c) *search* reading: looking for some specific piece of information.

(d) reading for *mastery*: to get detailed information or understanding of a topic.

(e) *critical* reading: reading for stimulus or to challenge and assess ideas, values or arguments.

3. Do not start at the beginning. Whichever type of reading you are doing, do a quick scan or survey of your material.

For overview reading, check the contents list, chapter headings and sub-headings, and the introduction and conclusion. This should be enough to gain a general understanding of what the material is about and for you to make a short list of key points. This may be all you want. If you go on to read all or part of the material, do it quickly, for you are only trying to get an overall impression. In reading cases, for example, you may only need to read through the headnote to get an overview.

For search reading, scan as in overview or use the index to identify the relevant section. Find and read the section quickly to check it has the details you want. If it has, re-read and note down the details you want. If it has not, go back to the index or try another source. Do not waste time by reading the whole book in the hope that you will find something else.

For mastery, try the "SQ3R" method. Start by scanning the material for an overall impression. Then, taking a paragraph, section or chapter at a time:

> SURVEY the passage, to get an idea of what it is about, (*e.g.* "the key elements of negligence").
>
> QUESTION by turning the statement into a question, (*e.g.* "What are the key elements of negligence?").
>
> READ the passage actively to find the answer to your question.
>
> RECITE what you find (this is best done in your own words).
>
> REVIEW or check to be sure that you understand accurately what you have read.

Reading actively like this helps your concentration and understanding. Don't take notes until the RECITE or REVIEW phases. By this time you should be clear about what are the major points and what are the minor ones. *Note only the major ideas*, and try to make them as brief as possible. Most students take too many notes. *Always try to use your own words*—if you cannot rephrase what you have read, you have probably not understood it. If you want to copy out a particular sentence, such as a key quotation from a judgement, make sure that you prune the quote to its essentials. Do not copy out long passages.

For *critical* reading the SQ3R method may also be useful for understanding the reading you are about to assess. In assessing reading, look for:

> * *arguments*: consider any assumptions or assertions that are made. Are they justified? Are the steps in the argument logical? Are there missing steps? Can you think of counter-arguments?
>
> * *evidence*: what exactly is the evidence relied on? Is it partial or distorted? Is more evidence needed? Do you know of any counter evidence?
>
> * *conclusions*: are they based on the evidence and arguments? Has the author made too much or too little of the material?

Taking notes from your reading

It should now be clear that you are likely to take different kinds of notes according to the reasons you have for reading the material. Here are some general points:

1. Start by making a note of the *title* of the book or article that you are reading. If it is in a library, you should also note the *classification number* in case you want to return to it later. If you are making a case note, write down the *reference* to the law report you are using. The reference that you make must be good enough to allow you to find the book, article or case again if you need to.

2. Do not take notes until you have skimmed the material and then read in full the sections which you have decided are important. Only then will you have a clear idea about the organisation of the ideas and the main points.

3. Make notes on your second reading. Keep your notes brief. Use your own words.

4. Reference your own notes with the relevant paragraph, page or chapter, so you can refer back to the place from which you took the note if necessary.

5. Add your comments and criticisms, clearly marked as either your own or from another source. Reference further sources.

6. Organise the notes you take: well laid out notes are easier to read, understand and remember at revision time. So, leave a wide margin and plenty of space between points, and use capitals, underlining, numbering or different colours to make points stand out. Keep your notes in a loose-leaf file so you can add to them later.

7. Some students prefer to underline and make notes in their own textbooks rather than to take notes from them. This can be useful in the short term but is not a good substitute for taking notes because:

    (a) you may be reading the book for one purpose now but want to use it for a different purpose later. Underlining is distracting when you are looking for different ideas or if you have changed your mind about what is important in the text.

    (b) marking a book avoids re-phrasing the main ideas. If you are aiming to master difficult ideas the best way of checking that you have understood is to explain them in your own words.

(c) you may want to sell the book.

LECTURES AND TAKING LECTURE NOTES

Lectures are the backbone of most law courses. They will indicate the syllabus to be covered, provide references and suggest aspects of the subject which are worth exploring further.

Lecturing styles vary a great deal. Some lecturers will aim to cover all of the course topics in detail. Others will give you a basic outline, and will select certain issues for particular attention or analysis. Often the choice depends on whether a textbook is available which covers the course topics at the desired depth of treatment. *If there is a recommended textbook, buy it and use it*. It is also a standard practice on many law courses to give detailed lecture handouts with the full references for any cases, sections of statutes or useful reading which will be mentioned in the lecture. This not only saves you time in note-taking, but is a valuable guide to the structure of the lectures and the course.

The best way to understand and remember what a lecture is about is to listen carefully and question mentally what the lecturer is saying. Note-taking is helpful in two ways: (a) it keeps you active in the lecture, helping you concentrate on the points that are made, and (b) it provides you with a written record to come back to later, for essay writing or revision. DO NOT TRY TO WRITE EVERYTHING DOWN: aim for structure and the main ideas, not a mass of detail.

Your lecturer will probably be working from notes that have been broken down into sections and sub-headings. Listen carefully for *key words and phrases* that indicate the organisation of the material. For example:

"There are four main points . . . Now . . . Then . . . Next . . . Finally"

These indicate a series of main points. These are often organised according to importance.

"Above all, Chief, Least important."

Major points are often followed by supporting points. These may back up what has been said,

"For instance, to illustrate."

or qualify what has been said,

"Yet, But, However."

Get ready for the end, which may be a last argument or general conclusion:

"Thus, consequently, in conclusion."

Most lecturers will try to help you by pausing before important points or new sections. If a point is stressed repeatedly, the lecturer wants you to remember it. Ask questions if you do not understand.

Organise your notes in the way suggested under "reading" on page 89. Leave lots of space for later additions and to increase visual impact, so that the key points "spring out of the page" on re-reading. It is easier to rearrange and add to your notes later if you use a loose-leaf file and write only on one side of the paper. After the lecture, review your notes as soon as possible (same day) to correct unclear sentences and add details which make the points clear.

WRITING ESSAYS

1. Understanding the task

Read the question carefully to make sure you understand what is required. Look carefully at the key words and phrases which indicate the sort of answer you are expected to give. For example:

* *What is the significance of . . . ?* Give a definition, followed by an outline of uses, consequences and implications.

* *Discuss.* Give facts and their interpretation from all sides of the argument. Try to arrive at a conclusion.

* *Contrast.* Set in opposition in order to bring out differences.

* *Criticise.* Give your views about the matter backing your judgment with a discussion of the evidence.

* *Evaluate.* Give your opinion of the worth of something in the light of its truth and usefulness.

* *Outline/Summarise.* Give the main points, leaving out details and emphasising structure.

2. Getting started

Now think about the question and how it could be answered. Work out what kind of information you will be looking for in your reading. You may already know some of the answers.

Example

"English law does not recognise a remedy in tort for invasion of privacy, although such recognition is long overdue." Discuss.

Tackle this by questioning the statement. Do not assume any statement quoted is accurate or that you will agree with it. So, you might ask:

Does English law recognise a remedy in tort for invasion of privacy? You will need to look for cases and statutes where such a remedy has been granted or denied to clarify the factual situation. Think of further questions at this stage: Suppose a remedy has been recognised, how wide or how limited is its application? Suppose it has not, is privacy protected in other ways?

Is such recognition overdue? If you already have ideas on the matter, jot them down. Look out for books, articles, textbook and case note analysis on whether the state of law is satisfactory. Look for arguments both for and against the proposition.

Next get hold of your sources. Check through your lecture notes, look up the topic in your textbook, follow up references in your textbook and from your reading list to find cases, statutes, articles, official reports or books on the matter. Use SEARCH reading techniques to find the information you want quickly, followed by MASTERY or CRITICAL reading when you find important passages. Then think about the question again in the light of what you know. It often helps at this stage to discuss the essay with other students.

3. Planning

You will have more material from your reading than you will use in your essay. The planning stage is important for identifying the main ideas and most relevant material and for weeding out less important material. Do not be tempted to throw in things just to show that you know about them or because you found them interesting. The test is, does the item help to answer the question?

Jot down the main ideas as they come to you, or, alternatively, use the brain pattern technique illustrated below. Take a large piece of paper, put the subject of the essay in the middle and circle it. Then jot down your facts and ideas radiating from the subject. Many people find it easier to see relationships in this way.

Then order your points in a logical sequence to form an essay plan.

4. Writing the essay

Check the length that is expected of the essay. At degree level this is usually about 4–6 sides of A4 paper in average handwriting. Before you start, summarise, in three to four sentences, what the essay is about. This is your brief answer. It will help you to keep to the point and you might use this summary later as your concluding paragraph.

The first paragraph should indicate what will follow and how you propose to approach the topic. In the middle part of the essay, make sure that you keep to the subject and that everything you say answers part of the question. Start a new paragraph for each main idea and try to write a whole paragraph at a time as this will help your writing "flow." Use short, clear sentences in preference to long, rambling ones. Try to support each main idea with examples, relevant facts or authorities, making clear where information or quotations you used came from. Do not make statements which invite the response "prove it." The last paragraph should sum up the main points, making clear your conclusions. It should not just be a précis of the essay.

Check the essay through to see that the sentences make sense and that spelling, grammar and punctuation are correct. Before you hand it in, show the essay to a friend or review it yourself. Put yourself in the position of your tutor. What criticisms would you make of your essay? Can you do anything about them?

5. Problem questions

In many law subjects you will be expected to write answers to "problem" questions. A hypothetical set of facts will be given and you will be asked to "discuss" the matter or "advise" one of the characters in the problem.

The preliminary stages in answering a problem question are much the same as in answering an essay question. Clarify what you have to do, pose questions and look for the answers in your reading. Like most essays, there will be one or two major points that will require extended discussion, together with a number of minor points which may or may not be included. However, many stu-

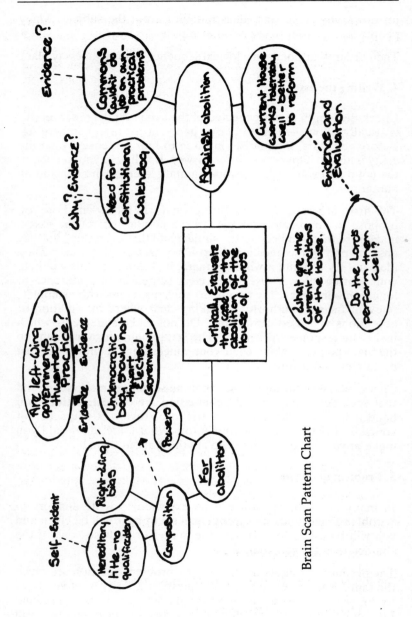

Brain Scan Pattern Chart

dents experience some difficulties with problem questions, in (a) identifying the range of potential issues; (b) selecting the most important; and (c) seeing the logical sequence in dealing with them. The potential issues and the logical sequence will depend upon the legal topic, and you should discuss this with your tutor. The most important points will vary according to the question set. Train yourself to develop a systematic approach to problems in the area of law you are studying, always bearing in mind that, for a particular problem set, you will probably need to concentrate on only one or two aspects.

Example

Ronald set fire to his house in order to claim an insurance premium. When he started the fire, he was not sure whether his tenant, Nancy, was on holiday or at home. In fact, Nancy was asleep in the house and was killed.

Discuss Ronald's criminal liability.

1. First, jot down all the offences Ronald may have committed. In this case, for example, arson, murder, if not murder, then manslaughter, etc.

2. Next identify what you think the main points for discussion will be. For example, had Ronald the requisite "malice aforethought" to be found guilty of murder.

3. Now do your reading. Make sure that the reading you do tells you what each of the legal elements of any issue are.

4. Now answer the problem. Order your material. Make sure you give more space to the more important points. Where several crimes must be considered, deal with the most serious first, unless guilt is very doubtful. In that case, start with the clearest crime. Make sure you discuss all the possible arguments.

COMMON MISTAKES IN WRITTEN WORK

1. Not answering the question set

The following are all variations of this basic mistake:

* regurgitation of lecture notes.

* plagiarism (copying sections from a book or article without attributing them to the author).

Apart from the element of cheating involved in both of the above, neither lecture notes nor a book or article are likely to precisely answer the question.

* discussing only one side of the question.

* not advising the party as asked in the question but, rather, producing a general outline of the law on the topic.

In both of the above, the mistake lies in failing to follow the instruction given. What is said in the answer may be very good but it will receive poor marks because it is not what was required.

* writing down everything known about a topic in the hope that some of it is relevant. This is a particular problem in examination answers.

* lengthy discussion of minor or irrelevant points.

Part of the skill demonstrated in any answer is the ability to identify that which is relevant. Answers with the above faults may be correct in what they say but will get poor marks because they do not show an ability to select the appropriate material. The person marking the script may suspect this is because the student does not know the correct material.

2. Structure and technique

Mistakes include:

* illogical order.

* inadequate introduction and conclusion.

* repetition.

* poor, or inappropriate, use of evidence and authority.

* a conclusion which does not follow from the evidence.

Law students often experience particular problems in the use of cases. It is important to remember that cases can be used in a number of different ways. A common mistake is to treat all cases in the same way. For example, an answer may imply that anything said in a judgment is a binding rule of law (failing to distinguish ratio and *obiter*). Be prepared to go into some cases, or some parts of cases, in depth and deal with others very briefly, according to the purpose the case is put to.

GROUP DISCUSSIONS: TUTORIALS AND SEMINARS

Discussion groups take a variety of forms. They are usually called tutorials, in the case of smaller groups, or seminars, in the case of larger groups.

Tutorials

These vary in size and objectives. In some institutions a tutorial will consist of one or two students meeting a tutor to discuss essays they have written. It is more common for tutorials to consist of groups of 4–8 students discussing a set assignment, such as an hypothetical legal problem or the arguments around a particular issue of importance in the law. A list of suggested reading will frequently be set by the tutor. Small groups give students the opportunity to sort out problems that have arisen in the course. They are also a way in which alternative views and arguments can be exchanged.

Tackling a tutorial assignment is rather like the first stage of preparing an essay.

1. Start with the assignment. What is going to be discussed? Jot down preliminary answers on the basis of what you already know. Before you start your reading, make sure you know what you are looking for.

2. Use SEARCH reading, then reading for MASTERY and CRITICISM on major points. Note down things you find difficult or confusing. These can then be raised in tutorial discussion.

3. Prepare a written answer to the assignment in note form. Select the main points and the relevant supporting material and organise them into a logical sequence.

4. In the tutorial, listen carefully to the opinions being expressed. Try to decide what evidence is being used to support them. Compare this with what you know. Be prepared to question inaccurate and illogical statements (including those made by your tutor).

5. Encourage others in the group who are having difficulty getting their ideas across. If you do not understand, ask for the matter to be further explained.

6. Put forward your own opinions for discussion. If they are sound, they will help others. If you are mistaken, it is

quite likely others will have made the same mistake, so any correction will help the group as a whole.

Seminars

These are larger groups than tutorials. They generally consist of 10–20 students, with one person presenting a paper to the group which then is discussed by everybody. Everyone in the group should come prepared to discuss the paper or the seminar will be of little value.

Presenting a seminar paper

1. Check the length that you will have to talk for. It will probably be about 10–15 minutes.
2. Begin by telling the group what you are trying to achieve. Build up arguments in clear, simple steps. Do try to mystify or impress. Remember your paper should be an interpretation of the material you have used, not just a précis.
3. End with a summary of the main points. Make some suggestions about the issues which you feel are worth discussing further.

Participants should prepare for the seminar in the same way that they would for a tutorial.

For all group discussions

It is not enough just to do the reading, attend and expect that a discussion will somehow materialise. Good discussion groups are based upon active participation by everybody in the group. If you are in a tutorial or seminar that is not going well, try and decide for yourself the reasons for this. Ask for 10 minutes at the end of the discussion to review how the group is working.

Try this exercise.

Ask the members of your discussion group to think back to the last discussion.
* What work was set? Did you do the reading? If not, why not?
* Did you prepare yourself in any other way? How?
* Who talked the most and who talked the least? What reasons can you give for this?

* Was the discussion helpful? Identify the kinds of discussion that took place, (*e.g.* questions, explanations, opinions, digressions) and decide how useful it was.
* Write a list of the ways to make the discussion more useful and enjoyable.
* Write a list of the behaviour which makes the discussion less useful and less enjoyable.
* What are you going to do about it?

EXAMINATIONS

Revision

For each course, make sure you know the syllabus of the course and what the examinable topics are. First try to get a good grasp of the major topics. After you have done this you can move on to the less important points. Remember almost all examinations aim to test, not just for knowledge of facts, but for understanding and the ability to use them. When revising ask

(a) What are the key points.

(b) What is the authority/evidence/argument for each proposition?

(c) Is there any counter evidence?

(d) Which aspects of this topic pose particular difficulty or are the subject of controversy?

(e) Test yourself by doing brief outline answers to questions from old examination papers.

Make a timetable, dividing up your revision into small units. Re-read the section on "Organising your time" on page 86. Time-limts and targets are particularly important in your revision programme. They help concentration. This, in turn, focusses your mind on something more constructive than panic. Many students worry because they do not "know everything" before they go into the examination room. No-one ever does. Whatever you revise, do it properly and actively, rather than sliding your eyes vaguely over your notes. Constantly remind yourself what you do know rather than concentrating on what you do not know.

Before the examination

Check the timetable to make sure you know all the details of the paper, including the way in which it is sub-divided. Check your equipment, making sure you have a spare pen, biro, pencil and rubber.

In the examination

1. Read quickly through the whole paper to get an idea of what questions there are.

2. Re-read the paper slowly and carefully and decide what each question is actually asking. Underline "key words" (see Essays) which indicate the kind of answer you should give. Then select the questions that you intend to answer.

3. Before writing anything, decide on the order you will tackle the questions. Choose the question that seems "easiest" first and work through to the "hardest." By answering the first question well you will gain confidence and be better able to tackle the more difficult ones.

4. Make notes for each question, jotting down all the ideas which come to mind. Try to make these brief notes for all the questions before you start writing. This gets you thinking about other questions even when you are writing your first question. In jotting down some ideas, questions that appeared impossible, to answer may become clearer. More ideas about other questions will come to you as you are answering the first one.

5. For each question, sort out the main points, weeding out irrelevancies. Answer the question set, not the one which you would like to have answered. Do not attempt to write down everything you know about the topic; expect to have to go into depth on only part of what you know.

6. Allocate your time properly. If each question bears an equal number of marks, spend an equal amount of time on each question. If the marks are different for different questions spend an approppriate proportion of your time on each question. If you use up your time-limit on a question, you will already have gained most of the marks that you are going to get. Another five or ten minutes writing is unlikely to get you many more marks. The same time concentrating on the key issues in a new question will earn you more marks. Remember that the first few marks in each question are the easiest ones to get.

7. If you miscalculate the time badly, finish the question in

note-form. This is better than nothing and may pick up a few valuable marks.

8. Always answer the right number of questions even if your last answer(s) are short and scrappy. The few marks which you gain may be vital for your final result.

REMEMBER

Read the exam paper through carefully before you begin writing.

When you write, be brief, be clear, be relevant.

Keep to the allocated time for each question.

Part 3

EXERCISES

This section of the book will test your understanding of the skills we have just described. Before attempting each exercise reread the appropriate chapter of this book. Each exercise is divided into two sections. Answers to Section A in each exercise are to be found at the back of this book. Do not look at these answers before you have tried to do the questions yourself. There are no answers to Section B in this book. You should discuss your answers to these questions with either your course tutor or with someone else you know who is studying law.

EXERCISE 1

Statutes I

Start by re-reading the appropriate parts of Chapter 5 and then look at the Human Organ Transplants Act 1989 which is reproduced below. Then answer the questions. When answering the questions, make sure that you include the correct statutory reference.

HUMAN ORGAN TRANSPLANTS ACT 1989

[Royal Seal]

(1989 c. 31)

An Act to prohibit commercial dealings in human organs intended for transplanting; to restrict the transplanting of such organs between persons who are not genetically related; and for supplementary purposes connected with those matters.

[27th July 1989]

Prohibition of commercial dealings in human organs

1.—(1) A person is guilty of an offence if in Great Britain he—

(a) makes or receives any payment for the supply of, or for an offer to supply, an organ which has been or is to be removed from a dead or living person and is intended to be transplanted into another person whether in Great Britain or elsewhere;

(b) seeks to find a person willing to supply for payment such an organ as is mentioned in paragraph (a) above or offers to supply such an organ for payment;

(c) initiates or negotiates any arrangement involving the making of any payment for the supply of, or for an offer to supply, such an organ; or

(d) takes part in the management or control of a body of persons corporate or unincorporate whose activities consist of or include the initiation or negotiation of such arrangements.

(2) Without prejudice to paragraph (b) of subsection (1) above, a person is guilty of an offence if he causes to be published or distributed, or knowingly publishes or distributes, in Great Britain an advertisement—

(a) inviting persons to supply for payment any such organs as are mentioned in paragraph (a) of that subsection or offering to supply any such organs for payment; or

(b) indicating that the advertiser is willing to initiate or negotiate any such arrangement as is mentioned in paragraph (c) of that subsection.

(3) In this section "payment" means payment in money or money's worth but does not include any payment for defraying or reimbursing—

(a) the cost of removing, transporting or preserving the organ to be supplied; or

(b) any expenses or loss of earnings incurred by a person so far as reasonably and directly attributable to his supplying an organ from his body.

(4) In this section "advertisement" includes any form of advertising whether to the public generally, to any section of the public or individually to selected persons.

(5) A person guilty of an offence under subsection (1) above is liable on summary conviction to imprisonment for a term not exceeding three months or a fine not exceeding level 5 on the standard scale or both; and a person guilty of an offence under subsection (2) above is liable on summary conviction to a fine not exceeding level 5 on that scale.

Restriction on transplants between persons not genetically related

2.—(1) Subject to subsection (3) below, a person is guilty of an offence if in Great Britain he—

(a) removes from a living person an organ intended to be transplanted into another person; or

(b) transplants an organ removed from a living person into another person,

unless the person into whom the organ is to be or, as the case may be, is transplanted is genetically related to the person from whom the organ is removed.

(2) For the purposes of this section a person is genetically related to—

(a) his natural parents and children;

(b) his brothers and sisters of the whole or half blood;

(c) the brothers and sisters of the whole or half blood of either of his natural parents; and

(d) the natural children of his brothers and sisters of the whole or half blood or of the brothers and sisters of the whole or half blood of either of his natural parents;

but persons shall not in any particular case be treated as related in any of those ways unless the fact of the relationship has been established by such means as are specified by regulations made by the Secretary of State.

(3) The Secretary of State may by regulations provide that the prohibition in subsection (1) above shall not apply in cases where—

>   (a) such authority as is specified in or constituted by the regulations is satisfied—
>
>> (i) that no payment has been or is to be made in contravention of section 1 above; and
>>
>> (ii) that such other conditions as are specified in the regulations are satisfied; and
>
>   (b) such other requirements as may be specified in the regulations are complied with.

(4) The expenses of any such authority shall be defrayed by the Secretary of State out of money provided by Parliament.

(5) A person guilty of an offence under this section is liable on summary conviction to imprisonment for a term not exceeding three months or a fine not exceeding level 5 on the standard scale or both.

(6) The power to make regulations under this section shall be exercisable by statutory instrument.

(7) Regulations under subsection (2) above shall be subject to annulment in pursuance of a resolution of either House of Parliament; and no regulations shall be made under subsection (3) above unless a draft of them has been laid before and approved by a resolution of each House of Parliament.

Information about transplant operations

3.—(1) The Secretary of State may make regulations requiring such persons as are specified in the regulations to supply to such authority as is so specified such information as may be so specified with respect to transplants that have been or are proposed to be carried out in Great Britain using organs removed from dead or living persons.

(2) Any such authority shall keep a record of information supplied to it in pursuance of the regulations made under this section.

(3) Any person who without reasonable excuse fails to comply with those regulations is guilty of an offence and liable on summary conviction to a fine not exceeding level 3 on the standard scale; and any person who, in purported compliance with those regulations, knowingly or recklessly supplies information which is false or misleading in a material respect is guilty of an offence and liable on summary conviction to a fine not exceeding level 5 on the standard scale.

(4) The power to make regulations under this section shall be exercisable by statutory instrument subject to annulment in pursuance of a resolution of either House of Parliament.

Offences by bodies corporate

4.—(1) Where an offence under this Act committed by a body corporate is proved to have been committed with the consent or connivance of, or to be attributable to any neglect on the part of, any director, manager, secretary or other similar officer of the body corporate or any person who was purporting to act in any such capacity, he as well as the body corporate is guilty of the offence and is liable to be proceeded against and punished accordingly.

(2) Where the affairs of a body corporate are managed by its members, subsection (1) above shall apply to the acts and defaults of a member in connection with his functions of management as if he were a director of the body corporate.

Prosecutions

5. No proceedings for an offence under section 1 or 2 above shall be instituted in England and Wales except by or with the consent of the Director of Public Prosecutions.

Northern Ireland

6. An Order in Council under paragraph 1(1)(b) of Schedule 1 to the Northern Ireland Act 1974 (legislation for Northern Ireland in the interim period) which contains a statement that it is made only for purposes corresponding to the purposes of this Act—
   (a) shall not be subject to paragraph 1(4) and (5) of that Schedule (affirmative resolution of both Houses of Parliament); but
   (b) shall be subject to annulment in pursuance of a resolution of either House of Parliament.

Short title, interpretation, commencement and extent

7.—(1) This Act may be cited as the Human Organ Transplants Act 1989.

(2) In this Act "organ" means any part of a human body consisting of a structured arrangement of tissues which, if wholly removed, cannot be replicated by the body.

(3) Section 1 above shall not come into force until the day after that on which this Act is passed and section 2(1) above shall not come into force until such day as the Secretary of State may appoint by an order made by statutory instrument.

(4) Except for section 6 this Act does not extend to Northern Ireland.

SECTION A

1. Does the Act create civil or criminal liability?

2. To which parts of the United Kingdom does the Act apply?

3. When did the Act come into force?

4. Jane pays Robert £50 for a pint of blood for use in a transplant operation. Does Jane commit an offence under the Act?

5. How would you find out if there had been any reported cases under this Act?

6. Usha sees Rachael buying a human liver from John. Usha knows Rachael intends to use the liver in a transplant operation. Usha decides that it is her public duty to prosecute Rachael for her action. Will Usha succeed?

7. Susan, a newsagent, puts a card in the window of her shop saying that Robert is willing to pay donors large sums of money, which he then intends to use for transplant operations. Has Susan committed an offence under the Act?

SECTION B

8. What is the short title of this Act?

9. Why do you think this Act was passed?

10. Jim buys a human kidney from Linda intending to dissect it. Has Jim committed an offence under the Act?

11. Akram agrees to donate his kidney for use in a transplant operation. He is given an air-ticket, hotel accommodation and the sum of £200. Is an offence under the Act committed?

12. Fiona invests a large sum of money in a firm whose sole business is obtaining human organs for transplants. The firm pays substantial fees for such organs. Fiona regularly visits the firm to see how her investment is doing. When she visits she is treated with great courtesy and, because she is a major investor in the firm, her opinion on various

points in the firm's policy is sought. Fiona finds this very embarrassing but, out of politeness, gives rather vague answers by way of reply. Has Fiona committed any offence under the Act?

EXERCISE 2

Statutes II

Mobile Homes Act 1983

CHAPTER 34

ARRANGEMENT OF SECTIONS

Mobile Homes Act 1983

[Royal Seal]

1983 CHAPTER 34

An Act to make new provision in place of sections 1 to 6 of the Mobile Homes Act 1975.   [13th May 1983]

BE IT ENACTED by the Queen's most Excellent Majesty, by and with the advice and consent of the Lords Spiritual and Temporal, and Commons, in this present Parliament assembled, and by the authority of the same, as follows:—

Particulars of agreements. 1.—(1) This Act applies to any agreement under which a person ("the occupier") is entitled—

(*a*) to station a mobile home on land forming part of a protected site; and

(*b*) to occupy the mobile home as his only or main residence.

(2) Within three months of the making of an agreement to which this Act applies, the owner of the protected site ("the owner") shall give to the occupier a written statement which—

(*a*) specifies the names and addresses of the parties and the date of commencement of the agreement;

(*b*) includes particulars of the land on which the occupier is entitled to station the mobile home sufficient to identify it;

(*c*) sets out the express terms of the agreement;

(*d*) sets out the terms implied by section 2(1) below; and

(*e*) complies with such other requirements as may be prescribed by regulations made by the Secretary of State.

(3) If the agreement was made before the day on which this Act comes into force, the written statement shall be given within six months of that day.

(4) Any reference in subsection (2) or (3) above to the making of an agreement to which this Act applies includes a reference to any variation of an agreement by virtue of which the agreement becomes one to which this Act applies.

(5) If the owner fails to comply with this section, the occupier may apply to the court for an order requiring the owner so to comply.

(6) Regulations under this section—

(*a*) shall be made by statutory instrument; and

(*b*) may make different provision with respect to different cases or descriptions of case, including different provision for different areas.

Terms of agreements. **2.**—(1) In any agreement to which this Act applies there shall be implied the terms set out in Part I of Schedule 1 to this Act; and this subsection shall have effect notwithstanding any express term of the agreement.

(2) The court may, on the application of either party made within six months of the giving of the statement under section 1(2) above, order that there shall be implied in the agreement terms concerning the matters mentioned in Part II of Schedule 1 to this Act.

(3) The court may, on the application of either party made within the said period of six months, by order vary or delete any express term of the agreement.

(4) On an application under this section, the court shall make such provision as the court considers just and equitable in the circumstances.

Successors in title. **3.**—(1) An agreement to which this Act applies shall be binding on and enure for the benefit of any successor in title of the owner and any person claiming through or under the owner or any such successor.

(2) Where an agreement to which this Act applies is lawfully assigned to any person, the agreement shall enure for the benefit of and be binding on that person.

(3) Where a person entitled to the benefit of and bound by an agreement to which this Act applies dies at a time when he is occupying the mobile home as his only or main residence, the agreement shall enure for the benefit of and be binding on—

    (*a*) any person residing with that person ("the deceased") at that time being—

        (i) the widow or widower of the deceased; or

        (ii) in default of a widow or widower so residing, any member of the deceased's family; or

    (*b*) in default of any such person so residing, the person entitled to the mobile home by virtue of the deceased's will or under the law relating to intestacy but subject to subsection (4) below.

(4) An agreement to which this Act applies shall not enure for the benefit of or be binding on a person by virtue of subsection (3)(*b*) above in so far as—

    (*a*) it would, but for this subsection, enable or require that person to occupy the mobile home; or

    (*b*) it includes terms implied by virtue of paragraph 5 or 9 of Part I of Schedule 1 to this Act.

Jurisdiction of the court. **4.** The court shall have jurisdiction to determine any question arising under this Act or any agreement to which it applies, and to entertain any proceedings brought under this Act or any such agreement.

Interpret-
ation.

5.—(1) In this Act, unless the context otherwise requires—
"the court" means—
    (*a*) in relation to England and Wales, the county court for the district in which the protected site is situated or, where the parties have agreed in writing to submit any question arising under this Act or, as the case may be, any agreement to which it applies to arbitration, the arbitrator;
    (*b*) in relation to Scotland, the sheriff having jurisdiction where the protected site is situated or, where the parties have so agreed, the arbiter;
"local authority" has the same meaning as in Part I of the Caravan Sites and Control of Development Act 1960;

1960 c. 62.

"mobile home" has the same meaning as "caravan" has in that Part of that Act;
"owner", in relation to a protected site, means the person who, by virtue of an estate or interest held by him, is entitled to possession of the site or would be so entitled but for the rights of any persons to station mobile homes on land forming part of the site;
"planning permission" means permission under Part III of the Town and Country Planning Act 1971 or Part III of the Town and Country Planning (Scotland) Act 1972;

1971 c. 78.
1972 c. 52.

"protected site" does not include any land occupied by a local authority as a caravan site providing accommodation for gipsies or, in Scotland, for persons to whom section 24(8A) of the Caravan Sites and Control of Development Act 1960 applies but, subject to that, has the same meaning as in Part I of the Caravan Sites Act 1968.

1968 c. 52.

(2) In relation to an agreement to which this Act applies—
    (*a*) any reference in this Act to the owner includes a reference to any person who is bound by and entitled to the benefit of the agreement by virtue of subsection (1) of section 3 above; and
    (*b*) subject to subsection (4) of that section, any reference in this Act to the occupier includes a reference to any person who is entitled to the benefit of and bound by the agreement by virtue of subsection (2) or (3) of that section.

(3) A person is a member of another's family within the meaning of this Act if he is his spouse, parent, grandparent,

child, grandchild, brother, sister, uncle, aunt, nephew or niece; treating—

(*a*) any relationship by marriage as a relationship by blood, any relationship of the half blood as a relationship of the whole blood and the stepchild of any person as his child; and

(*b*) an illegitimate person as the legitimate child of his mother and reputed father;

or if they live together as husband and wife.

Short title, repeals, commencement and extent. **6.**—(1) This Act may be cited as the Mobile Homes Act 1983.

(2) The enactments mentioned in Schedule 2 to this Act are hereby repealed to the extent specified in the third column of that Schedule.

(3) This Act shall come into force on the expiry of the period of one week beginning with the day on which it is passed.

(4) This Act does not extend to Northern Ireland.

SCHEDULES

Section 2.

SCHEDULE 1

AGREEMENTS UNDER ACT

PART I

TERMS IMPLIED BY ACT

Duration of agreement

1. Subject to paragraph 2 below, the right to station the mobile home on land forming part of the protected site shall subsist until the agreement is determined under paragraph 3, 4, 5 or 6 below.

2.—(1) If the owner's estate or interest is insufficient to enable him to grant the right for an indefinite period, the period for which the right subsists shall not extend beyond the date when the owner's estate or interest determines.

(2) If planning permission for the use of the protected site as a site for mobile homes has been granted in terms such that it will expire at the end of a specified period, the period for which the right subsists shall not extend beyond the date when the planning permission expires.

(3) If before the end of a period determined by this paragraph there is a change in circumstances which allows a longer period, account shall be taken of that change.

Termination by occupier

3. The occupier shall be entitled to terminate the agreement by notice in writing given to the owner not less than four weeks before the date on which it is to take effect.

Termination by owner

4. The owner shall be entitled to terminate the agreement forthwith if, on the application of the owner, the court—

(a) is satisfied that the occupier has breached a term of the agreement and, after service of a notice to remedy the breach, has not complied with the notice within a reasonable time; and

(b) considers it reasonable for the agreement to be terminated.

5. The owner shall be entitled to terminate the agreement forthwith if, on the application of the owner, the court is satisfied that the occupier is not occupying the mobile home as his only or main residence.

6.—(1) The owner shall be entitled to terminate the agreement at the end of a relevant period if, on the application of the owner, the court is satisfied that, having regard to its age and condition, the mobile home—

(a) is having a detrimental effect on the amenity of the site; or

(b) is likely to have such an effect before the end of the next relevant period.

(2) In sub-paragraph (1) above "relevant period" means the period of five years beginning with the commencement of the agreement and each succeeding period of five years.

Recovery of overpayments by occupier

7. Where the agreement is terminated as mentioned in paragraph 3, 4, 5 or 6 above, the occupier shall be entitled to recover from the owner so much of any payment made by him in pursuance of the agreement as is attributable to a period beginning after the termination.

Sale of mobile home

8.—(1) The occupier shall be entitled to sell the mobile home, and to assign the agreement, to a person approved of by the owner, whose approval shall not be unreasonably withheld.

(2) Where the occupier sells the mobile home, and assigns the agreement, as mentioned in sub-paragraph (1) above, the owner shall be entitled to receive a commission on the sale at a rate not exceeding such rate as may be specified by an order made by the Secretary of State.

(3) An order under this paragraph—
  (*a*) shall be made by statutory instrument which shall be subject to annulment in pursuance of a resolution of either House of Parliament; and
  (*b*) may make different provision for different areas or for sales at different prices.

Gift of mobile home

9. The occupier shall be entitled to give the mobile home, and to assign the agreement, to a member of his family approved by the owner, whose approval shall not be unreasonably withheld.

Re-siting of mobile home

10. If the owner is entitled to require that the occupier's right to station the mobile home shall be exercisable for any period in relation to other land forming part of the protected site—
  (*a*) that other land shall be broadly comparable to the land on which the occupier was originally entitled to station the mobile home; and
  (*b*) all costs and expenses incurred in consequence of the requirement shall be paid by the owner.

PART II

MATTERS CONCERNING WHICH TERMS MAY BE IMPLIED BY COURT

1. The right of the occupier to quiet enjoyment or, in Scotland, undisturbed possession of the mobile home.

2. The sums payable by the occupier in pursuance of the agreement and the times at which they are to be paid.

3. The review at yearly intervals of the sums so payable.

4. The provision or improvement of services available on the protected site, and the use by the occupier of such services.

5. The preservation of the amenity of the protected site.

6. The maintenance and repair of the protected site by the owner, and the maintenance and repair of the mobile home by the occupier.

7. Access by the owner to the land on which the occupier is entitled to station the mobile home.

SCHEDULE 2 — Section 6.

REPEALS

Chapter	Short title	Extent of repeal
1975 c. 49.	The Mobile Homes Act 1975.	Sections 1 to 6. In section 9, in subsection (1), all definitions except those of "the Act of 1960", "the Act of 1968" and "mobile home", and subsection (2).

SECTION A

1. To what parts of the United Kingdom does this Act apply?

2. What is the long title of this statute?

3. Robert and Meena are lovers. They live together but have no intention of marrying. If Robert dies, is Meena part of his family for the purposes of section 3(3)(*a*)(ii) of the Act?

4. Paragraph 8 of Part 1 of Schedule 1 to the Act gives the Secretary of State power to set a rate for the commission that a site owner is entitled to receive on any sale, by an occupier, of their mobile home. How would you find what that rate is?

5. Ronald is the owner of a protected site. Barbara owns a mobile home which she moved on to Ronald's site four months ago. Barbara is troubled by her neighbour Cyril who has just moved his mobile home on to what she thought was part of her site. When she asked Ronald what the boundaries of her site were he was vague in his response. Is there anything the Act that will help Barbara?

6. Florence has decided to give her mobile home to Rupert, her illegitimate son. David, the owner of the site on which the home is presently situated, says that he will not give his approval because other occupants of the site disapprove of Florence having an illegitimate son and do not wish to have him as a neighbour. Can the Act assist Florence in any way?

SECTION B

7. Does this Act apply to Northern Ireland?

8. Margaret wants to take action under the Act. Which court should she go to?

9. Felicity is the owner of a protected site. She told Christine that she could station her mobile home on Felicity's site. Felicity told Christine that if she signed a document agreeing to waive her rights under Part 1 of Schedule 1 to the Act Christine's rent would be reduced by 10 per cent. Christine did sign. Christine now regrets her action. Is there anything that she can now do?

10. Clayton, the owner of a mobile home, concluded an agreement, to which the 1983 Act applies, with Ruth, the owner of a site. Raymond has now bought the site from Ruth. Raymond insists that it is necessary for Clayton to enter into a new agreement with him. Is he right?

11. Vera, the owner of a protected site, has told two of her older residents that they must leave immediately because their mobile homes are too old. She has also shown them a clause in the agreement with them which gives her the power to order any occupier of any home to leave at any time for any reason. Both residents suspect that the real reason that Vera is ordering them to leave is because she heard them being rude about her hair-style. Under the Act, is Vera entitled to end their agreement?

12. *Drafting Exercise* Impressed by the success of the Mobile Homes Act, the Secretary of State asks you to draft similiar legislation to apply to houseboats. However, the Secretary of State wishes to exclude from the ambit of the legislation marinas which simply cater for pleasure-craft. Provide a statutory definition of "houseboat" and "marina" suitable for inclusion in the legislation.

EXERCISE 3

Cases I

a   # Greenwich London Borough Council v Powell and another

HOUSE OF LORDS
LORD BRIDGE OF HARWICH, LORD TEMPLEMAN, LORD GRIFFITHS, LORD ACKNER AND LORD LOWRY
7, 8 NOVEMBER, 8 DECEMBER 1988

b

Local authority – Caravan sites – Provision of caravan sites – Duty of local authority – Duty to provide accommodation for gipsies – Gipsies occupying caravans on site seasonally as main or only residence – Whether sites 'protected sites' – Whether occupants entitled to security of tenure – Caravan Sites Act 1968, s 6 – Mobile Homes Act 1983, s 5(1).

c   A caravan site provided by a local authority in the discharge of its duty under s 6[a] of the Caravan Sites Act 1968 to accommodate those whom it bona fide believes to be gipsies because they are nomadic for part of the year is not a 'protected site' within s 5(1)[b] of the Mobile Homes Act 1983 thereby entitling the occupants to security of tenure under that Act, notwithstanding that they may occupy the caravans as their main or only residence and may establish a permanent residence on the site by returning from year to year.
d   Moreover, even if the occupants give up their erstwhile nomadic way of life entirely such a site will still not become a protected site unless the local authority adopts a policy of offering vacancies on the site to static residents who have fixed full-time employment (see p 69 *j* to p 70 *a d e* and p 71 *b c f* to *h*, post).

Notes
e   For the powers of local authorities with respect to the provisions of caravan sites, see 29 Halsbury's Laws (4th edn) para 118.
    For the Caravan Sites Act 1968, s 6, see 32 Halsbury's Statutes (4th edn) 503.
    For the Mobile Homes Act 1983, s 5, see ibid 517.

f   **Cases referred to in opinions**
Mills v Cooper [1967] 2 All ER 100, [1967] 2 QB 459, [1967] 2 WLR 1343, DC.
West Glamorgan CC v Rafferty, R v Secretary of State for Wales, ex p Gilhaney [1987] 1 All ER 1005, [1987] 1 WLR 457, CA.

Appeal
g   Greenwich London Borough Council appealed with leave of the Appeal Committee of the House of Lords given on 9 June 1988 against the decision of the Court of Appeal (Purchas LJ and Heilbron J) on 23 February 1988 allowing an appeal by the defendants, George Powell and Harriett Powell, against the order of his Honour Judge James sitting in the Woolwich County Court on 3 November 1988 whereby, on the application of the council under CCR Ord 24, he ordered that the Powells give up possession of pad J1 at
h   the Thistlebrook Caravan Site, Harrow Manorway, London SE2, owned by the council. The facts are set out in the opinion of Lord Bridge.

John R Macdonald QC and *C P L Braham* for the council.
Nigel Pascoe QC and *David Wade* for the Powells.

j   **LORD BRIDGE OF HARWICH.** My Lords, the appellants are the local authority for the London borough of Greenwich. I shall refer to them as 'the council'. The respondents are Mr and Mrs Powell. I shall refer to them as 'the Powells'. The council own a caravan

---

a   Section 6, so far as material, is set out at p 67 *a b*, post
b   Section 5(1), so far as material, is set out at p 68 *b*, post

site known as the Thistlebrook Caravan Site at Abbey Wood, London SE2. The Powells
occupy part of the site known as pad J1, on which they are permitted to station two   *a*
caravans pursuant to the terms of an agreement with the council. In October 1986 the
council gave the Powells four weeks' notice to quit and in November 1986 they instituted
proceedings for possession. The Powells pleaded in defence that the Thistlebrook site was
a 'protected site' as defined by s 5(1) of the Mobile Homes Act 1983. An agreement under
which a person is entitled to station a caravan on a protected site and to occupy it as his
only or main residence may only be terminated as provided by Sch 1 to the 1983 Act.   *b*
The Powells' agreement has never been so terminated and there is no dispute that they
occupy the caravans as their only or main residence. Hence the only issue in the case is
whether the Thistlebrook site is a 'protected site' as defined by s 5(1). On 3 November
1987 his Honour Judge James at the Woolwich County Court held that it was not and
made an order for possession. On 23 February 1988 the Court of Appeal (Purchas LJ and
Heilbron J) held that it was and allowed the Powells' appeal. The council now appeal by   *c*
leave of your Lordships' House.
    The issue raised is one of great importance for local authorities. It can only be
understood in the context of the historical development of the legislation governing
caravan sites.
    In the 1950s the mushrooming of residential caravan sites to alleviate the acute
shortage of conventional housing presented many problems to local planning authorities   *d*
which their powers under the Town and Country Planning Acts were inadequate to
resolve. The first direct statutory control over caravan sites as such was imposed by the
Caravan Sites and Control of Development Act 1960. This established a system of
licensing of caravan sites by local authorities which gave effective control over both the
establishment of new sites and the conditions under which sites were required to be
operated. Section 24 of the Act gave power to local authorities themselves to provide   *e*
both residential and holiday sites within their areas and to acquire land compulsorily for
the purpose. Sites provided by local authorities, since they were themselves the licensing
authorities, were not required to be licensed: see para 11 of Sch 1.
    Part I of the Caravan Sites Act 1968 introduced for the first time a very limited form
of statutory security of tenure for the occupier of a residential caravan on a 'protected site'   *f*
as defined by s 1(2), either as licensee of a pitch on which to station his own caravan or as
occupier of a caravan belonging to the site owner. In each case his contractual right could
only be determined by four weeks' notice and he could only be evicted by court order.
The court was given power to suspend enforcement of an eviction order 'for such period
not exceeding 12 months from the date of the order as the court thinks reasonable' and
from time to time to extend the period of suspension for not more than 12 months at a   *g*
time: see s 4. This limited protection I shall refer to as 'the 1968 security of tenure'. A
'protected site' is defined by s 1(2), which provides:

> 'For the purposes of this Part of this Act a protected site is any land in respect of
> which a site licence is required under Part I of the Caravan Sites and Control of
> Development Act 1960 or would be so required if paragraph 11 of Schedule 1 to
> that Act (exemption of land occupied by local authorities) were omitted, not being   *h*
> land in respect of which the relevant planning permission or site licence—(*a*) is
> expressed to be granted for holiday use only; or (*b*) is otherwise so expressed or
> subject to such conditions that there are times of the year when no caravan may be
> stationed on the land for human habitation.'

The effect of this definition is that the 1968 security of tenure is available to all occupiers   *j*
of residential caravans on local authority sites as well as on privately owned sites.
    Part II of the 1968 Act, which came into force on 1 April 1970, attempted to resolve
the problem of providing orderly caravan sites to accommodate the gipsy community
and of controlling unauthorised gipsy encampments. By the definition in s 16—

> '"gipsies" means persons of nomadic habit of life, whatever their race or origin,

a but does not include members of an organised group of travelling showmen, or of persons engaged in travelling circuses, travelling together as such.'

Section 6 imposes a duty on local authorities—

'to exercise their powers under section 24 of the Caravan Sites and Control of Development Act 1960 (provision of caravan sites) so far as may be necessary to provide adequate accommodation for gipsies residing in or resorting to their area.'

b Sections 10 to 12 impose a system of control of the unauthorised stationing of gipsies' caravans in the area of any local authority which is dependent on the designation of that area by the minister under s 12 as an area to which s 10 applies. The condition to justify designation under s 12 is that it must appear to the minister—

c 'either that adequate provision is made in the area for the accommodation of gipsies residing in or resorting to the area, or that in all the circumstances it is not necessary or expedient to make any such provision.'

(See s 12(3).)

Within a designated area it is an offence under s 10 for a gipsy to station a caravan on land within the boundaries of a highway, on other unoccupied land or on occupied land d without the consent of the occupier. Section 11 provides machinery for the expeditious removal by order of a magistrates' court of unauthorised gipsy caravans stationed in a designated area.

The policy underlying Pt II of the 1968 Act is, if I may say so, admirably described by Ralph Gibson LJ in *West Glamorgan CC v Rafferty* [1987] 1 All ER 1005 at 1010, [1987] 1 WLR 457 at 463:

e 'First, adequate accommodation is to be provided for gipsies in the area of the local authority in the interest of the gipsies themselves, giving them sites to which they can lawfully go and which will be supplied with facilities and supervised so that the sites will be maintained in decent order. Given some security of accommodation their children are more likely to get effective instruction in school. Any gipsies not complying with the regulations of the site may be ejected. Such f sites will be better both for the travelling people who use them and for those who live near the sites. The second purpose of the legislation is plain from ss 10 and 12 of the 1968 Act.'

Ralph Gibson LJ then summarised the effect of ss 10 to 12 and continued ([1987] 1 All ER 1005 at 1010–1011, [1987] 1 WLR 457 at 463):

g 'The rest of the community is thus to an extent protected from visitation by gipsies trespassing on land, and camping on unregulated sites so as to cause nuisance, and sometimes damage, to those areas in which they trespass and the people living there.'

h The Mobile Homes Act 1975 gave greatly enhanced security of tenure to a person stationing his own caravan on a licensed caravan site for occupation as his only or main residence. The detailed provisions are elaborate and have now been superseded. It is sufficient, therefore, to say that, in substance, they gave the occupier statutory security of tenure for five years, renewable for a further three years. This I will call 'the 1975 security of tenure'. The 1975 Act, however, by its own definition of 'protected site', which I need not set out, deliberately excluded from the benefit of the 1975 security of tenure j occupiers of caravans on all local authority sites.

The Mobile Homes Act 1983 replaced the main provisions of the 1975 Act and still further enhanced the security of tenure enjoyed by a person stationing his own caravan on an authorised site for occupation as his only or main residence. Subject to exceptions which are immaterial for present purposes, this security (the 1983 security of tenure) in substance continues indefinitely and is transmissible by sale or gift of the caravan. The occupier cannot be evicted except by court order which may only be made on the grounds, put shortly, (1) that the occupier is in breach of agreement and that it is *a* reasonable for the agreement to be terminated, (2) that the occupier is not occupying the caravan as his only or main residence, (3) that the condition of the caravan is detrimental to the amenity of the site (see Sch 1, Pt I, paras 4, 5 and 6). For present purposes, the all-important change effected by the 1983 Act, as compared with the 1975 Act, is to extend the 1983 security of tenure to caravans stationed on all local authority sites except gipsy sites. This change is effected by the definition in s 5(1) of the 1983 Act, which reads: *b*

'"protected site" does not include any land occupied by a local authority as a caravan site providing accommodation for gipsies . . . but, subject to that, has the same meaning as in Part I of the Caravan Sites Act 1968.'

The question on which this case turns is whether the Thistlebrook site is occupied by the council 'as a caravan site providing accommodation for gipsies'. It is common ground *c* that the question must be answered by reference to the site as a whole, not by reference to individual pads or pitches.

The facts may not have been investigated at the trial as fully as they might have been if the issues canvassed in the Court of Appeal and before your Lordships had been fully anticipated. But the essential primary facts are not, I think, in dispute. The Thistlebrook site was acquired by the council by compulsory purchase in 1967 under s 24 of the 1960 *d* Act. Before acquisition the site was occupied by a number of caravan dwellers who may or may not have been persons of nomadic habit of life. The trial judge gave an interesting account of the historical background leading to the compulsory purchase, but treated it, as I think rightly, as irrelevant to the issues. In the Court of Appeal there was produced for the first time the report of the inspector who held an inquiry into objections to the council's compulsory purchase order and this report was admitted without objection as *e* additional evidence. The Court of Appeal seem to have attached some importance to it, but there are two reasons why I find it difficult to draw any relevant inferences from the case made for the council in support of the compulsory purchase order as reported by the inspector. First, the acquisition was effected long before the council had any statutory duty to provide accommodation for gipsies. Second, the evidence is silent as to what *f* happened to the site between 1967 and 1972. The most the inspector's report proved of possible relevance was that a few of the caravan dwellers now resident on the site had been there before 1967 and objected to the compulsory purchase order.

The evidence of the principal witness for the council, which the judge accepted, was that the site was opened in three stages between October 1972 and December 1973 as a site to provide accommodation for gipsies in discharge of the council's duty under s 6 of *g* the 1968 Act. The Powells were among the first to come on the site after it was opened. The site had 54 pads, of which some, like that occupied by the Powells, accommodated more than one caravan. In May 1974 the Secretary of State for the Environment made the Gipsy Encampments (Designation of the London Borough of Greenwich) Order 1974, SI 1974/920. The order recites that it appears to the Secretary of State that adequate provision is made in the London borough of Greenwich for the accommodation of *h* gipsies residing in or resorting to that area and designates it as an area to which s 10 of the 1968 Act applies. The order must necessarily be read as referring to the Thistlebrook site as this was the only caravan site provided for by the council, and hence the only site in the borough purporting to provide accommodation for gipsies.

The Powells both gave evidence which the judge accepted. Mr Powell said that he was a gipsy by race and proud of it. Their evidence was that they did seasonal work fruit- *j* picking away from the Thistlebrook site which had usually been for four to five months a year. In 1987 they had been absent for three months. They had one residential caravan (presumably left permanently at Thistlebrook) and one mobile caravan (presumably used on their travels). Their pattern of life was typical of many others resident on the

Thistlebrook site. They and all the other occupants of the site had their permanent
a residence there and many others, like the Powells, had been there for many years.

The council's principal witness produced in evidence a helpful schedule, again accepted
by the judge, showing absences from the site in 1986 and 1987. A substantial number of
occupants of pads on the site had been absent from the site for periods up to five months
in each year and for longer than could reasonably be accounted for as holiday absences.
The clear inference from this evidence taken together with the Powells' evidence was
b that these occupiers were seasonal workers like the Powells who went on their travels in
their caravans for substantial periods of the year moving from place to place to find work.
It is not without significance that the site rules which were incorporated in occupiers'
agreements with the council allowed occupiers to be absent from the site for up to 20
weeks in any one year (or for longer if agreed in writing with the council) and to retain
their right to return by paying for the weeks of absence half the fixed weekly payments
c provided for in their agreements. This appears to have been designed to make provision
for persons following just such a pattern of life as the Powells.

The judge held that the character of the site was determined by the purpose of the
council to occupy it as a site providing accommodation for gipsies and that this was
affirmed by the order made by the Secretary of State for the Environment in 1974 under
s 12 of the 1968 Act designating the London borough of Greenwich as an area to which
d s 10 applies. He had no material to indicate any subsequent change in the council's
purpose. On this view he did not find it necessary to decide whether those presently
occupying the site were persons of nomadic habit of life. On the evidence, in particular
the schedule of absences in 1986 and 1987, he indicated that 'it would if applicable have
been my conclusion that none of those now occupying Thistlebrook are at the present
time of nomadic habit of life'. The Court of Appeal held that the status of the site was
e determined by the character of those presently occupying the site and that none were
persons of nomadic habit of life. Hence the site was a 'protected site' as defined by s 5(1)
of the 1983 Act and the Powells' agreement giving them the right to occupy had never
been determined.

In *Mills v Cooper* [1967] 2 All ER 100, [1967] 2 QB 459 the Divisional Court had to
consider the meaning of the word 'gipsy' in s 127 of the Highways Act 1959 without the
f aid of any statutory definition. The section provides:

'If, without lawful authority or excuse . . . (c) . . . a gipsy pitches a booth, stall or
stand, or encamps, on a highway, he shall be guilty of an offence . . .'

Lord Parker CJ said ([1967] 2 All ER 100 at 103, [1967] 2 QB 459 at 467):

g   'I think that, in this context, "gipsy" means no more than a person leading a
nomadic life with no, or no fixed, employment and with no fixed abode.'

Diplock LJ indicated his view that 'gipsy' in the section bore—

'its popular meaning, which I would define as a person without fixed abode who
leads a nomadic life, dwelling in tents or other shelters, or in caravans or other
h   vehicles.'

(See [1967] 2 All ER 100 at 104, [1967] 2 QB 459 at 468.)

Both Lord Parker CJ and Diplock LJ rejected the argument that 'gipsy' in the context
referred only to a person of Romany race.

It is difficult to think that the draftsman of the 1968 Act did not have these passages in
j mind when he provided the definition of 'gipsies' in s 16. He could have defined them as
'persons of nomadic habit of life and of no fixed abode', but he did not. Moreover, the
duty imposed by s 6(1) is to provide accommodation 'for gipsies *residing in* or resorting to
their area'. I am inclined to conclude from these indications alone that a person may be
within the definition if he leads a nomadic life only seasonally and notwithstanding that

he regularly returns for part of the year to the same place where he may be said to have a
fixed abode or permanent residence.   *a*
   But we are only concerned with the definition of 'gipsies' in s 16 of the 1968 Act, so to
speak, at one remove. What we have directly to construe is the definition of 'protected
site' in the 1983 Act. It was for this reason that I thought it necessary to trace the
legislative history in some detail. This made it clear that from 1968 to 1983 the only
security of tenure enjoyed by a caravan resident on any local authority site was the 1968
security of tenure. Meanwhile, from 1970 to 1983 local authorities up and down the   *b*
country, and in particular London boroughs, were doing their best to discharge their
duty under s 6 of the 1968 Act to provide sites for gipsies in accordance with policy
guidance issued to them by the Department of the Environment. Likewise, local
authority areas were being designated under s 12 of the 1968 Act, in order to make
available the important powers of control over unauthorised gipsy caravans under ss 10
and 11, in accordance with the view then taken as to what could amount to 'adequate   *c*
provision . . . for the accommodation of gipsies residing in or resorting to' the local
authority area.
   It was only when the 1983 Act came into force that it became important to distinguish
between local authority sites 'providing accommodation for gipsies' and other local
authority sites, because it was then for the first time that the crucial distinction between
the security of tenure enjoyed by caravan residents on the two classes of site was   *d*
introduced. The Bill which became the 1983 Act was a government Bill and it would be
quite unrealistic not to recognise that the distinction between the two classes of site made
in the statute must have been made with full knowledge of the policy which had been
followed since 1970 with regard to the performance by local authorities of their duty
under s 6 of the 1968 Act. That policy, whilst technically inadmissible as an aid to the
construction of the definition of 'gipsies' in s 16 of the 1968 Act, is, in my opinion, fully   *e*
cognisable as a powerful pointer to the intention of the legislature in excluding local
authority sites 'providing accommodation for gipsies' from the definition of 'protected
site' in the 1983 Act.
   The available indications of the relevant policy are twofold. First, your Lordships have
had the advantage of seeing Department of Environment circular 28/77 issued to local   *f*
authorities in England on 25 March 1977. The appendix to that circular is headed 'Gipsy
Caravan Sites. Notes for the Guidance of Local Authorities in the Implementation of Part
II of the Caravan Sites Act 1968'. Paragraph 5 of the notes observes perspicaciously:

   'The criterion "nomadic habit of life" leads to a certain ambiguity, especially in
   relation to gipsies who settle for lengthy periods on authorised sites.'

But later passages in the notes firmly grasp the nettle of this ambiguity and encourage   *g*
local authorities to provide sites to accommodate gipsies in four categories as follows: (1)
emergency stopping places (paras 55 and 56); (2) transit or short-stay sites (para 57); (3)
residential sites (paras 58–60); (4) permanent sites for long-term residential use (paras 61–
65). The last of these categories can only have had in contemplation sites such as that at
Thistlebrook to which gipsies return year after year as their permanent residence but   *h*
from which they set forth at certain seasons to pursue their traditional nomadic way of
life.
   Second, there is ample evidence that the policy advocated in the circular with regard
to permanent sites for long-term residential use had been recognised by the Secretary of
State as an appropriate criterion before 1977 for application under s 12 of the 1968 Act
in deciding whether adequate provision had been made in a local authority area for the   *j*
accommodation of gipsies to justify designation of the area. The undisputed evidence of
the council's principal witness at the trial, which the judge accepted, was that 17 other
London boroughs besides Greenwich had been designated under s 12 on the basis that
they had made adequate provision for the accommodation of gipsies on sites which were
operated on similar lines to the Thistlebrook site, ie by providing permanent

accommodation for gipsies as a home base from which they pursued their nomadic habit
a of life only seasonally. At least eight of these designation orders were made by statutory
instruments dated between 1973 and 1975.

These considerations confirm me in the opinion that, even if there is an ambiguity in
the definition of 'gipsies' in s 16 of the 1968 Act, the intention of the legislature in the
1983 Act was clearly to exclude from the definition of 'protected site' sites such as that at
Thistlebrook provided by local authorities in discharge of their duty under s 6 of the
b 1968 Act to accommodate those whom they bona fide believe to be gipsies because they
are nomadic for part of the year, notwithstanding that they may establish a permanent
residence on the site by returning from year to year. Such a site will not become a
'protected site' even if some of the erstwhile nomads, as well they may, give up their
nomadic way of life entirely. It would be different, of course, if the local authority
adopted a policy of offering vacancies on the site to static residents with fixed full-time
c employment, but this is hardly ever likely to happen.

Any other construction of 'protected site' in s 5(1) of the 1983 Act would, it seems to
me, cause great difficulties both for local authorities and for most of the gipsy community
and would undo much of the good work which has been done in this difficult field.
Those already established on sites like Thistlebrook would, of course, enjoy full 1983
security of tenure. But local authorities in the position of the council would need to start
d de novo to discharge their duty under s 6 of the 1968 Act. Many existing designations
under s 12 would have to be revoked or would perhaps be automatically invalidated.
Your Lordships were told that, on the strength of the Court of Appeal's decision, some
proceedings had already been instituted seeking judicial review of existing orders made
under s 12. For the future, local authorities establishing new sites providing
accommodation for gipsies would have to be vigilant to prevent their residence acquiring
e any degree of permanency. This, I think, they could in practice only do by applying a
short rule-of-thumb limit of stay, which would be quite contrary to the interests of the
gipsy community.

I would accordingly allow the appeal, set aside the order of the Court of Appeal and
restore the order of the Woolwich County Court.

f **LORD TEMPLEMAN.** My Lords, for the reasons given by my noble and learned
friend Lord Bridge, I would allow this appeal.

LORD GRIFFITHS. My Lords, I agree that this appeal should be allowed for the
reasons given in the speech of my noble and learned friend Lord Bridge.

g **LORD ACKNER.** My Lords, I have had the advantage of reading the speech of my
noble and learned friend Lord Bridge, and I would allow this appeal.

LORD LOWRY. My Lords, I have had the advantage of reading in draft the speech of
my noble and learned friend Lord Bridge. I respectfully agree with it and for the reasons
h given by him I would allow the appeal.

Appeal allowed.

Solicitors: *Colin Roberts* (for the council); *Thos Boyd Whyte*, Bexleyheath (for the Powells).

Mary Rose Plummer   Barrister.

SECTION A

1. Who started the proceedings in *Greenwich London Borough Council* v. *Powell*?

2. Are there any other cases on the Mobile Homes Act 1983?

3. Give a short statement of the facts of the case. Try to exclude as many irrelevant facts as possible.

4. (i) Were these criminal or civil proceedings?
   (ii) In which courts was the case heard?
   (iii) What was the decision at first instance?
   (iv) Was the decision of the first instance judge overturned on appeal?
   (v) Was the first instance decision reported?

5. What point of law did the judges in *Greenwich London Borough Council* v. *Powell* have to consider?

6. Did Lords Templeman, Griffiths, Ackner and Lowry agree with Lord Bridge?

7. Why was Lord Bridge concerned to trace the "legislative history" underlying the Mobile Homes Act 1983?

SECTION B

8. Find alternative references to *Greenwich London Borough Council* v. *Powell*.

9. Has *Greenwich London Borough Council* v. *Powell* been cited in any subsequent case?

10. What use did Lord Bridge make of the case of *West Glamorgan CC* v. *Rafferty*?

11. Find out what kind of proceedings Lord Bridge is referring to when he says (at p. 71 d) that: "Your Lordships were told that, on the strength of the Court of Appeal's decision, some proceedings had already been instituted seeking judicial review of existing orders made under s.12."

12. Write a short statement giving the *ratio* of the case.

13. The Sunnysea Urban District Council has established a caravan site to provide accommodation for the many gypsies who pass through the area, especially during the summer holiday periods. What is the status of that site in the following circumstances:

(a) The Council only permits mobile home owners to stay on the site for a maximum of three months at a time, or a maximum of six months in any one calendar year.

(b) The Council operates a policy of allowing occupants of the site to remain for a maximum of six months at a time, but has been prepared to relax the enforcement of that policy to permit former occupants to remain permanently at the site on reaching the age of 65.

(c) The Council makes 20 plots on the site available to accommodate construction workers and their families who have arrived in the area to participate in the building of a new power station.

(d) In order to save money, the Council closes the site every year between 1st November and the following 1st March.

EXERCISE 4

Cases II(i)

798   All England Law Reports   **[1989] 1 All ER**

Caparo Industries plc v Dickman and others

COURT OF APPEAL, CIVIL DIVISION   *d*
O'CONNOR, BINGHAM AND TAYLOR LJJ
25, 26, 27, 28, 29 APRIL, 3 MAY, 29 JULY 1988

Negligence – Information or advice – Knowledge third party might rely on information – Auditor – Preparation of company's accounts – Duty to shareholder – Duty to prospective investor – Plaintiffs owning shares in public company – Plaintiffs making successful take-over bid for **e** *company in reliance on audited accounts of company – Accounts showing profit instead of loss – Whether reasonably foreseeable that shareholders and potential investors might rely on auditor's report when dealing in company's shares – Whether sufficient proximity between auditor and shareholders or potential investors – Whether just and reasonable to impose duty of care on auditor – Whether auditor owing duty of care to shareholders or potential investors to carry out* **f** *audit with reasonable care and skill.*

The plaintiffs owned shares in a public company, F plc, and were interested in making a take-over bid for it. As shareholders the plaintiffs were entitled to receive the audited accounts of F plc and after receipt of the accounts for the year ended 31 March 1984 they purchased more shares in F plc and later that year made a successful take-over bid. Following the take-over, the plaintiffs brought an action against, inter alios, the auditors **g** of F plc, alleging that they had made their bid in reliance on F plc's audited accounts and that the auditors had been negligent in auditing the accounts, which instead of showing a reported profit of £1·3m should have shown a loss of £0·46m. On the trial of a preliminary issue, the judge held that the auditors owed no duty of care to the plaintiffs either as shareholders or as potential investors. The plaintiffs appealed to the Court of **h** Appeal.

Held (O'Connor LJ dissenting) – The auditor of a public company owed a duty of care to individual shareholders to carry out his audit of the company using reasonable care and skill and, since it was reasonably foreseeable that shareholders and potential investors in the company might rely on the auditor's report in considering whether and how to deal **j** in the company's shares, there was sufficient proximity between the auditor and the shareholders arising out of the close and direct relationship between an auditor and the shareholders and the fact that the auditor voluntarily assumed direct responsibility to individual shareholders, and it was just and reasonable to impose a duty of care on the auditor. However, although such a duty was owed to a shareholder in respect of the purchase of further shares in the company, it was not owed to potential investors in, or *a* take-over bidders for, the company, having regard to the lack of proximity between the auditor and potential investor and the fact that it would not be just and reasonable to impose a duty on the auditor to non-shareholding investors. Accordingly, if the plaintiffs could show that the auditors had failed to exercise the ordinary skill and care of a reasonable and competent auditor and that they had relied on the audited accounts of F plc and had suffered damage as a result, they were entitled to succeed in their claim against them. The appeal would therefore be allowed to that extent (see p 806 *b* to *d*, *b* p 807 *h* to p 808 *b*, p 809 *h*, p 811 *j* to p 812 *a f* to *h*, p 813 *a*, p 815 *h*, p 816 *c d*, p 819 *f g*, p 820 *a* to *d f j*, p 821 *g j* to p 822 *a d e* and p 830 *h j*, post).

Ministry of Housing and Local Government v Sharp [1970] 1 All ER 1009, dicta of Lord Salmon in *Anns v Merton London Borough* [1977] 2 All ER 492 at 512–513, of Lord Keith in *Govenors of the Peabody Donation Fund v Sir Lindsay Parkinson & Co Ltd* [1984] 3 All ER 529 at 534 and of Lord Keith *Yuen Kun-yeu v A-G of Hong Kong* [1987] 2 All ER 705 at 710 *c* applied.

Scott Group Ltd v McFarlane [1978] 1 NZLR 553, *Twomax Ltd v Dickson M'Farlane & Robinson* 1982 SC 113 and *JEB Fasteners Ltd v Marks Bloom & Co (a firm)* [1983] 1 All ER 583 considered.

Notes

d For auditors' duties and auditors' reports, see 7(1) Halsbury's Laws (4th edn reissue) paras 905, 912–914 and for cases on the subject, see 9 Digest (Reissue) 601–607, 3593–3614.

For negligence in relation to statements by professional men, see 34 Halsbury's Laws (4th edn) para 53, and for cases on the subject, see 36(1) Digest (Reissue) 49–50, *149–158*.

Cases referred to in judgments

e *Anns v Merton London Borough* [1977] 2 All ER 492, [1978] AC 728, [1977] 2 WLR 1024, HL.
Bolam v Friern Hospital Management Committee [1957] 2 All ER 118, [1957] 1 WLR 582.
Candler v Crane Christmas & Co [1951] 1 All ER 426, [1951] 2 KB 164, CA.
Candlewood Navigation Corp Ltd v Mitsui OSK Lines Ltd, The Mineral Transporter, The Ibaraki Maru [1985] 2 All ER 935, [1986] AC 1, [1985] 3 WLR 381, PC.
f *Cann v Willson* (1888) 39 Ch D 39.
Citizens State Bank v Timm Schmidt & Co (1983) 113 Wis 2d 376, Wis SC.
Courteen Seed Co v Hong Kong and Shanghai Banking Corp (1927) 245 NY 377, NY Ct of Apps.
Credit Alliance Corp v Arthur Andersen & Co (1985) 65 NY 2d 536, NY Ct of Apps.
Donoghue (or M'Alister) v Stevenson [1932] AC 562, [1932] All ER Rep 1, HL.
g *Glanzer v Shepard* (1922) 233 NY 236, NY Ct of Apps.
Goldberg v Housing Authority of Newark (1962) 38 NJ 578, NJ SC.
Greater Nottingham Co-op Society Ltd v Cementation Piling and Foundations Ltd [1988] 2 All ER 971, [1989] QB 71, [1988] 3 WLR 396, CA.
Haig v Bamford (1976) 72 DLR (3d) 68, Can SC.
h *Hedley Byrne & Co Ltd v Heller & Partners Ltd* [1963] 2 All ER 575, [1964] AC 465, [1963] 3 WLR 101, HL.
Hill v Chief Constable of West Yorkshire [1988] 2 All ER 238, [1989] AC 53, [1988] 2 WLR 1049, HL.
Home Office v Dorset Yacht Co Ltd [1970] 2 All ER 294, [1970] AC 1004, [1970] 2 WLR 1140, HL.
j *Ingram Industries Inc v Nowicki* (1981) 527 F Supp 683, ED Ky.
JEB Fasteners Ltd v Marks Bloom & Co (a firm) [1981] 3 All ER 289; affd [1983] 1 All ER 583, CA.
Junior Books Ltd v Veitchi Co Ltd [1982] 3 All ER 201, [1983] 1 AC 520, [1982] 3 WLR 477, HL.
Kingston Cotton Mill Co, Re [1896] 1 Ch 6, CA.
Le Lievre v Gould [1893] 1 QB 491, CA.

London and General Bank, Re (No 2) [1895] 2 Ch 673, [1895–9] All ER Rep 953, CA.
McLoughlin v O'Brian [1982] 2 All ER 298, [1983] 1 AC 410, [1982] 2 WLR 982, HL.   *a*
Ministry of Housing and Local Government v Sharp [1970] 1 All ER 1009, [1970] 2 QB 223, [1970] 2 WLR 802, CA.
Muirhead v Industrial Tank Specialities Ltd [1985] 3 All ER 705, [1986] QB 507, [1985] 3 WLR 993, CA.
Mutual Life and Citizens' Assurance Co Ltd v Evatt [1971] 1 All ER 150, [1971] AC 793, [1971] 2 WLR 23, PC.   *b*
Peabody Donation Fund (Governors) v Sir Lindsay Parkinson & Co Ltd [1984] 3 All ER 529, [1985] AC 210, [1984] 3 WLR 953, HL.
Rhode Island Hospital Trust National Bank v Swartz Bresenoff Yavner & Jacobs (1972) 455 F 2d 847, US Ct of Apps, 5th Cir.
Rosenblum (H) Inc v Adler (1983) 93 NJ 324, NJ SC.
Ross v Caunters (a firm) [1979] 3 All ER 580, [1980] Ch 297, [1979] 3 WLR 605.   *c*
Rowling v Takaro Properties Ltd [1988] 1 All ER 163, [1988] AC 473, [1988] 2 WLR 418, PC.
Saif Ali v Sydney Mitchell & Co (a firm) [1978] 3 All ER 1033, [1980] AC 198, [1978] 3 WLR 849, HL.
SCM (UK) Ltd v W J Whittall & Son Ltd [1970] 3 All ER 245, [1971] 1 QB 337, [1970] 3 WLR 694, CA.   *d*
Scott Group Ltd v McFarlane [1978] 1 NZLR 553, NZ CA; *affg* [1975] 1 NZLR 582, NZ SC.
Simaan General Contracting Co v Pilkington Glass Ltd (No 2) [1988] 1 All ER 791, [1988] QB 758, [1988] 2 WLR 761, CA.
Spartan Steel and Alloys Ltd v Martin & Co (Contractors) Ltd [1972] 3 All ER 557, [1973] QB 27, [1972] 3 WLR 502, CA.   *e*
State Street Trust Co v Ernst (1938) 278 NY 104, NY Ct of Apps.
Sutherland Shire Council v Heyman (1985) 60 ALR 1, Aust HC.
Twomax Ltd v Dickson M'Farlane & Robinson 1982 SC 113, Outer House; *rvsd by consent* 1984 SLT 424, Inner House.
Ultramares Corp v Touche (1931) 255 NY 170, NY Ct of Apps.   *f*
W (an infant), Re [1971] 2 All ER 49, [1971] AC 682, [1971] 2 WLR 1011, HL.
Weller & Co v Foot and Mouth Disease Research Institute [1965] 3 All ER 560, [1966] 1 QB 569, [1965] 3 WLR 1082.
Yuen Kun-yeu v A-G of Hong Kong [1987] 2 All ER 705, [1988] AC 175, [1987] 3 WLR 776, PC.

Cases also cited   *g*
Cattle v Stockton Waterworks Co (1875) LR 10 QB 453, [1874–80] All ER Rep 220, DC.
Clarke v Bruce Lance & Co (a firm) [1988] 1 All ER 364, [1988] 1 WLR 881, CA.
Harris v Wyre Forest DC [1988] 1 All ER 691, [1988] QB 835, CA.
Hickman v Kent or Romney Marsh Sheepbreeders' Association [1915] 1 Ch 881, [1914–15] All ER Rep 900.   *h*
Leigh & Sillavan Ltd v Aliakmon Shipping Co Ltd, The Aliakmon [1986] 2 All ER 145, [1986] AC 785, HL.
Newton v Birmingham Small Arms Co Ltd [1906] 2 Ch 378.

Interlocutory appeal
The plaintiffs, Caparo Industries plc (Caparo), by writ dated 24 July 1985 brought an   *j*
action against the first and second defendants Stephen Graham Dickman and Robert
Anthony Dickman, who were the directors of Fidelity plc, and the third defendants,
Touche Ross & Co (the auditors), claiming damages against the first and second defendants
for fraud and against the auditors for negligence. The statement of claim alleged that in
July 1983 the directors of Fidelity plc forecast that the company's profits for the year

ended 31 March 1984 would be £2·2m. On 1 March 1984 the company's share price was

a 143p. On 22 May the company announced profits for the year ended 31 March 1984 of £1·3m and by 1 June the share price had fallen to 63p. Caparo purchased 100,000 shares in the company at 70p on 8 June and 50,000 shares at 73p on 12 June. On 12 June the audited accounts for the year ended 31 March 1984 were released to shareholders and in reliance on the information contained in the accounts Caparo purchased further shares in the company and by 6 July held 29·9% of the company's stock. On 4 September

b Caparo made a take-over bid for the company at 120p per share which was later increased to 125p per share at which price the directors of the company, including the first and second defendants, recommended shareholders to accept the offer. The bid was successful by 25 October. By para 7 of the statement of claim it was alleged that the accounts overstated the profits of the company by including non-existent stock, making under-provision for obsolete stock and making under-provision in respect of after-date sales

c credits. It was alleged that the true position of the comany was that it had made a loss of at least £465,000 and it was claimed that if Caparo had known the true position it would not have made its take-over bid for the company at the price it did or at all. It was alleged that the first and second defendants had forged stock sheets, had included as sales transactions which were not sales at all and had misrepresented the company's position to Caparo, and it was further alleged that the auditors had been negligent in failing to

d discover the forgery and other irregularities perpetrated by the first and second defendants when carrying out the audit of the accounts. Caparo claimed that the auditors knew or ought to have known that the company required financial assistance and ought to have foreseen that the company was vulnerable to a take-over and that persons such as Caparo might well rely on the accounts for the purpose of making a take-over and might well suffer loss if the accounts were inaccurate. By order of Sir Neil Lawson, sitting as a judge

e of the High Court in the Queen's Bench Division in chambers the question whether on the facts alleged the auditors owed a duty of care to Caparo as (a) potential investors in the company or (b) shareholders in the company in respect of the audit of the company's accounts for the year ended 31 March 1984 was tried as a preliminary issue. On the trial of that issue Sir Neil Lawson ([1988] BCLC 387) held that the auditors did not owe a duty of care to Caparo either as potential investors or as shareholders in the company. Caparo

f appealed.

Christopher Bathurst QC and *Michael Brindle* for Caparo.
Peter Goldsmith QC and *Stephen Moriarty* for the auditors.

g   *Cur adv vult*

29 July. The following judgments were delivered.

BINGHAM LJ (giving the first judgment at the invitation of O'Connor LJ).

h   'It is not easy, or perhaps possible, to find a single proposition encapsulating a comprehensive rule to determine when persons are brought into a relationship which creates a duty of care upon those who make statements towards those who may act upon them and when persons are not brought into such a relationship.'

Thus said the Lord Ordinary (Stewart) in *Twomax Ltd v Dickson M'Farlane & Robinson* 1982 SC 113 at 122. Others have spoken to similar effect. In *Hedley Byrne & Co Ltd v*

j *Heller & Partners Ltd* [1963] 2 All ER 575 at 601, [1964] AC 465 at 514 Lord Hodson said:

       'I do not think that it is possible to catalogue the special features which must be found to exist before the duty of care will arise in a given case . . .'

and Lord Devlin said ([1963] 2 All ER 575 at 611, [1964] AC 465 at 529–530):

'I do not think it possible to formulate with exactitude all the conditions under
which the law will in a specific case imply a voluntary undertaking, any more than   *a*
it is possible to formulate those in which the law will imply a contract.'

In *Mutual Life and Citizens' Assurance Co Ltd v Evatt* [1971] 1 All ER 150 at 162, [1971] AC
793 at 810 Lord Reid and Lord Morris said:

'In our judgment it is not possible to lay down hard and fast rules as to when a
duty of care arises in this or in any other class of case where negligence is alleged.'   *b*

In *Rowling v Takaro Properties Ltd* [1988] 1 All ER 163 at 172, [1988] AC 473 at 501 Lord
Keith, emphasising the need for careful analysis case by case, said:

'It is at this stage that it is necessary, before concluding that a duty of care should
be imposed, to consider all the relevant circumstances. One of the considerations
underlying certain recent decisions of the House of Lords (*Governors of the Peabody*   *c*
Donation Fund v Sir Lindsay Parkinson & Co Ltd [1984] 3 All ER 529, [1985] AC 210)
and of the Privy Council (*Yuen Kun-yeu v A-G of Hong Kong* [1987] 2 All ER 705,
[1988] AC 175) is the fear that a too literal application of the well-known observation
of Lord Wilberforce in *Anns v Merton London Borough* [1977] 2 All ER 492 at 498,
[1978] AC 728 at 751–752 may be productive of a failure to have regard to, and to   *d*
analyse and weigh, all the relevant considerations in considering whether it is
appropriate that a duty of care should be imposed. Their Lordships consider that
question to be of an intensely pragmatic character, well suited for gradual
development but requiring most careful analysis. It is one on which all common
law jurisdictions can learn much from each other, because, apart from exceptional
cases, no sensible distinction can be drawn in this respect between the various   *e*
countries and the social conditions existing in them. It is incumbent on the courts
in different jurisdictions to be sensitive to each other's reactions; but what they are
all searching for in others, and each of them striving to achieve, is a careful analysis
and weighing of the relevant competing considerations.'

The many decided cases on this subject, if providing no simple ready-made solution to
the question whether or not a duty of care exists, do indicate the requirements to be   *f*
satisfied before a duty is found.

The first is foreseeability. It is not, and could not be, in issue between these parties that
reasonable foreseeability of harm is a necessary ingredient of a relationship in which a
duty of care will arise: see *Yuen Kun-yeu v A-G of Hong Kong* [1987] 2 All ER 705 at 710,
[1988] AC 175 at 192. It is also common ground that reasonable foreseeability, although
a necessary, is not a sufficient condition of the existence of a duty. This, as Lord Keith   *g*
observed in *Hill v Chief Constable of West Yorkshire* [1988] 2 All ER 238 at 241, [1989] AC
53 at 60, has been said almost too frequently to require repetition.

The second requirement is more elusive. It is usually described as proximity, which
means not simple physical proximity but extends to—

'... such close and direct relations that the act complained of directly affects a   *h*
person whom the person alleged to be bound to take care would know would be
directly affected by his careless act.'

(See *Donoghue v Stevenson* [1932] AC 562 at 581, [1932] All ER Rep 1 at 12 per Lord
Atkin.) Sometimes the alternative expression 'neighbourhood' is used, as by Lord Reid
in the *Hedley Byrne* case [1963] 2 All ER 575 at 580, [1964] AC 465 at 483 and Lord   *j*
Wilberforce in *Anns v Merton London Borough* [1977] 2 All ER 492 at 498, [1978] AC 728
at 751, with more conscious reference to Lord Atkin's speech in the earlier case.
Sometimes, as in the *Hedley Byrne* case, attention is concentrated on the existence of a
special relationship. Sometimes it is regarded as significant that the parties' relationship
is 'equivalent to contract' (see the *Hedley Byrne* case [1963] 2 All ER 575 at 610, [1964] AC

465 at 529 per Lord Devlin) or falls 'only just short of a direct contractual relationship'
a (see *Junior Books Ltd v Veitchi Co Ltd* [1982] 3 All ER 201 at 204, [1983] 1 AC 520 at 533
per Lord Fraser) or is 'as close as it could be short of actual privity of contract' (see the
Junior Books case [1982] 3 All ER 201 at 214, [1983] 1 AC 520 at 546 per Lord Roskill). In
some cases, and increasingly, reference is made to the voluntary assumption of
responsibility: see *Muirhead v Industrial Tank Specialities Ltd* [1985] 3 All ER 705 at 715,
[1986] QB 507 at 528 per Robert Goff LJ, *Yuen Kun-yeu v A-G of Hong Kong* [1987] 2 All
b ER 705 at 711, 714, [1988] AC 175 at 192, 196, *Simaan General Contracting Co v Pilkington
Glass Ltd (No 2)* [1988] 1 All ER 791 at 803, 805, [1988] QB 758 at 781, 784 and *Greater
Nottingham Co-op Society Ltd v Cementation Piling and Foundations Ltd* [1988] 2 All ER 971
at 984, 989, 990, [1989] QB 71 at 100, 106, 107. Both the analogy with contract and the
assumption of responsibility have been relied on as a test of proximity in foreign courts
as well as our own: see *Glanzer v Shepard* (1922) 233 NY 236, *Ultramares Corp v Touche*
c (1931) 255 NY 170 at 182–183, *State Street Trust Co v Ernst* (1938) 278 NY 104 at 111–
112 and *Scott Group Ltd v McFarlane* [1978] 1 NZLR 553 at 566. It may very well be that
in tortious claims based on negligent misstatement these motions are particularly
apposite. The content of the requirement of proximity, whatever language is used, is
not, I think, capable of precise definition. The approach will vary according to the
particular facts of the case, as is reflected in the varied language used. But the focus of the
d inquiry is on the closeness and directness of the relationship between the parties. In
determining this, foreseeability must, I think, play an important part: the more obvious
it is that A's act or omission will cause harm to B, the less likely a court will be to hold
that the relationship of A and B is insufficiently proximate to give rise to a duty of care.
    The third requirement to be met before a duty of care will be held to be owed by A to
B is that the court should find it just and reasonable to impose such a duty: see *Governors
e of the Peabody Donation Fund v Sir Lindsay Parkinson & Co Ltd* [1984] 3 All ER 529 at 534,
[1985] AC 210 at 241 per Lord Keith. This requirement, I think, covers very much the
same ground as Lord Wilberforce's second stage test in *Anns's* case [1977] 2 All ER 492 at
498, [1978] AC 728 at 752 and what in cases such as *Spartan Steel and Alloys Ltd v Martin
& Co (Contractors) Ltd* [1972] 3 All ER 557, [1973] QB 27 and *McLoughlin v O'Brian* [1982]
2 All ER 298, [1983] 1 AC 410 was called policy. It was considerations of this kind which
f Lord Fraser had in mind when he said in *Candlewood Navigation Corp Ltd v Mitsui OSK
Lines Ltd, The Mineral Transporter, The Ibaraki Maru* [1985] 2 All ER 935 at 945, [1986]
AC 1 at 25:

        '... some limit or control mechanism has to be imposed on the liability of a
        wrongdoer towards those who have suffered economic damage in consequence of
g   his negligence.'

The requirement cannot, perhaps, be better put than it was by Weintraub CJ in *Goldberg
v Housing Authority of Newark* (1962) 38 NJ 578 at 583:

        'Whether a *duty* exists is ultimately a question of fairness. The inquiry involves a
        weighing of the relationship of the parties, the nature of the risk, and the public
h   interest in the proposed solution.' (Weintraub CJ's emphasis.)

If the imposition of a duty on a defendant would be for any reason oppressive, or would
expose him, in Cardozo CJ's famous phrase in *Ultramares Corp v Touche* 255 NY 170 at
179—

        'to a liability in an indeterminate amount for an indeterminate time to an
j   indeterminate class...'

that will weigh heavily, probably conclusively, against the imposition of a duty (if it has
not already shown a fatal lack of proximity). On the other hand, a duty will be the more
readily found if the defendant is voluntarily exercising a professional skill for reward, if
the victim of his carelessness has (in the absence of a duty) no means of redress, if the

duty contended for (as in *McLoughlin v O'Brian*) arises naturally from a duty which already exists or if the imposition of a duty is thought to promote some socially desirable *a* objective.

At the heart of this case lies the role of the statutory auditor. That role is, I think, without close analogy. Its peculiar characteristics derive from the nature of the public limited liability company. The members, or shareholders, of the company are its owners. But they are too numerous, and in most cases too unskilled, to undertake the day-to-day management of that which they own. So responsibility for day-to-day management of *b* the company is delegated to directors. The shareholders, despite their overall powers of control, are in most companies for most of the time investors and little more. But it would, of course, be unsatisfactory and open to abuse if the shareholders received no report on the financial stewardship of their investment save from those to whom the stewardship had been entrusted. So provision is made for the company in general meeting to appoint an auditor (Companies Act 1985, s 384) whose duty is to investigate *c* and form an opinion on the adequacy of the company's accounting records and returns and the correspondence between the company's accounting records and returns and its accounts (s 237). The auditor has then to report to the company's members (among other things) whether in his opinion the company's accounts give a true and fair view of the company's financial position (s 236). In carrying out his investigation and informing his opinion the auditor necessarily works very closely with the directors and officers of the *d* company. He receives his remuneration from the company. He naturally, and rightly, regards the company as his client. But he is employed by the company to exercise his professional skill and judgment for the purpose of giving the shareholders an independent report on the reliability of the company's accounts and thus on their investment. Vaughan Williams J said in *Re Kingston Cotton Mill Co* [1896] 1 Ch 6 at 11:
e
'No doubt he is acting antagonistically to the directors in the sense that he is appointed by the shareholders to be a check upon them.'

The auditor's report must be read before the company in general meeting and must be open to inspection by any member of the company (s 241). It is attached to and forms part of the company's accounts (ss 238(3) and 239). A copy of the company's accounts *f* (including the auditor's report) must be sent to every member (s 240). Any member of the company, even if not entitled to have a copy of the accounts sent to him, is entitled to be furnished with a copy of the company's last accounts on demand and without charge (s 246).

It is pointed out, quite correctly, that the primary duty in and about the preparation of accounts is that of the directors. It is the duty of the company to keep proper *g* accounting records (s 221). It is the duty of the directors to prepare an annual profit and loss account and balance sheet (s 227) complying with the statutory requirements (s 228). It is the duty of the directors to lay the accounts before the company in general meeting (s 241(1)) and to deliver a copy to the registrar of companies (s 241(3)), who must make them available for inspection by any person (s 709). It is the directors who are criminally liable for breach of the statutory accounting requirements (s 245). The auditor's role is *h* secondary and accessory. His task is to vet the accounts, not to draw them up in the first place or carry out the detailed accounting work necessary to draw them up.

These provisions show, as I think, a plain parliamentary intention that shareholders in a public company shall receive independent and reliable information on the financial standing of the company (and thus of their investment): see *Re London and General Bank (No 2)* [1895] 2 Ch 673 at 682, [1895–9] All ER Rep 953 at 956 per Lindley LJ. For what *j* purpose is this required? The company lawyer's answer would, I think, be: to enable the members to make an informed judgment whether, and if so how, they should exercise the powers of control enjoyed by them as members. The commercial man's answer would more probably be: to enable each shareholder to make an informed judgment whether he should retain or reduce or increase his holding of shares in the company. I *a* see no reason to reject either of these answers. Successive Companies Acts have promulgated a detailed code designed to ensure that the ultimate powers of decision are vested in the members. But it is a truism that possession of adequate information is a necessary condition of effective decision-making. It would not be realistic to expect shareholders to exercise their powers of control on the basis only of such information as the directors chose to give them. But I think these provisions also reflect a wider and more commercial intention. The growth and development of limited liability companies

b over a relatively very short period have been phenomenal. Their proliferation and expansion have depended on their acceptance by the investing public as an advantageous and (on the whole) reliable medium of investment. The statutory requirements that companies account to their members and that auditors express an independent opinion to shareholders on the truth and accuracy of company accounts are in my view designed (in part at least) to fortify confidence in the holding of shares as a medium of investment

c by enabling shareholders to make informed investment decisions. There are obvious reasons, both economic and social, why this end should be regarded as desirable.

The requirement that a company make its accounts available for inspection by members of the public who are not shareholders is imposed for reasons which are in part the same and in part different from those just considered. Submission of accounts to the registrar could be required for purposes of official supervision and regulation, but this

d would not of itself require the accounts to be available for inspection by the public. This additional requirement must in my view be imposed (in part at least) for the protection of those dealing with the company as contracting parties, creditors, lenders and even, perhaps, defendants in litigation. But again I think that wider commercial considerations play a part. It would not be conducive to a flourishing and orderly market in company shares, which is plainly thought to be desirable, if reliable information of a company's

e performance were restricted to its shareholders, directors and employees. The publication of accounts must limit, if it cannot eliminate, the scope for rumour-inspired speculation and thus promote an informed and orderly market. It enables prospective investors, like shareholders, to make informed decisions. For such prospective investors the independent opinion of the auditor has the same significance as for existing shareholders.

f It is common ground between the parties that an auditor owes a duty to the company which appoints him to exercise reasonable care and skill in conducting the audit and making his audit report. Such a duty is plainly to be implied into the contract between auditor and company. A coincident duty in tort will also arise. If the auditor breaches his duty he will be liable to the company for any reasonably foreseeable loss the company suffers as a result of his breach. Helpful examples were given. Thus, for example, the

g company may have a good claim if an auditor's negligence allows a dishonest employee to continue defrauding it or fails to alert the company to the need to take steps to improve performance or eliminate losses. But this duty will not of course avail a shareholder or investor who makes a mistaken investment decision on the strength of a negligent audit report, because that will cause no loss to and therefore support no claim by the company.

The judge held that the auditor owes no duty of care to the shareholders as a body or

h class. For reasons which will appear when I consider the position of individual shareholders, I doubt the correctness of this conclusion, unless it be that damage to the shareholders as a class is not reasonably foreseeable. In almost any situation in which damage has been suffered by the shareholders as a class, damage will also have been suffered by the company and in the ordinary way the company will then be the appropriate plaintiff. Counsel suggested only one case in which damage would be

j suffered by the shareholders as a class but not by the company: where a parent company, in reliance on a negligent report by the auditor of its subsidiary, sold its shareholding in the subsidiary at an undervalue. No doubt other examples could be elaborated. But this example depends on the singularity of the shareholders as a class and it seems clear that a duty owed to shareholders as a class, if existing at all, would be of minimal practical significance.

So I turn to consider the first major question arising on this appeal, which is whether the auditor of a public company owes any, and if so what, duty of care to individual shareholders (as distinct from shareholders as a class). This is a question to be answered by applying to the special facts of this relationship the three requirements which I mentioned at the outset.

The judge held that the foreseeability of economic loss to Caparo Industries plc (Caparo) as a shareholder was present when the auditors' report was published. This finding has not been challenged. It was therefore common ground that Caparo could satisfy the first and necessary requirement of foreseeability. I have no doubt this conclusion is correct. The auditors of course knew that their report would be communicated to those who were registered as shareholders when the accounts were sent to members under s 240 or when the report was read in general meeting under s 241. They must have known that some shareholders might rely on the report and accounts in making investment decisions. They must have known that an unqualified report, negligently made, might cause individual shareholders to suffer loss by selling if the accounts undervalued the company's worth or buying if the accounts overvalued the company's worth. These findings are, I think, inherent in the conclusion that economic loss to Caparo as a shareholder was foreseeable by the auditors as a result of any failure to exercise reasonable care in conducting their audit and reporting to the shareholders.

It was on the second requirement of proximity that major battle between the parties was joined. Caparo's case was simple. Auditors are appointed for the important and specific purpose of reporting to the shareholders. A private report to the directors will not suffice (see *Re London and General Bank Ltd (No 2)* [1895] 2 Ch 673, [1895–9] All ER Rep 953). The 1985 Act requires a copy of the report to reach the breakfast table or desk of every shareholder and the report itself to be read before the company in general meeting and to be opened to inspection by any member. Relations between auditor and shareholder are both close and direct. A lack of care will directly affect the very person whose interest the auditor is engaged to protect. *Hedley Byrne & Co Ltd v Heller & Partners Ltd* [1963] 2 All ER 575, [1964] AC 465 shows that the relationship of A and B may be sufficiently proximate if, independently of contract, A assumes the responsibility of giving B deliberate advice; if A engages B contractually to give advice to C, the relationship of B and C is no less proximate, however that expression is interpreted.

Counsel for the auditors sought to rebut Caparo's argument on proximity by a sustained and closely reasoned submission. Most of this was specifically directed to the auditors' relationship with investors who are not shareholders but the principal points applied equally to shareholders. The starting point of the argument was that the law treats negligent words differently from negligent acts. The peculiar character of words has led to insistence on closer proximity between the parties before a duty of care can arise than is required where physical injury or damage is in issue. That this is so emerges, I think, clearly from the *Hedley Byrne* case itself [1963] 2 All ER 575 at 580, 613 [1964] AC 465 at 482, 534 esp per Lord Reid and Lord Pearce. The trend of authority over the last 25 years shows considerable wariness in upholding claims for economic loss divorced from physical injury or damage, although lack of proximity has not usually proved the plaintiff's undoing.

The fundamental submission of counsel for the auditors was that voluntary assumption of direct responsibility to the plaintiff (and thus, here, to Caparo as shareholder) in circumstances equivalent to contract is the touchstone of proximity in cases such as this. This requires that the auditor should deliberately accept a particular responsibility to the shareholder in addition to the responsibility already existing to the company. This also requires that the statement should be made for the very purpose of a particular transaction of which the auditor knows, that the shareholder should be the person (or a member of a small and determinate class) for whom the statement is made and that there should be some communication or conduct linking the auditor to the shareholder so as to show his acceptance of special responsibility to the shareholder. Judged by these tests the *a* relationship between auditor and shareholder (it was said) lacks the proximity necessary before a duty of care can arise.

I think that at this stage of the inquiry it is important to concentrate on the substance of what one is investigating, which is the degree of closeness between the parties. It is only too easy to be mesmerised by expressions used in other cases which, however apt in those cases, provide no universally applicable yardstick. The language used in other cases guides but does not govern.

b Thus 'voluntary assumption of responsibility', although a very useful expression, does not provide a single, simple litmus test of proximity. In *Ministry of Housing and Local Government v Sharp* [1970] 1 All ER 1009 at 1018–1019, [1970] 2 QB 223 at 268–269 Lord Denning MR said:

> *c* 'Counsel for the defendants submitted to us, however, that the correct principle did not go to that length. He said that a duty to use due care (where there was no contract) only arose when there was a voluntary assumption of responsibility. I do not agree. He relied particularly on the words of Lord Reid in *Hedley Byrne & Co Ltd v Heller & Partners Ltd* [1963] 2 All ER 575 at 583, [1964] AC 465 at 487, and of Lord Devlin ([1963] 2 All ER 575 at 610–611, [1964] AC 465 at 529). I think they used those words because of the special circumstances of that case (where the bank
> *d* disclaimed responsibility). But they did not in any way mean to limit the general principle. In my opinion the duty to use due care in a statement arises, not from any voluntary assumption of responsibility, but from the fact that the person making it knows, or ought to know, that others, being his neighbours in this regard, would act on the faith of the statement being accurate. That is enough to bring the duty into being. It is owed, of course, to the person to whom the certificate is issued
> *e* and who he knows is going to act on it, see the judgment of Cardozo J in *Glanzer v Shepard* (1922) 233 NY 236. But it is also owed to any person who he knows or ought to know, will be injuriously affected by a mistake, such as the incumbrancer here.'

Salmon LJ said ([1970] 1 All ER 1009 at 1027–1028, [1970] 2 QB 223 at 279):

> *f* 'I do not accept that, in all cases, the obligation to take reasonable care necessarily depends on a voluntary assumption of responsibility.'

Cross LJ added ([1970] 1 All ER 1009 at 1038, [1970] 2 QB 223 at 291):

> 'It is true that the phrase "voluntary assumption of risk" occurs frequently in the speeches in the *Hedley Byrne* case, but I agree with the judge that that case did not
> *g* purport to lay down any metes and bounds within which legal liability in tort for false statements, on which the parties to whom they are made rely, has to be confined. (See in particular per Lord Devlin ([1963] 2 All ER 575 at 611, [1964] AC 465 at 530–531).) I see no sufficient reason why in an appropriate case the liability should not extend to cases in which the defendant is obliged to make the statement which proves to be false.'

h If, however, one asks whether the auditors here voluntarily assumed direct responsibility to individual shareholders it seems to me inescapable that they did. They did not have to accept appointment as auditors. Their work was not in reality unrewarded. They undertook it, no doubt, in the ordinary course of professional practice in order to earn a fee and, perhaps, obtain additional work from the company. But they knew that the end-

j product of their audit was a report to shareholders on which they knew any shareholder might rely. It would, I think, be surprising if in those circumstances the auditors were said not voluntarily to have assumed a responsibility to each shareholder.

There is, of course, no contract between the shareholders (either as a class or individually) and the auditor. But certainly as between the shareholders as a class and the auditor the relationship seems to me to be very close indeed to contract. The auditor's contract is made with the company, but it is a contract made on the company's behalf by the shareholders; the auditor's fee is paid out of company funds otherwise available (in part) for distribution to the shareholders; and the object of the contract is to obtain a report to shareholders made independently of the company itself. As between the shareholders individually and the auditor the analogy with contract is less compelling, but in my view it remains close. If a company engaged a doctor to examine and advise its senior employees, I would regard the relationship between the doctor and each individual employee as equivalent to contract for all except strictly legal purposes. The relationship between auditor and individual shareholder is less close, but not in my opinion critically so.

In *Candler v Crane Christmas & Co* [1951] 1 All ER 426 at 435, [1951] 2 KB 164 at 183 Denning LJ confined the duty which he upheld to—

'cases where the accountant prepares his accounts and makes his report for the guidance of the very person in the very transaction in question.'

In *Glanzer v Shepard* (1922) 233 NY 236 a buyer who paid his seller on the faith of an erroneous certificate of weight given by a public weigher succeeded in a claim against the weigher because use of the certificate by the buyer for the purpose of paying the seller was, as the weigher knew, 'the end and aim of the transaction'. These cases must be read in context. Denning LJ was naturally concerned to make his departure from binding authority as narrow as possible, and did not wish to be thought to give his blessing to the foundation of liability on a careless misstatement made to the world at large. Thus immediately after the words quoted above he continued:

'That is sufficient for the decision of this case. I can well understand that it would be going too far to make an accountant liable to any person in the land who chooses to rely on the accounts in matters of business, for that would expose him ... to ... "liability in an indeterminate amount for an indeterminate time to an indeterminate class."'

When, in *Ultramares Corp v Touche* (1931) 255 NY 170, Cardozo CJ came to comment on his earlier decision in *Glanzer v Shepard* he also was at pains to disavow the possibility of liability at large. But he approved an earlier statement by Pound J in *Courteen Seed Co v Hong Kong and Shanghai Banking Corp* (1927) 245 NY 377 at 381 that—

'negligent words are not actionable unless they are uttered directly, with knowledge or notice that they will be acted on, to one to whom the speaker is bound by some relation of duty, arising out of public calling, contract or otherwise, to act with care if he acts at all.'

(See 255 NY 170 at 185.)

This formulation would not exclude the finding of a sufficiently proximate relationship in the present case if the words 'will be acted on' are replaced, as in English law I think they should be, by 'may be acted on'.

All these cases are concerned to insist on the need for a clear and close nexus between the author and the victim of the allegedly careless misstatement. In cases of physical injury or damage the nexus rarely causes a problem. It is enough that the plaintiff chances to be (out of the whole world) the person with whom the defendant collided or who purchased the offending ginger beer. Where careless words causing economic loss are complained of, more is required to establish proximity than the fortuity of suffering damage. Thus in recent consideration of *Cann v Willson* (1888) 39 Ch D 39, *Le Lievre v Gould* [1893] 1 QB 491 and *Candler's* case, and in cases such as those I consider at the end of this judgment, attention has been concentrated on the author's knowledge of the victim's intention to rely on the statement complained of in a particular way. But none of the cases involved relations between a shareholder and a statutory auditor. None was a case in which the author was subject to a statutory duty to report to the victim in a

capacity in which the victim sues. Even in the absence of a statutory duty, and without
a regard to an accountant's statutory liability (with or without negligence) for
misstatements in a prospectus, Lord Salmon in *Anns v Merton London Borough* [1977] 2 All
ER 492 at 512–513, [1978] AC 728 at 769 plainly regarded the relationship of certifying
accountant and subscriber as sufficiently proximate to give rise ot a duty of care and he
said:

b   'There are a wide variety of instances in which a statement is negligently made by
          a professional man which he knows will be relied on by many people besides his
          client, eg a well-known firm of accountants certifies in a prospectus the annual
          profits of the company issuing it and unfortunately, due to negligence on the part
          of the accountants, the profits are seriously overstated. Those persons who invested
          in the company in reliance on the accuracy of the accountants' certificate would
c   have a claim for damages against the accountants for any money they might have
          lost as a result of the accountants' negligence: see the *Hedley Byrne* case.'

I do not regard the relationship Lord Salmon had in mind as more proximate than the
present. A prospectus, of course, solicits investment whereas an auditor's report appended
to a company's accounts does not. But the recipient of a prospectus (foreseeably) may or
d may not subscribe. The shareholder receiving a company's accounts and auditor's report
(foreseeably) may or may not base an investment decision on them. The greatest
difference is that the class of potential subscribers is in all probability larger and less
determinate than the class of shareholders.
     It is true, as counsel for the auditors argued, that in some of the authorities (as for
example *Haig v Bamford* (1976) 72 DLR (3d) 68 at 75, 80) reference is made to the victim's
e membership of a 'limited class' as a test of proximity. By 'limited', it was said, one should
understand 'small and determinate'. I have little doubt that a victim of a careless misstatement falling within Cardozo CJ's 'indeterminate class' would fail to show sufficient
proximity, as recognised by Lord Wilberforce in *Anns* [1977] 2 All ER 492 at 504, [1978]
AC 728 at 758 when he referred to the possible objection that an endless, indeterminate
class of potential plaintiffs may be called into existence.' Again the emphasis was on the
f need for a clear and close nexus between the author and the victim of the allegedly
careless misstatement. But the class of shareholders to whom an auditor reports is not
indeterminate. The composition of the class changes but the members of it can at any
instant be precisely identified. It cannot be predicted who within that class will rely on
the report, but that does not make indeterminate the class to whose members the duty is
owed but only the identity of the potential claimant. The class may of course, in a large
g public company, be very numerous. That is a relevant consideration when deciding
whether it is just and reasonable and whether as a matter of policy a duty should be
imposed, but I do not think it can deprive of proximity a relationship otherwise having
that quality. Lord Salmon cannot have thought so.
     Weighing the competing submissions on proximity in the light of the many
     authorities cited, I am left in no real doubt but that there is a sufficiently proximate
h relationship between the statutory auditor and the shareholder to whom he reports to
sustain a duty of care which it is otherwise right to impose.
     I come, therefore, to the third requirement to be satisfied by Caparo, that it is in all the
circumstances just and reasonable to impose a duty of care on a statutory auditor towards
individual shareholders. Caparo's case was again simple. The duty contended for obliges
j an auditor to do nothing which he is not already obliged to do under his contract with
the company. The existing obligation is one from which the auditor cannot be excused
(see s 310 of the 1985 Act). The duty contended for would simply extend a right of
redress, if the auditor failed to perform his duties with reasonable care and skill, from the
company, which would rarely have a claim, to shareholders, who foreseeably would. It is
just and in principle desirable that those who fail to perform their professional duties in

accordance with professional standards should compensate those foreseeably injured by their failure.

The auditors relied on a number of matters as showing that it would not be just or politic to impose the duty contended for. Where a shareholder suffered loss by relying on misleading accounts, the primary responsibility lay with the directors, who might well be fraudulent. But the directors would usually lack the means to satisfy a large claim against them. So the tendency would be to add the auditor as a party in order to gain the benefit of the auditor's insurance cover, even where no defect in the audit procedure could at the outset be identified. There was, however, already extreme difficulty in obtaining professional indemnity cover. If it could not be obtained, an auditor's personal fortune would be at risk, perhaps through the error of his partner or employee. If it could be obtained, the cost would be high and this would necessarily be reflected in the cost of audit work to the prejudice of the great mass of shareholders. An undesirably defensive and self-protective attitude would moreover be encouraged. Reliance was placed on Lord Keith's observations in *Rowling v Takaro Properties Ltd* [1988] 1 All ER 163 at 173, [1988] AC 473 at 502:

'The third is the danger of overkill. It is to be hoped that, as a general rule, imposition of liability in negligence will lead to a higher standard of care in the performance of the relevant type of act; but sometimes not only may this not be so, but the imposition of liability may even lead to harmful consequences. In other words, the cure may be worse than the disease. There are reasons for believing that this may be so in cases where liability is imposed on local authorities whose building inspectors have been negligent in relation to the inspection of foundations, as in the *Anns* case itself, because there is a danger that the building inspectors of some local authorities may react to that decision by simply increasing, unnecessarily, the requisite depth of foundations, thereby imposing a very substantial and unnecessary financial burden on members of the community. A comparable danger may exist in cases such as the present, because, once it became known that liability in negligence may be imposed on the ground that a minister has misconstrued a statute and so acted ultra vires, the cautious civil servant may go to extreme lengths in ensuring that legal advice, or even the opinion of the court, is obtained before decisions are taken, thereby leading to unnecessary delay in a considerable number of cases.'

The duty would, it was said, if imposed, expose auditors to claims indeterminate in number and unquantifiable in amount for periods which could not be calculated. Rather than incur this burden accountants might decline to undertake audit work. It was no answer to say that auditors would usually defeat claims made against them because they would still have the burden and expense of defending themselves, with the inevitable risk of damage to their professional reputation. This was all unnecessary: if shareholders were dissatisfied with the auditor's performance they could remove him.

This argument amounted to much more than a simple submission that a decision in favour of Caparo would open the floodgates to an uncontrollable inrush of claims against auditors. But certain features of the argument, in particular concerning insurance, are hard to assess in the absence of evidence or inquiry. I think that certain conclusions can none the less be reached. (1) The removal of an auditor gives no adequate redress to a shareholder who has suffered loss through his negligence. It is not in any event a remedy open to a minority shareholder or one who has sold his shareholding in reliance on a negligent audit report. (2) Given the duty which already exists, I do not think recognition of a duty to individual shareholders would lead to any significant change in audit practice. (3) Given the duty which already exists, I do not think recognition of a duty to shareholders would lead competent accountants to decline audit work, at any rate unless there were comparable alternative work available which did not expose them to potential liability. (4) I do not think it realistic to envisage auditors being subjected to hundreds or

thousands of claims, as a pharmaceutical manufacturer might be. The reality is that the
a greater the number of claims the smaller each must necessarily be, and the smaller the
claim the smaller the chance that the shareholder will embark on an expensive action.
The probability is that action will be brought, if at all, by one large shareholder, as here,
or by a handful of large shareholders. The quantification of damage would not, I think,
be more problematical than in many tortious situations. The odds are that the auditor's
error, if any, will come to light fairly soon; it is unlikely to lie undiscovered for years, as
b may happen with a negligently designed building or bridge. (5) The shareholder's claim
will in the ordinary way be a very hard claim to establish.

This last point deserves a little elaboration. As in any other claim of professional
negligence the claimant must show that the defendant failed to exercise the ordinary
skill of an ordinary competent man exercising his particular art: see *Bolam v Friern
Hospital Management Committee* [1957] 2 All ER 118, [1957] 1 WLR 582. Lord Diplock
c said in *Saif Ali v Sydney Mitchell & Co (a firm)* [1978] 3 All ER 1033 at 1043, [1980] AC
198 at 220:

> 'No matter what profession it may be, the common law does not impose on those
> who practice it any liability for damage resulting from what in the result turns out
> to have been errors of judgment, unless the error was such as no reasonably well-
> informed and competent member of that profession could have made.'
d

These principles afford special protection to auditors, whose task is not to draw the
accounts nor to turn every stone and open every cupboard but to exercise their very
considerable skill and judgment in carrying out checks and investigations in accordance
with complex but none the less detailed and explicit professional standards. Many entries
in the accounts will depend on the directors' judgment, and here it is for the auditors not
e to satisfy themselves that the judgment is correct but that it is reasonable. Lord Hailsham
LC said in *Re W (an infant)* [1971] 2 All ER 49 at 56, [1971] AC 682 at 700:

> 'Two reasonable parents can perfectly reasonably come to opposite conclusions on
> the same set of facts without forfeiting their title to be regarded as reasonable . . .
> Not every reasonable exercise of judgment is right, and not every mistaken exercise
f > of judgment is unreasonable.'

If, despite these obstacles, the shareholder can show a failure to exercise ordinary skill
and care he must still show that he relied on the auditor's report. Most shareholders will
not do so. Woolf J in *JEB Fasteners Ltd v Marks Bloom & Co (a firm)* [1981] 3 All ER 289 at
297 said:

g > 'The longer the period which elapses prior to the accounts being relied on, from
> the date on which the auditor gave his certificate, the more difficult it will be to
> establish that the auditor ought to have foreseen that his certificate would, in those
> circumstances, be relied on.'

If that obstacle also is overcome, the shareholder must then prove damage. That he can
h do only if the negligence complained of has had a significant effect on the share price. It
is not every oversight or blunder, even if negligent, which will have that effect. Some
error having a real and palpable effect on the value of the company will be called for.

Not many claims by shareholders will, I think, fulfil these stringent requirements. If a
shareholder can prove these things, I think it just and reasonable that he should obtain
redress. I am not persuaded that any compelling consideration of policy should deny
j him. It may be that to begin with auditors will be put to the burden and expense of
defending some bad claims, but the problems facing plaintiffs will be quickly appreciated
and the liability for costs is likely to be an effective deterrent. I simply do not think that
a decision in principle in favour of Caparo will lead to an uncontrollable inrush of claims.

I accordingly conclude that the auditor of a public company does owe individual
shareholders a duty to exercise reasonable care in carrying out his audit and making his

audit report. But that does not conclude even this part of the appeal. For the auditors submitted that if, contrary to their primary contention, an auditor owes a shareholder *a* any duty of care the duty is owed to him as shareholder only, not investor; thus a claim might lie for loss sustained by selling or retaining shares in reliance on a negligent audit report but not for loss sustained by buying, because in buying the shareholder would be acting not as such but as an investor. This distinction is not without a logical basis. The shareholder receives the report by virtue of his existing shareholding and as a report on the stewardship of his existing shareholding. But I have to say (with respect to those who *b* think otherwise) that I do not consider this a sensible place at which to draw the line. There is no distinction to be drawn between selling and retaining on the one hand and buying on the other in terms of foreseeability or proximity. Nor does any consideration of what is just and reasonable or of what policy demands lead me to conclude that a duty imposed in the one situation should be denied in the other. In reality the shareholder is an investor in each situation, whether he is selling, retaining or buying, as the auditor *c* well knows. Nor can it sensibly be said that a duty is owed if a shareholder, in reliance on the audit report, buys a small number of additional shares but not if he buys a large number or seeks to buy all the shares he does not already hold. Any such distinction would in my view deserve Lord Devlin's eloquent denunciation in the *Hedley Byrne* case [1963] 2 All ER 575 at 602–603, [1964] AC 465 at 517.

If I am right so far, the question whether the auditors owed Caparo a duty of care as an *d* investor, irrespective of their capacity as a shareholder, by virtue of the facts pleaded in para 16 of the statement of claim (assumed for purposes of the issue to be true) does not strictly arise. But the question has been very fully argued. It is one of considerable importance. It is appropriate to express a conclusion.

The judge held that a buyer who was not a shareholder could show the foreseeability of economic damage caused by reliance on a negligent audit report. It was, he said, *e* foreseeable that a negligent misstatement in the auditors' report, referring to an annexed account, would cause economic loss to investors. This conclusion was not challenged. So, at any rate on the facts pleaded in para 16, a non-shareholder buyer can satisfy the requirement of foreseeability.

When, however, one turns to the second requirement, of proximity, it is in my view *f* apparent that the relationship between the auditors and Caparo on the facts assumed (but on the assumption that Caparo is not a shareholder) is very much less proximate than that of auditor and shareholder. There is here no statutory duty. The auditor is not engaged by the company to report to such a buyer, even though it is known that the report will be available for his inspection. Such a buyer may be, almost literally, anyone in the world. He may inspect the report and accounts in the public company file. More probably he will obtain a copy from his stockbroker or financial adviser. There is no *g* knowing. Only in a loose sense could the auditor be said to have assumed a responsibility towards him. The relationship falls far short of contract. The nexus or link between the parties is tenuous. If the report were a dangerous chattel likely to cause physical injury the requisite proximity might be found, but the relationship does not in my view satisfy the more stringent standards required of negligent misstatement. In truth, Caparo's case *h* on proximity rests on foreseeability alone and foreseeability alone is not enough.

If, contrary to my view, Caparo can show sufficient proximity I should none the less conclude that it could not on the facts assumed satisfy the third requirement. It is true that the obligation to make the report and accounts available for public inspection, and the general commercial considerations to which I earlier referred, would weigh in favour of a duty not limited to shareholders. It could be said with force to be anomalous that a *j* duty is owed to one who is registered as a shareholder at the date of the general meeting but not to one who becomes a shareholder thereafter and exercises his right to obtain a copy of the accounts under s 246. To extend the duty to non-shareholding investors adds nothing to the substance of what the auditor is in practical terms required to do. It merely increases his potential liability. But this would be a large extension of potential

liability. Time and experience may show such an extension to be desirable or necessary.
a It is, however, preferable that analogical developments of this kind should be gradual and cautious. I am not at present persuaded that it would be just and reasonable, or politic, that the law should be extended so as to impose a duty when no more is shown than the facts Caparo has pleaded.

I consider this conclusion to be broadly consistent with the law as developed in other common law jurisdictions, to which (in deference to Lord Keith's injunction cited at the
b outset) I should make brief reference.

(1) The most far-reaching statement of principle in this immediate field in any English case is, I think, that of Woolf J in *JEB Fasteners Ltd v Marks Bloom & Co (a firm)* [1981] 3 All ER 289 at 296. He relied on Lord Wilberforce's oft-quoted statement in *Anns* in particular and applied what was in substance a foreseeability test. He described (at 293) the facts before him as in some respects similar to those in *Candler v Crane Christmas &*
c *Co* [1951] 1 All ER 426, [1951] 2 KB 164, but it seems to me that they were in principle scarcely distinguishable. The plaintiffs on 23 June 1975 acquired the share capital of BG Fasteners Ltd. The defendants were BG's auditors and (by Mr Marks) its accountant and financial adviser. Well before the acquisition Mr Marks knew that financial support was being sought in various forms (at 298). In August 1974 Mr Marks wrote to BG enclosing draft accounts for the period November 1973 to July 1974, indicating that BG would
d require these for dealing with the plaintiffs. He thought the plaintiffs would want further information and offered to help (at 298). In April 1975 he sent BG a fair copy of the (uncertified) accounts for the year ended 31 October 1974 so that BG could visit the bank with the figures. He also sent a copy to the bank (at 298). After the accounts were certified a proposal was made that the plaintiffs should take over BG. Mr Marks was fully aware of the progress of the negotiations thereafter, on which he advised BG. He also
e supplied information to the plaintiffs (at 299). On the day following the acquisition he submitted a bill which included a charge (albeit modest) for corresponding with the plaintiffs and advising them on the telephone (at 299). The audited accounts were not, therefore, certified with the plaintiffs' take-over specifically in view, but the plaintiffs' interest was known and it was readily to be inferred that after certification the defendants impliedly represented the accuracy of their report and the accounts which they had (I
f think) themselves prepared. I respectfully doubt whether any extension of *Candler* or *Hedley Byrne* principles was called for in order to resolve the duty of care issue in favour of the plaintiffs.

(2) The facts in *Twomax Ltd v Dickson M'Farlane & Robinson* 1982 SC 113 were less strong than in *JEB Fasteners* but still stronger than here. The Lord Ordinary (Stewart) said (at 125):
g

'Mr M'Farlane's state of knowledge when he audited the 1973 accounts included a number of matters which I consider relevant to an assessment of what he should reasonably have foreseen. He was aware that Kintyre was suffering from a shortage of capital. He was aware during the summer months of 1973 that a director, Mr Anderson, wished to dispose of his shareholding. He was aware that this shareholding
h was substantial, amounting to 10,000 shares. The defenders had in fact advertised in the newspaper under a box number on behalf of Mr Anderson. He knew for certain that the accounts were being made available to lenders in so far as he knew they were lodged with the company's bank. He knew that auditors' certificates, when they were "clean" certificates, were commonly relied on by shareholders, potential investors, and potential lenders. In the whole circumstances I consider that
j Mr M'Farlane should have foreseen before he certified the 1973 accounts that these accounts might be relied on by a potential investor for the purpose of deciding whether or not to invest. The situation was such that I would have thought it an inevitable inference that Mr M'Farlane should have realised by the time he came to grant his audit certificate that there would shortly be some dealings in the issued

shares of Kintyre and might well be fresh shares issued in order to inject new capital
into the company.'   *a*

In reaching his decision the Lord Ordinary (Stewart) relied on Lord Wilberforce's
statement in *Anns* and Woolf J's statement in *JEB Fasteners*. Even so, I think it questionable
whether he would have reached a decision in favour of the plaintiffs on the bare facts
pleaded here.
   (3) In *Haig v Bamford* (1976) 72 DLR (3d) 68 a very similar question was considered by   *b*
the Supreme Court of Canada. Accountants of a company (who claimed to have carried
out an audit but who had not in fact done so) were held to owe a duty of care to an
investor in the company who relied on a negligent financial statement. The crucial
finding (to which three of the judges in particular attached importance) was (at 70):

> 'Instructions were issued to the firm of R. L. Bamford & Co. (the accountants), of
> whom the respondents (defendants) were partners, to prepare the required financial   *c*
> statement and Scholler began a search for an outside investor. He made it known to
> the accountants that he was seeking an investor. The trial Judge, MacPherson, J.,
> made a crucial finding, not disturbed by the Court of Appeal for Saskatchewan, that
> the accountants knew, prior to completion of the financial statement, dated June 18,
> 1965, at the root of the present litigation, that the statement would be used by   *d*
> Sedco, by the bank with whom the Company was doing business, and by a potential
> investor in equity capital.'

Without that finding, stronger than the facts assumed here, the plaintiffs' claim would, I
think, have failed for want of proximity.
   (4) The case which perhaps gives Caparo most assistance is *Scott Group Ltd v McFarlane*
[1978] 1 NZLR 553. The plaintiffs relied on accounts audited by the defendants to take   *e*
over John Duthie Holdings Ltd. This company was rich in assets but unimpressive in
earnings and thus, as Cooke J put it (at 582), 'a classic case for a takeover or merger'. But
when the defendants carried out their audit and signed their report they had no
knowledge of any intention by the plaintiffs or anyone else to make a take-over offer. At
first instance Quilliam J held that the auditors owed the plaintiffs no duty of care because
on the facts there was no special relationship between them (see [1975] 1 NZLR 582). On   *f*
appeal Richmond P agreed with him, relying in particular on the restrictive statements
on principle in the *Hedley Byrne* case and *Candler's* case. But on this point the other two
members of the Court of Appeal disagreed. Woodhouse J held that a relationship of
sufficient, indeed 'close' (at 575), proximity existed. He attached particular importance
(at 575–576) to the publicity requirements in the New Zealand Companies Act 1955 (a
point which also caused Richmond P some concern (at 568)). But he limited his decision   *g*
to the case of a take-over related to the value of shareholders' funds (at 575). The reasoning
of Cooke J followed similar lines. He also regarded the publicity requirements as
important (at 581), and he also concerned himself with the position of a party taking
over a company, reserving his opinion on the position of an ordinary market purchaser
who buys in reliance on the audited accounts. Plainly Caparo is assisted by the conclusions   *h*
of these two distinguished judges. But there was, overall, an equal division of judicial
opinion. The majority view may, in the wake of *Anns*, have been unduly coloured by the
finding of foreseeability. And I do not, with respect, think the distinction between
buying a limited number of shares and buying enough to take the company over is
convincing: recognition that a company is ripe for take-over would, after all, be good
enough reason for a shrewd investor to buy some shares in the company even if he could   *j*
not take it over himself. So I am not shaken in my view that English law should not, yet,
advance to this position. I am, however, reassured by what I take to be an implicit
assumption by all three members of the Court of Appeal that a duty of care is owed by
auditors to shareholders (see [1978] 1 NZLR 553 at 555, 568, 575, 581).
   (5) The United States cases do not present a consistent picture. In *Ultramares Corp v*

Touche (1931) 255 NY 170 the accountants knew that the accounts when certified would
be used to raise money and for that purpose supplied 32 certified and serially numbered
a copies (at 173–174). On the faith of one of those copies, given to it on its demand, the
plaintiff lent the company money. The audit was found to be negligent. A claim in
negligence failed on the ground that the auditors owed the plaintiff no duty of care, there
being no sufficiently proximate relationship. A requirement of privity, not of contract
but of relationship, was laid down. This rule appears still to be the rule in New York: see
b *Credit Alliance Corp v Arthur Andersen & Co* (1985) 65 NY 2d 536. Other states also adhere
to it. But a much less restrictive rule has been followed elsewhere: see for example
H Rosenblum Inc v Adler (1983) 93 NJ 324 1, in which account was taken of the *Hedley
Byrne* and *JEB Fasteners* cases, and *Citizens State Bank v Timm Schmidt & Co* (1983) 113 Wis
2d 376. In *Rhode Island Hospital Trust National Bank v Swartz Bresenoff Yavner & Jacobs*
(1972) 455 F 2d 847 at 851 the United States Court of Appeals, applying Rhode Island
c law, applied the rule that an accountant should be liable in negligence for careless
financial misrepresentations relied on by actually foreseen and limited classes of persons.
In *Ingram Industries Inc v Nowicki* (1981) 527 F Supp 683 a federal judge applying the law
of Kentucky relied on the American Law Institute's Restatement of the Law, Second,
Torts 2d (1977) §552, pp 126–127. This is perhaps as close as one can come to a concensus
of opinion in the United States. Section 552 provides:

d
> 'Information Negligently Supplied for the Guidance of Others   (1) One who, in
> the course of his business, profession or employment, or in any other transaction in
> which he has a pecuniary interest, supplies false information for the guidance of
> others in their business transactions, is subject to liability for pecuniary loss caused
> to them by their justifiable reliance upon the information, if he fails to exercise
> reasonable care or competence in obtaining or communicating the information.
e
> (2) Except as stated in Subsection (3), the liability stated in Subsection (1) is
> limited to loss suffered (a) by the person or one of a limited group of persons for
> whose benefit and guidance he intends to supply the information or knows that the
> recipient intends to supply it; and (b) through reliance upon it in a transaction that
> he intends the information to influence or knows that the recipient so intends or in
f > a substantially similar transaction.
> (3) The liability of one who is under a public duty to give the information
> extends to loss suffered by any of the class of persons for whose benefit the duty is
> created, in any of the transactions in which it is intended to protect them.'

It would be unprofitable to discuss at length whether this statement accords or should
accord with English law. It would not, I think, support a claim by Caparo otherwise than
g as a shareholder, but subsection (3) would appear to me to cover its claim as shareholder.
The auditors argue that it would be absurd for the important issue of duty or no duty
to turn on the holding of a single share. But that is because, in the ordinary way and
leaving non-commercial considerations aside, it is absurd to hold a single share. The mass
of investors in public companies hold more than a single share, and once one accepts
multiple shareholding as the norm it does not seem to me absurd that the issue of duty
h or no duty should turn on whether a party misled does or does not belong to the specific
class to whom the auditor was engaged to report.
I would allow the appeal against the decision of the judge that the auditors owed no
duty of care to Caparo as a shareholder but dismiss it against his decision that they owed
Caparo no duty of care as a non-shareholding buyer.

j   **TAYLOR LJ.** This case raises an important question of principle. To whom do auditors
of a company owe a duty of care in respect of their report made pursuant to s 236 of the
Companies Act 1985 and what is the scope of that duty? The judge dealt with this
question as a preliminary issue. He held that the only duty was to the company itself.
Caparo's case is put on alternative footings. Primarily, they contend that auditors owe

a duty not only· to the company but also to individual investors, whether existing
shareholders or potential shareholders and whether the investment relates to a few shares ***a***
or to a take-over of the company. Secondly, even if the duty does not extend to all
potential investors, where the company is vulnerable to take-over, it does extend to a
potential 'suitor' (a word used to define a legal entity seeking to take-over the company).
Thirdly, at the very least counsel for Caparo argues that the duty extends to existing
shareholders.

The judge held that three factors must be present to establish a duty of care in the field ***b***
of negligent misstatement: firstly, foreseeability of loss; secondly, proximity of the
plaintiff to the defendant; and, thirdly, the court must be satisfied that it is fair, just and
reasonable that the defendant should owe a duty to the plaintiff. The judge incorporated
the element of public policy in his third factor, whereas the auditors treat it as a separate
element. Subject to that, there is no real issue between the parties as to the correctness of
the judge's three-part test.   ***c***

It is agreed that in the present case the element of foreseeability was present in relation
to both shareholders and potential investors. When the auditors issued their report it was
foreseeable to them that shareholders and potential investors might rely on it in
considering whether and how to deal in the company's shares. Moreover, it is conceded
by counsel for Caparo that proof of such foreseeability although essential is not enough,
even if qualified by the fair, just and reasonable test. There must be present the second ***d***
of the judge's three factors, which he called proximity. This is now settled law. The
much-quoted passage from Lord Wilberforce's speech in *Anns v Merton London Borough*
[1977] 2 All ER 492 at 498–499, [1978] AC 728 at 751–752 has been held not to have
laid down any universal rule to the contrary. Thus, in *Governors of the Peabody Donation
Fund v Sir Lindsay Parkinson & Co Ltd* [1984] 3 All ER 529 at 534, [1985] AC 210 at 240
Lord Keith, after quoting Lord Wilberforce, said: ***e***

> 'There has been a tendency in some recent cases to treat these passages as being
> themselves of a definitive character. This is a temptation which should be resisted.
> The true question in each case is whether the particular defendant owed to the
> particular plaintiff a duty of care having the scope which is contended for, and
> whether he was in breach of that duty with consequent loss to the plaintiff. A ***f***
> relationship of proximity in Lord Atkin's sense must exist before any duty of care
> can arise, but the scope of the duty must depend on all the circumstances of the
> case.'

In *Yuen Kun-yeu v A-G of Hong Kong* [1987] 2 All ER 705 at 710, [1988] AC 175 at 192
Lord Keith, giving the advice of the Privy Council, said: ***g***

> 'Foreseeability of harm is a necessary ingredient of such a relationship, but it is
> not the only one. Otherwise there would be a liability in negligence on the part of
> one who sees another about to walk over a cliff with his head in the air, and forbears
> to shout a warning. *Donoghue v Stevenson* [1932] AC 562, [1932] All ER Rep 1
> established that the manufacturer of a consumable product who carried on business
> in such a way that the product reached the consumer in the shape in which it left ***h***
> the manufacturer, without any prospect of intermediate examination, owed the
> consumer a duty to take reasonable care that the product was free from defect likely
> to cause injury to health. The speech of Lord Atkin stressed not only the requirement
> of foreseeability of harm but also that of a close and direct relationship of proximity.'

Lord Keith then quoted the famous passage from Lord Atkin's speech in *Donoghue v* ***j***
Stevenson [1932] AC 562 at 580, [1932] All ER Rep 1 at 11 beginning: 'Who, then, in law
is my neighbour? . . .' He continued as follows ([1987] 2 All ER 705 at 711, [1988] AC
175 at 192):

> 'Lord Atkin clearly had in contemplation that all the circumstances of the case,

a
not only the foreseeability of harm, were appropriate to be taken into account in determining whether a duty of care arose.'

The main arguments in the present case have been addressed to the following issues. (1) What amounts to proximity in the context of negligent misstatement? (2) Was the judge right in concluding such proximity did not exist between the auditors and Caparo (a) as shareholders and (b) as investors? (3) Was he right in concluding further that to impose on auditors the duty contended for by Caparo would not be fair, just and
b
reasonable?

1. *Proximity*

Counsel for the auditors in his admirable argument sought to identify the criteria for establishing proximity. His main submission was that there must be by the defendant a
c
voluntary assumption of responsibility towards the individual plaintiff in circumstances akin to contract. That test was propounded in *Hedley Byrne & Co Ltd v Heller & Partners Ltd* [1963] 2 All ER 575, [1964] AC 465. It was applied in *Muirhead v Industrial Tank Specialities Ltd* [1985] 3 All ER 705, [1986] QB 507, in *Simaan General Contracting Co v Pilkington Glass Ltd (No 2)* [1988] 1 All ER 791, [1988] QBD 758 and in *Greater Nottingham Co-op Society Ltd v Cementation Piling and Foundations Ltd* [1988] 2 All ER 971, [1989] QB
d
71. However, in each of those cases there could have been no nexus creating proximity between the parties in the absence of a voluntary assumption of responsibility by the defendant to the plaintiff.

In the *Hedley Byrne* case the plaintiffs and defendants had no reason to know of each other's existence. The plaintiffs, via their bankers, sought a reference for a company which banked with the defendants. The defendants gave the reference negligently
e
knowing that reliance would or might be placed on it by a customer of the inquiring bank and, had they not issued a disclaimer, it was held they would have been liable. That was because they would voluntarily have assumed responsibility to the plaintiff. In that case, proximity could only be established by such a voluntary assumption. There was nothing else.

The other authorities cited above were not negligent misstatement cases. Each was a
f
case in which there was a chain of contracts but no relevant direct contract between the parties. In each case it was sought unsuccessfully to establish liability for economic loss by reliance on the *Hedley Byrne* principle. In the *Simaan* case [1988] 1 All ER 791 at 805, [1988] QB 758 at 784 Dillon LJ said:

'If, however, foreseeability does not automatically lead to a duty of care, the duty
g
in a Hedley Byrne type of case must depend on the voluntary assumption of responsibility towards a particular party giving rise to a special relationship, as Lord Keith held in *Yuen Kun-yeu v A-G of Hong Kong* [1987] 2 All ER 705, [1988] AC 175 . . .' (My emphasis.)

The latter case was somewhat closer on its facts to the present one. The Commissioner of
h
Deposit-taking Companies was responsible for registering such companies under an ordinance. One company so registered went into liquidation. The plaintiffs lost money which they had deposited with the company and alleged negligence against the commissioner since he should have known the company was suspect and the plaintiffs had relied on the registration as showing the company to be sound. Lord Keith referred to the *Hedley Byrne* case and *Junior Books Ltd v Veitchi Co Ltd* [1982] 3 All ER 201, [1983] 1
j
AC 520 and continued ([1987] 2 All ER 705 at 714, [1988] AC 175 at 196):

'These decisions turned on the voluntary assumption of responsibility towards a particular party, giving rise to a special relationship. Lord Devlin in the *Hedley Byrne* case [1963] 2 All ER 575 at 611, [1964] AC 465 at 530 proceeded on the proposition that wherever there is a relationship equivalent to a contract, there is a duty of care.

In the present case there was clearly no voluntary assumption by the commissioner
of any responsibility towards the appellants in relation to the affairs of the company. *a*
It was argued, however, that the effect of the ordinance [Deposit-taking Companies
Ordinance 1976] was to place such a responsibility on him. Their Lordships consider
that the ordinance placed a duty on the commissioner to supervise deposit-taking
companies in the general public interest, but no special responsibility towards
individual members of the public.'

Because in a *Hedley Byrne* type of case a voluntary assumption of responsibility is necessary *b*
to establish proximity, it does not follow that such an assumption is necessary in every
case. There may be some other nexus sufficient to create proximity. In *Yuen Kun-yeu's*
case Lord Keith considered the argument that the ordinance might suffice. Their
Lordships rejected that argument, not because of any necessity for a voluntary assumption
of responsibility, but because the ordinance did not create a special responsibility to any
individual member of the public. That liability might exist without voluntary *c*
assumption of risk where the defendant was under an obligation to make a statement
was clearly envisaged by Cross LJ in *Ministry of Housing and Local Government v Sharp*
[1970] 1 All ER 1009 at 1038, 2 QB 223 at 291. He said:

> 'It is true that the phrase "voluntary assumption of risk" occurs frequently in the
> speeches in the *Hedley Byrne* case, but I agree with the judge that that case did not *d*
> purport to lay down any metes and bounds within which legal liability in tort for
> false statements, on which the parties to whom they are made rely, has to be
> confined. (See in particular per Lord Devlin ([1963] 2 All ER 575 at 611, [1964] AC
> 465 at 530–531).) I see no sufficient reason why in an appropriate case the liability
> should not extend to cases in which the defendant is obliged to make the statement
> which proves to be false.' *e*

In the same case the other members of the court also indicated that voluntary assumption
of responsibility is not essential to create a duty. Thus, Lord Denning MR said ([1970] 1
All ER 1009 at 1018, [1970] 2 QB 223 at 268):

> '[Counsel for the defendants] said that a duty to use due care (where there was no *f*
> contract) only arose when there was a voluntary assumption of responsibility. I do
> not agree. He relied particularly on the words of Lord Reid in *Hedley Byrne & Co Ltd
> v Heller & Partners Ltd* [1963] 2 All ER 575 at 583, [1964] AC 465 at 487, and of
> Lord Devlin ([1963] 2 All ER 575 at 610–611, [1964] AC 465 at 529). I think they
> used those words because of the special circumstances of that case (where the bank
> disclaimed responsibility). But they did not in any way mean to limit the general
> principle. In my opinion the duty to use due care in a statement arises, not from *g*
> any voluntary assumption of responsibility, but from the fact that the person
> making it knows, or ought to know, that others, being his neighbours in this regard,
> would act on the faith of the statement being accurate.'

In using the phrase 'being his neighbours' Lord Denning MR was clearly referring to
'neighbours' in the sense in which the word was used by Lord Atkin, implying proximity *h*
not merely foreseeability. Salmon LJ said ([1970] 1 All ER 1009 at 1027–1028, [1970] 2
QB 223 at 279):

> 'I do not accept that, in all cases, the obligation to take reasonable care necessarily
> depends on a voluntary assumption of responsibility.'

Counsel for the auditors went on to consider other possible touchstones of proximity. *j*
He suggested there must be a special relationship between the parties, that the negligent
statement must have been made for the very purpose for which reliance was placed on
it, that the plaintiff must be a member of a small limited class and that there must be
some communing between the plaintiff and the defendant. It is unnecessary to cite the

cases relied on in support of these several tests. Clearly, in appropriate cases it will be
a relevant to have regard to all or some of them. I do not accept, however, that any one or
group of them can be regarded as definitive of the requisite proximity. As Bingham LJ
said in the *Simaan* case [1988] 1 All ER 791 at 803, [1988] QB 758 at 782:

> 'However attractive it may theoretically be to postulate a single principle capable
> of embracing every kind of case, that is not how the law has developed. It would of
b course be unsatisfactory if (say) doctors and dentists owed their patients a different
> duty of care. I do not, however, think it unsatisfactory or surprising if, as I think, a
> banker's duty towards the recipient of a credit reference and an industrial glass
> manufacturer's duty towards a main contractor, in the absence of any contract
> between them, differ.'

c   In my judgment it is not possible to lay down one precise test or set of tests applicable
in every situation to show whether the necessary proximity is established. In each case
the court must inquire how close and direct a relationship exists between the parties and
whether the defendant should have had the plaintiff in contemplation as a person who
would or might rely on the relevant statement.

d 2(a). *Caparo as shareholders*
Primarily, the duty of auditors is to the company whose accounts they audit. But,
under the Companies Act 1985, they are appointed by the shareholders in general
meeting (s 384). They have a duty to report to the shareholders whether, inter alia, the
company's accounts give a true and fair view of its financial position (s 236). A report
made by auditors to the directors rather than to the shareholders is not a proper
e compliance with that duty (see *Re London and General Bank (No 2)* [1895] 2 Ch 673 at 682,
684–685, [1895–9] All ER Rep 953 at 956–958). By s 240 a copy of the company's
accounts together with the auditor's report must be sent to every shareholder. Further,
the auditor's report must be read at a general meeting of the company's shareholders
(s 241). These provisions show that, although the legal entity which contracts with and
pays the auditors and to which the auditors owe a statutory duty is the company,
f Parliament entrusted the appointment of auditors to the shareholders and required the
auditors to render their report to the shareholders rather than the directors, so that those
owning the company's shares should receive an independent account of its financial state.
Auditors have thus in my judgment a close and direct relationship with the
shareholders. Once auditors accept appointment they know that their report has to be
sent to each shareholder as a named individual who will or may act on it. It is argued
g that the shareholders of a company are a constantly changing body; but, at the relevant
time when the report goes out, their identity is ascertainable and has to be ascertained.
In this context some observations of Megarry V-C in *Ross v Caunters (a firm)* [1979] 3 All
ER 580 at 587, [1980] Ch 297 at 308 are relevant and helpful:

> '. . . the question is whether a solicitor owes a duty of care to a beneficiary under a
h will that he makes for a client, and, if so, on what basis that duty rests. This is, of
> course, the central core of the case. In considering this, three features of the case
> before me seem to stand out. First, there is the close degree of proximity of the
> plaintiff to the defendants. There is no question of whether the defendants could
> fairly have been expected to contemplate the plaintiff as a person likely to be affected
> by any lack of care on their part, or whether they ought to have done so: there is no
j "ought" about the case. This is not a case where the only nexus between the plaintiff
> and the defendants is that the plaintiff was the ultimate recipient of a dangerous
> chattel or negligent misstatement which the defendants had put into circulation.
> The plaintiff was named and identified in the will that the defendants drafted for
> the testator. Their contemplation of the plaintiff was actual, nominate and direct. It

was contemplation by contract, though of course, the contract was with a third party, the testator.'   *a*

Auditors' contemplation of an individual registered shareholder is also 'actual, nominate and direct'. They know of the shareholder's actual existence; they know his nominate identity; and they send directly to that shareholder the report on which his reliance is foreseeable. Here too one has 'contemplation by contract'. True, the contract is with the company and not the shareholders but the auditors' appointment by them and duty to report to them creates a nexus close to contract. Indeed, the only reason there is no contract with the shareholders derives from the rule giving a limited liability company a legal identity separate from that of its members.   *b*

Even if one were to apply the voluntary assumption of responsibility test, it would in my view be satisfied here. In the *Hedley Byrne* case, the House of Lords clearly indicated that a voluntary assumption might be implied rather than express (see [1963] 2 All ER 575 esp at 611, [1964] AC 465 esp at 529–530 per Lord Devlin). Auditors are not obliged to accept appointment. If they do so voluntarily, then they assume (as the statute requires) the duty to report to each shareholder individually knowing that he may well act in reliance on the report. In those circumstances, I would hold that a voluntary assumption of responsibility arises by implication. For these reason, I conclude that there was the requisite proximity between Caparo as shareholders and the auditors.   *c*

d

2(b). *Caparo as investors*

The position of a potential investor is very different. He plays no role in the statutory scheme relating to auditors. He has no part in appointing them; he does not receive their report directly from them. He may, of course, be shown the accounts and the report by others. A copy of those documents has to be delivered to the registrar of companies (s 241(3)) and they must be available for inspection by anyone (s 709). But the right to inspect them and the option to buy shares are enjoyed by the world at large. Within the auditors' contemplation there is no focus on any person or class of person who may decide to invest. All they can foresee is that some unidentified investor or investors may inspect their report and act on it. By the same token other unascertained persons may also do so, eg a bank contemplating the grant to the company of a loan or its suppliers or creditors. In none of these instances is there any close or direct relationship with the auditors. Foreseeability of reliance is conceded but the element of proximity is in my judgment lacking.   *e*

f

Counsel for Caparo argued that where, as pleaded here, a company is vulnerable to take-over the auditors owe a duty to a suitor in respect of their statutory report. He submits that especially in the case of an unwelcome suitor the only information available consists of the published accounts and auditors' report. Ex hypothesi the company will not itself vouchsafe information. Whereas a duty to investors generally would or could be owed to vast numbers, there can he submits be only one successful suitor in a take-over so that liability would be restricted.   *g*

Apart from the difficulty which would arise from the vague and elusive nature of vulnerability as a test, I can see no reason in principle to distinguish between a suitor (welcome or otherwise) and any other investor. Assuming the company was vulnerable to take-over in the present case, it may have been more readily foreseeable that a suitor might rely on the auditors' report. However, I do not see how the argument for proximity is any stronger. I therefore conclude that investors even if they are suitors are not owed any duty of care by the auditors.   *h*

j

3. *Fair, just and reasonable?*

The principal concern in this class of case is that casting too wide a duty on a potential defendant may result in a liability which is intolerably onerous. The courts have therefore been reluctant to extend the scope of liability for economic loss arising from negligent

misstatement. The fear is well summarised in the much-quoted observation of Cardozo
a CJ in *Ultramares Corp v Touche* (1931) 255 NY 170 at 179:

> '... liability in an indeterminate amount for an indeterminate time to an
> indeterminate class.'

Counsel for the auditors submits that those words would obviously and incontrovertibly
apply if auditors owed a duty to the world of investors at large. But he maintains they
b also apply even if the duty extends no further than to shareholders.

I do not, however, think shareholders can be described as an indeterminate class. The
class may well be very large in the case of a major public company, but its members are
ascertainable. Again, as to time, the period during which reliance could reasonably be
placed on the report would in practice be limited. It is right to say that liability could be
for a large amount. On the other hand, a plaintiff shareholder would have a number of
c hurdles to clear before he could recover damages. He would first have to establish that
the auditors were negligent. It would by no means follow, for example, that failure to
expose deliberate and well concealed fraud on the part of a company's directors would
amount to negligence by the auditors. They are not insurers. They would be judged by
reasonable professional standards. Reliance on the report would have to be proved, as
would damage. These considerations and the risk of having to bear the costs of an
d unsuccessful claim would in my view be sufficient to deter all but the stout-hearted and
seriously aggrieved from bringing proceedings.

It is contended that auditors would find it difficult and cripplingly expensive to obtain
insurance cover. It is even suggested that accountants might decline to be appointed as
auditors. No evidence was adduced on this aspect of the case and if I am right about the
difficulties and disincentives affecting possible claimants the insurance problem should
e not be insurmountable. It would always be open to Parliament to intervene should
limitation of liability be considered necessary.

Counsel for Caparo emphasises that the auditors already have a duty to the company
to prepare their report with proper professional skill and care. No additional work or
different standard would be required of them should their duty extend not merely to the
company but also to the shareholders. It is, he submits, only fair and reasonable that they
f should have a remedy if the auditors they appoint report to them negligently and they
in consequence act to their detriment. The judge said their remedy was to get rid of the
auditors but, as counsel for the auditors accepted, that is no remedy at all. At best the
threat of removal might be some sanction against carelessness. But those shareholders
who have shed their total holdings would have no power to remove the auditors; neither
would a minority. In the unlikely event of a majority of shareholders exercising the
g power, they would merely be shutting the stable door. They would not recoup their
losses.

Balancing the factors urged on both sides, I conclude it is fair, just and reasonable that
an individual shareholder should have a remedy against a negligent auditor. I do not
consider that the reasons advanced against the existence of the duty are of sufficient
cogency to outweigh those in favour.
h
But what should be the scope of the duty? Here again fairness and public policy are
the tests. Counsel for the auditors submits that at highest the duty should only apply to
a shareholder in respect of his existing shareholding. It should not extend to his purchase
of further shares in reliance on the report. He submits the only distinction between a
shareholder and any other investor is that the former already owns some shares. In
j respect of any further shares bought he is in no different position from that of any other
investor and should be so treated.

In my view, once proximity to the shareholder is established, the auditor ought prima
facie to be liable for any loss suffered in foreseeable reliance on the report; prima facie,
that is, unless such liability be unfair, unjust or unreasonable. There is no logical basis
for distinguishing between reliance for the purpose of selling shares and reliance in

purchasing more. It is, therefore, necessary to analyse the possible situations which could occur.   *a*

A negligent report can result in misrepresentation only of two broad kinds: either an overvalue or an undervalue of the company's shares. A shareholder relying on the report can act only in one of three ways. He may sell; he may retain his holding; or he may buy more shares. If the report undervalues, a shareholder who buys has no complaint. If he retains his shares he has neither lost nor gained by the error. Only if he sells at an undervalue will he have sustained loss. He would then be entitled to claim from the *b* auditors the difference between what he received and the true value. However, since this would involve dealing with his existing shareholding it does not bear on the issue under consideration. Take the converse situation, where the negligent report shows an overvalue. The shareholder who sells will gain and one who simply retains his holding will neither gain nor lose. Only he who buys will suffer damage. This last would therefore be the only instance of liability occurring as a result of extending the duty to *c* all dealings by shareholders and not otherwise. The claim would be for the difference between what the shareholder paid and the true value. I do not consider the liability of the auditors to that extent in that one situation would be unfair, unjust or unreasonable. To exclude it would be illogical and arbitrary. Accordingly, I would hold that the auditors' duty to individual shareholders was not limited to their existing shareholding.

Bingham LJ has considered in detail *JEB Fasteners Ltd v Marks Bloom & Co* [1981] 3 All *d* ER 289 and *Twomax Ltd v Dickson M'Farlane & Robinson* 1982 SC 113 and has also reviewed the American and Commonwealth authorities. I entirely agree with his analysis and cannot usefully add to it.

I, too, would allow this appeal as to the auditors' duty to Caparo qua shareholder and dismiss it against the judge's decision that they owed no duty to Caparo as a non-shareholding investor.   *e*

O'CONNOR LJ. In 1984 the plaintiffs (Caparo) made a successful take-over bid for Fidelity plc (Fidelity). At all material times the defendants, Touche Ross & Co (the auditors), were auditors of Fidelity. In July 1985 Caparo commenced this action in which they claim damages for fraud against two directors of Fidelity and damages for negligence *f* against the auditors. Caparo alleged that they made their bid in reliance on the accounts of Fidelity for the year ending 31 March 1984. These were signed by the auditors in May with a clean certificate, sent to shareholders in June, read and approved at the annual general meeting on 4 July. Broadly, Caparo say that so far from giving a true and fair view of the state of affairs of Fidelity the accounts gave a false picture in that the reported profit of £1·3m should have been a loss of £0·46m.   *g*

In July 1987 an order was made for the trial of a preliminary issue:

'. . . whether on the facts set out in paragraphs 4 and 6 and in sub-paragraphs (1) and (2) of paragraph 16 of the Statement of Claim herein, the Third Defendants, Touche Ross & Co., owed a duty of care to the Plaintiffs Caparo Industries PLC . . .'

That issue was tried by Sir Neil Lawson in December 1987. He decided that the auditors *h* owed no duty of care. Caparo appeal to this court.

I set out para 4 of the statement of claim:

'In June 1984 Caparo began to purchase Fidelity shares in the open market and purchased 100,000 shares at 70 pence each on 8th June 1984. On 12th June 1984, the date on which the Accounts for the period ended 31st March 1984 were issued to shareholders, including Caparo, a further 50,000 shares were purchased at 73 *j* pence each.'

Paragraph 6 sets out the details of the take-over transaction; the material fact averred is that Caparo acted in reliance on the information contained in the accounts.

I set out para 16 in full:

a   'Touche Ross, as auditors of Fidelity carrying out their functions as auditors and certifiers of the Accounts in April and May 1984, owed a duty of care to investors and potential investors, and in particular to Caparo, in respect of the audit and certification of the Accounts. In support of that duty of care Caparo will rely upon the following matters:—(1) Touche Ross knew or ought to have known (a) that in early March 1984 a press release had been issued stating that profits for the financial year would fall significantly short of £2·2m (b) that Fidelity's share price fell from *b*   143 pence per share on 1st March 1984 to 75 pence per share on 2nd April 1984 (c) that Fidelity required financial assistance. (2) Touche Ross therefore ought to have foreseen that Fidelity was vulnerable to a take-over bid and that persons such as Caparo might well rely on the Accounts for the purpose of deciding whether to take over Fidelity and might well suffer loss if the Accounts were inaccurate.'

c   Caparo claim to have lost the cost of the take-over, £13m. This may be small in the context of take-over bids ranging up to a billion pounds or more but it is obvious that the decision in this case is of great importance to all accountants who act as auditors.

I must make it clear that the auditors strongly deny that they were negligent in any way and that it is only for the purposes of deciding the point of law that we have to assume that the clean certificate was a negligent misstatement. Once more we have to *d*   consider possible liability for economic loss caused by negligent misstatement. The law has developed rapidly since 1963, when the House of Lords opened the door to such liability in *Hedley Bryne & Co Ltd v Heller & Partners Ltd* [1963] 2 All ER 575, [1964] AC 465. What emerges from the cases is that, in a case such as this, in deciding whether a duty of care exists it is also necessary to consider its scope: see *Rowling v Takaro Properties Ltd* [1988] 1 All ER 163 at 172, [1988] AC 473 at 501. In the same case Lord Keith said *e*   ([1988] 1 All ER 163 at 172, [1988] AC 473 at 501):

> 'It is at this stage that it is necessary, before concluding that a duty of care should be imposed, to consider all the relevant circumstances. One of the considerations underlying certain recent decisions of the House of Lords (*Governors of the Peabody Donation Fund v Sir Lindsay Parkinson & Co Ltd* [1984] 3 All ER 529, [1985] AC 210) and of the Privy Council (*Yuen Kun-yeu v A-G of Hong Kong* [1987] 2 All ER 705, *f*   [1988] AC 175) is the fear that a too literal application of the well-known observation of Lord Wilberforce in *Anns v Merton London Borough* [1977] 2 All ER 492 at 498, [1978] AC 728 at 751–752 may be productive of a failure to have regard to, and to analyse and weigh, all the relevant considerations in considering whether it is appropriate that a duty of care should be imposed. Their Lordships consider that question to be of an intensely pragmatic character, well suited for gradual *g*   development but requiring most careful analysis. It is one on which all common law jurisdictions can learn much from each other, because, apart from exceptional cases, no sensible distinction can be drawn in this respect between the various countries and the social conditions existing in them. It is incumbent on the courts in different jurisdictions to be sensitive to each other's reactions; but what they are *h*   all searching for in others, and each of them striving to achieve, is a careful analysis and weighing of the relevant competing considerations.'

In *Yuen Kun-yeu v A-G of Hong Kong* [1987] 2 All ER 705 at 710, [1988] AC 175 at 191–192 Lord Keith said:

> 'Their Lordships venture to think that the two-stage test formulated by Lord *j*   Wilberforce for determining the existence of a duty of care in negligence has been elevated to a degree of importance greater than it merits, and greater perhaps than its author intended. Further, the expression of the first stage of the test carries with it a risk of misinterpretation. As Gibbs CJ pointed out in *Sutherland Shire Council v Heyman* (1985) 60 ALR 1 at 13 there are two possible views of what Lord Wilberforce meant. The first view, favoured in a number of cases mentioned by Gibbs CJ, is that

he meant to test the sufficiency of proximity simply by the reasonable contemplation
of likely harm. The second view, favoured by Gibbs CJ himself, is that Lord
Wilberforce meant the expression "proximity or neighbourhood" to be a composite
one, importing the whole concept of necessary relationship between plaintiff and
defendant described by Lord Atkin in *Donoghue v Stevenson* [1932] AC 562 at 580,
[1932] All ER Rep 1 at 11. In their Lordships' opinion the second view is the correct
one. As Lord Wilberforce himself observed in *McLoughlin v O'Brian* [1982] 2 All ER
298 at 303, [1983] 1 AC 410 at 420, it is clear that foreseeability does not of itself,
and automatically, lead to a duty of care. There are many other statements to the
same effect. The truth is that the trilogy of cases referred to by Lord Wilberforce
each demonstrate particular sets of circumstances, differing in character, which were
adjudged to have the effect of bringing into being a relationship apt to give rise to a
duty of care. Foreseeability of harm is a necessary ingredient of such a relationship,
but it is not the only one. Otherwise there would be liability in negligence on the
part of one who sees another about to walk over a cliff with his head in the air, and
forbears to shout a warning.'

In *Hill v Chief Constable of West Yorkshire* [1988] 2 All ER 238 at 241, [1989] AC 53 at
60. Lord Keith said:

'It has been said almost too frequently to require repetition that foreseeability of
likely harm is not in itself a sufficient test of liability in negligence. Some further
ingredient is invariably needed to establish the requisite proximity of relationship
between the plaintiff and defendant, and all the circumstances of the case must be
carefully considered and analysed in order to ascertain whether such an ingredient
is present. The nature of the ingredient will be found to vary in a number of
different categories of decided cases.'

The question in this case is: did the auditors owe a duty of care to someone who, relying
on the certified accounts, bought shares in the company?
    The Companies Act 1985 requires every company to appoint auditors at its annual
general meeting to hold office for a year (s 384). The directors are required to lay before
the company in general meeting copies of the accounts (s 241). The accounts must
contain the auditors' report (s 239). The requirements for the auditors' report are found
in s 236:

'(1) A company's auditors shall make a report to its members on the accounts
examined by them, and on every balance sheet and profit and loss account, and on
all group accounts, copies of which are to be laid before the company in general
meeting during the auditors' tenure of office.
    (2) The auditors' report shall state—(a) whether in the auditors' opinion the
balance sheet and profit and loss account and (if it is a holding company submitting
group accounts) the group accounts have been properly prepared in accordance with
this Act; and (b) without prejudice to the foregoing, whether in their opinion a true
and fair view is given—(i) in the balance sheet, of the state of the company's affairs
at the end of the financial year, (ii) in the profit and loss account (if not framed as a
consolidated account), of the company's profit or loss for the financial year, and (iii)
in the case of group accounts, of the state of affairs and profit or loss of the company
and its subsidiaries dealt with by those accounts, so far as concerns members of the
company.'

Auditors' duties and powers are set out in s 237:

'(1) It is the duty of the company's auditors, in preparing their report, to carry
out such investigations as will enable them to form an opinion as to the following
matters—(a) whether proper accounting records have been kept by the company
and proper returns adequate for their audit have been received from branches not

visited by them, (b) whether the company's balance sheet and (if not consolidated)
a   its profit and loss account are in agreement with the accounting records and returns.
(2) If the auditors are of opinion that proper accounting records have not been
kept, or that proper returns adequate for their audit have not been received from
branches not visited by them, or if the balance sheet and (if not consolidated) the
profit and loss account are not in agreement with the accounting records and
returns, the auditors shall state that fact in their report.
b   (3) Every auditor of a company has a right of access at all times to the company's
books, accounts and vouchers, and is entitled to require from the company's officers
such information and explanations as he thinks necessary for the performance of
the auditor's duties.
(4) If the auditors fail to obtain all the information and explanations which, to
the best of their knowledge and belief, are necessary for the purposes of their audit,
c   they shall state that fact in their report.
(5) If the requirements of Parts V and VI of Schedule 5 and Parts I to III of
Schedule 6 are not complied with in the accounts, it is the auditors' duty to include
in their report, so far as they are reasonably able to do so, a statement giving the
required particulars.
(6) It is the auditors' duty to consider whether the information given in the
d   directors' report for the financial year for which the accounts are prepared is
consistent with those accounts; and if they are of opinion that it is not, they shall
state that fact in their report.'

A copy of the accounts must be sent to every member of the company not less than 21
days before the date of the meeting at which they are to be laid (s 240).
e   Section 241(2) provides:

'The auditors' report shall be read before the company in general meeting, and be
open to the inspection of any member of the company.'

The result of these statutory provisions is that auditors are employed by the company
and it is an implied term of the contract that they will carry out their duties with the
f   care and skill expected from reasonably competent auditors. If they fail to do their audit
with the requisite care and skill they may fail to discover some irregularity in the
accounts which they ought to have discovered. If the irregularity is such that the auditors
ought not to have certified that a true and fair view of the state of the company's affairs is
given in the accounts it must follow that the accounts either understate or overstate the
true state of affairs. The company itself cannot suffer any loss from the over- or
g   understatement of its affairs, but may suffer loss from the failure of the auditors to
discover the irregularity.
Counsel for Caparo submitted that auditors know, or at least must be taken to know,
that investors considering buying shares in the company may rely on the accuracy of the
accounts certified by the auditors, which are readily available to investors. If the investor
was considering a take-over bid he would rely on the certified accounts in making his
h   decision. If as a result of negligent audit the auditors had failed to discover that the
accounts overstated the true position of the company, they could foresee that an investor
might suffer loss because he would be paying more for the shares than they were really
worth.
Counsel for Caparo accepted that foreseeability of damage was not sufficient to impose
a duty on the auditors but he submitted that the matters pleaded in para 16 of the
j   statement of claim introduced a sufficient degree of proximity. In support of that
contention he relied on the judgment of Woolf J in JEB Fasteners Ltd v Marks Bloom & Co
(a firm) [1981] 3 All ER 289. That was a take-over case, as appears from the opening
paragraphs of the judgment (at 291):

'... the plaintiffs acquired the entire share capital of that company. They contend that they would not have purchased the company if they had known its true financial position, but that they did so relying on its audited accounts for the year ending 31st October 1974, prepared by the defendants, which did not give a true and fair view of the state of the company. The plaintiffs allege that they have suffered substantial loss and damage as a result of the purchase of the company. Before going into the facts in great detail it is desirable if I indicate my views as to the legal issues involved which have been in dispute before me. In order to succeed in this case, the plaintiffs have to establish as a matter of law that the defendants owed them a duty of care so as to give rise to liability if they were negligent in the preparation of the accounts. It is not alleged that at the time the accounts were audited the defendants knew that the accounts would be relied on by the plaintiffs. Indeed, no takeover was then contemplated, and counsel for both the plaintiffs and the defendants agree that there is no direct English authority on the question whether the defendants owe such a duty in those circumstances.'

Woolf J then reviewed the authorities and as his decision on them is crucial to the argument for Caparo in the present case I must look a little more closely at the build up to his conclusion.

He began with the dissenting judgment of Denning LJ in *Candler v Crane Christmas & Co* [1951] 1 All ER 426 at 434, [1951] 2 KB 164 at 180–181 approved by the House of Lords in *Hedley Byrne & Co Ltd v Heller & Partners Ltd* [1963] 2 All ER 575, [1964] AC 465. In that case the accountants had been asked by the company to prepared accounts expressly for the purpose of being shown to the plaintiff, who was proposing to invest money in the company. Denning LJ asked himself to whom accountants owed a duty and said:

'They owe the duty, of course, to their employer or client, and also, I think, to any third person to whom they themselves show the accounts, or to whom they know their employer is going to show the accounts so as to induce him to invest money or take some other action on them. I do not think, however, the duty can be extended still further so as to include strangers of whom they have heard nothing and to whom their employer without their knowledge may choose to show their accounts. Once the accountants have handed their accounts to their employer, they are not, as a rule, responsible for what he does with them without their knowledge or consent.'

After further citation Woolf J said ([1981] 3 All ER 289 at 293):

'In *Candler*, although the facts are in some respects similar to those in the present case, it was clear that the accountants concerned had knowledge that the accounts were to be supplied to the plaintiffs, and of the specific purpose for which they were required. It is therefore understandable that Denning LJ, having dealt with liability of accountants who had such knowledge and the position of strangers to the accountants to whom their employer without their knowledge chose to show their accounts, did not deal specifically with the position where the accountants had no actual knowledge that the accounts would be shown to a particular person, but should reasonably have foreseen that the accounts could be shown to a third person who would rely on them.'

Woolf J then referred to the well-known passage from the judgment of Cardozo CJ in *Ultramares Corp v Touche* (1931) 255 NY 170 at 179:

'If liability for negligence exists, a thoughtless slip or blunder, the failure to detect a theft or forgery beneath the cover of deceptive entries, may expose accountants to a liability in an indeterminate amount for an indeterminate time to an indeterminate class. The hazards of a business conducted on these terms are so extreme as to enkindle doubt whether a flaw may not exist in the implication of a duty that exposes to these consequences.'

Woolf J then said that if the law had stood there he would have felt constrained to hold
a that there was no general duty based on foreseeability, but the law had not stood there
and he cited next the oft-cited passage from the speech of Lord Wilberforce in *Anns v
Merton London Borough* [1977] 2 All ER 492 at 498–499, [1978] AC 728 at 751:

'Through the trilogy of cases in this House, *Donoghue v Stevenson* [1932] AC 562,
[1932] All ER Rep 1, *Hedley Byrne & Co Ltd v Heller & Partners Ltd* [1963] 3 All ER
575, [1964] AC 465 and *Home Office v Dorset Yacht Co Ltd* [1970] 2 All ER 294, [1970]
b AC 1004, the position has now been reached that in order to establish that a duty of
care arises in a particular situation, it is not necessary to bring the facts of that
situation within those of previous situations in which a duty of care has been held
to exist. Rather the question has to be approached in two stages. First one has to ask
whether, as between the alleged wrongdoer and the person who has suffered damage
c there is a sufficient relationship of proximity or neighbourhood such that, in the
reasonable contemplation of the former, carelessness on his part may be likely to
cause damage to the latter, in which case a prima facie duty of care arises. Secondly,
if the first question is answered affirmatively, it is necessary to consider whether
there are any considerations which ought to negative, or to reduce or limit the scope
of the duty or the class of person to whom it is owed or the damages to which a
d breach of it may give rise (see the *Dorset Yacht* case [1970] 2 All ER 294 at 297–298,
[1970] AC 1004 at 1027, per Lord Reid). Examples of this are *Hedley Byrne & Co Ltd
v Heller & Partners Ltd* where the class of potential plaintiffs was reduced to those
shown to have relied on the correctness of statements made, and *Weller & Co v Foot
and Mouth Disease Research Institute* [1965] 3 All ER 560, [1960] 1 QB 569 and (I cite
these merely as illustrations, without discussion) cases about "economic loss" where,
e a duty having been held to exist, the nature of the recoverable damages was limited
(see *SCM (United Kingdom) Ltd v W J Whittall & Son Ltd* [1970] 3 All ER 245, [1971]
1 QB 337, *Spartan Steel and Alloys Ltd v Martin & Co (Contractors) Ltd* [1972] 3 All ER
557, [1973] QB 27).'

Woolf J also cited a passage from the speech of Lord Salmon ([1977] 2 All ER 492 at 512–
f 513, [1978] AC 728 at 769):

'There are a wide variety of instances in which a statement is negligently made by
a professional man which he knows will be relied on by many people besides his
client, eg a well-known firm of accountants certifies in a prospectus the annual
profits of the company issuing it and unfortunately, due to negligence on the part
of the accountants, the profits are seriously overstated. Those persons who invested
g in the company in reliance on the accuracy of the accountants' certificate would
have a claim for damages against the accountants for any money they might have
lost as a result of the accountants' negligence: see the *Hedley Byrne* case.'

Next he examined the New Zealand Court of Appeal's decision in *Scott Group Ltd v
McFarlane* [1978] 1 NZLR 553. That was another take-over case; the court was divided
h but Woolf J extracted from the judgments that two members of the court, applying the
foreseeability test from *Anns*, thought that a sufficient degree of proximity existed to
impose liability notwithstanding the fact that the auditors had no direct knowledge of
the plaintiffs or that a take-over from any quarter was contemplated.
Lastly he relied on certain passages in the judgment of Megarry V-C in *Ross v Caunters
(a firm)* [1979] 3 All ER 580, [1980] Ch 297. This is yet another case where the straight
j foreseeability test from *Anns* was used to impose a duty of care on a solicitor to the
beneficiary in a client's will.
After this review of the case law Woolf J said ([1981] 3 All ER 289 at 296–297):

'Without laying down any principle which is intended to be of general application,
on the basis of the authorities which I have cited, the appropriate test for establishing

whether a duty of care exists appears in this case to be whether the defendants knew or reasonably should have foreseen at the time the accounts were audited that a *a* person might rely on those accounts for the purpose of deciding whether or not to take over the company and therefore could suffer loss if the accounts were inaccurate. Such an approach does place a limitation on those entitled to contend that there has been a breach of duty owed to them. First of all, they must have relied on the accounts and, second, they must have done so in circumstances where the auditors either knew that they would or ought to have known that they might. If the *b* situation is one where it would not be reasonable for the accounts to be relied on, then, in the absence of express knowledge, the auditor would be under no duty. This places a limit on the circumstances in which the audited accounts can be relied on and the period for which they can be relied on. The longer the period which elapses prior to the accounts being relied on, from the date on which the auditor gave his certificate, the more difficult it will be to establish that the auditor ought to *c* have foreseen that his certificate would, in those circumstances, be relied on.'

The *JEB Fasteners* case was relied on and followed in a case in the Outer House in *Twomax Ltd v Dickson M'Farlane & Robinson* 1982 SC 113. In that case the three pursuers had bought shares in a company relying on the audited accounts. The Lord Ordinary (Stewart) found as a fact that Mr M'Farlane, the auditor, did not know that any of the *d* three pursuers were potential investors when he audited the accounts but, applying the approach suggested by Woolf J, held that the auditors did owe a duty of care. It is instructive to see how the judge did this. He said (at 125):

'Mr M'Farlane's state of knowledge when he audited the 1973 accounts included a number of matters which I consider relevant to the assessment of what he should reasonably have foreseen. He was aware that Kintyre was suffering from a shortage *e* of capital. He was aware during the summer months of 1973 that a director, Mr Anderson, wished to dispose of his shareholding. He was aware that this shareholding was substantial, amounting to 10,000 shares. The defenders had in fact advertised in the newspaper under a box number on behalf of Mr Anderson. He knew for certain that the accounts were being made available to lenders in so far as he knew they were lodged with the company's bank. He knew that auditors' certificates, *f* when they were "clean" certificates, were commonly relied on by shareholders, potential investors, and potential lenders. In the whole circumstances I consider that Mr M'Farlane should have foreseen before he certified the 1973 accounts that these accounts might be relied on by a potential investor for the purpose of deciding whether or not to invest. The situation was such that I would have though it an *g* inevitable inference that Mr M'Farlane should have realised by the time he came to grant his audit certificate that there would shortly be some dealings in the issued shares of Kintyre and might well be fresh shares issued in order to inject new capital into the company. While he did not know then about Twomax and Mr Gordon he should, in my view, reasonably have foreseen that there would be incorporations or individuals who would be interested potential investors either in the sense of *h* purchasing shares already issued or of taking up any fresh issue. To these, the latest audited accounts of the company would be of very great importance in influencing them whether or not to invest and at what price. I, therefore, consider that in respect of Twomax and Mr Gordon, both being in the class of persons who were potential investors, Mr M'Farlane owed a *prima facie* duty of care in the auditing of the 1973 accounts. That answers affirmatively the first question posed by Lord Wilberforce *j* in *Anns*.'

I think that the judges in these two cases, *JEB Fasteners* and *Twomax*, understood the first stage of the test in *Anns* in the first sense referred to by Lord Keith in *Yuen Kun-yeu v A-G of Hong Kong* [1987] 2 All ER 705 at 710, [1988] AC 175 at 191. They appreciated the conflict with what I may call 'the *Ultramares* control' and sought to resolve it by confining

foreseeability. Now that the later development of the law has uncoupled proximity from
_a_ foreseeability it is no longer necessary to attempt what I regard as an artificial constriction
of foreseeability. Assume that auditors know, as a result of their professional skill and
experience, that the state of the company is such that a take-over bid may be made, I do
not think that, if a bid is made, that knowledge alone creates a sufficient proximity
between bidder and auditor to impose a duty of care on the auditor. In any given case
the fact that the number of potential take-over bidders is less, or far less if you like, than
_b_ the number of potential share buyers does not produce proximity. In my judgment
there has to be something linking the auditor to the person relying on his certificate
other than knowledge that some person or persons may rely on the certificate. The
linkage which I regard as necessary has sometimes been identified in the cases as
'assumption of responsibility' or 'a special relationship', but I think that it is the same
concept. Obvious examples were given by Denning LJ in _Candler's_ case where it will be
_c_ remembered the accounts had been produced for the express purpose of being shown to
an identified would-be investor. I do not regard it as necessary or desirable to say more as
to what facts may provide the necessary linkage.
    In the present case, if one disregards the fact that Caparo were shareholders, I am
satisfied that on the facts pleaded the auditors did not owe any duty of care to Caparo.
    Caparo were in fact shareholders: see para 4 of the statement of claim. Counsel for
_d_ Caparo submitted that that fact alone was sufficient to satisfy the requirement of
proximity. I must examine that submission.
    Although auditors are employed by the company, the statutory provisions focus on
the report which they are required to make to the shareholders and I have no doubt that
they are under a like duty to exercise care and skill in making their report. Similar
provisions in the Companies Act 1879 were considered in this court in _Re London and_
_e_ _General Bank (No 2)_ [1895] 2 Ch 673, [1895-9] All ER Rep 953. In that case the auditors
made a report to the directors pointing out in detail the unsatisfactory nature of the
bank's main asset, 'loans to customers and other securities'. They ended saying that in
their opinion no dividend should be paid for the year. They were persuaded by the
chairman to omit that last sentence from the report before it went to the board. Their
_f_ certificate, as laid before shareholders, concluded: 'The value of the assets as shewn on the
balance-sheet is dependent upon realisation.' As originally drafted it had gone on to say
'And on this point we have reported specifically to the board', but again the chairman
prevailed on them to withdraw that sentence. At the general meeting, on the chairman's
proposal, a dividend was declared. It turned out that the dividend could only be paid and
was paid out of capital. When the bank was wound up the liquidator claimed the sum
_g_ paid out as dividend from the auditors. Lindley LJ said ([1895] 2 Ch 673 at 682, [1895-
9] All ER Rep 953 at 956-957):

> 'It is impossible to read s. 7 of the Companies Act, 1879, without being struck
> with the importance of the enactment that the auditors are to be appointed by the
> shareholders, and are to report to them directly, and not to or through the directors.
> The object of this enactment is obvious. It evidently is to secure to the shareholders
_h_ > independent and reliable information respecting the true financial position of the
> company at the time of the audit. The articles of this particular company are even
> more explicit on this point than the statute itself, and remove any possible ambiguity
> to which the language of the statute taken alone may be open if very narrowly
> criticised. It is no part of an auditor's duty to give advice, either to directors or
> shareholders, as to what they ought to do. An auditor has nothing to do with the
_j_ > prudence or imprudence of making loans with or without security. It is nothing to
> him whether the business of a company is being conducted prudently or
> imprudently, profitably or unprofitably. It is nothing to him whether dividends are
> properly or improperly declared, provided he discharges his own duty to the
> shareholders. His business is to ascertain and state the true financial position of the
> company at the time of the audit, and his duty is confined to that.'

The court held that the auditors had failed to discharge their duty to the shareholders.

There is a further passage in the judgment of Lindley LJ to which I must refer. He *a* said ([1895] 2 Ch 673 at 688, [1895–9] All ER Rep 953 at 959–960):

> 'A point was made that the form of the order was wrong. But there is nothing in this. Mr. Theobald could obviously be sued alone in an action at law for breach of his statutory duty as auditor, and for damages resulting from the breach of duty, and the measure of damages would be the sum which he has been ordered to pay.'   *b*

In my judgment the proper analysis of that case is that the shareholders in general meeting took a decision, which but for the breach of duty of the auditors they would not have taken, and that decision caused loss to the company which it could have brought an action to recover. The court was not considering whether any duty was owed by the auditors to the shareholders in their individual capacities. Indeed, in their individual capacities so far from suffering any loss each had gained to the extent of the dividend *c* received.

The statutory duty owed by auditors to shareholders is, I think, a duty owed to them as a body. I appreciate that it is difficult to see how the overstatement of the accounts can cause damage to the shareholders as a body: it will be the underlying reasons for the overstatement which cause damage, for example fraudulent abstraction of assets by directors or servants, but such loss is recoverable by the company. I am anxious to limit *d* the present case to deciding whether the statutory duty operates to protect the individual shareholder as a potential buyer of further shares. If I am wrong in thinking that under the statute no duty is owed to shareholders as individuals, then I think that the duty must be confined to transactions in which the shareholder can only participate because he is a shareholder. The statute imposes a duty to shareholders as a class and the duty should not extend to an individual save as a member of the class in respect of some class activity. *e* Buying shares in a company is not such an activity. Selling shares may be, for only a shareholder can sell shares. (I disregard certain stock exchange short-term gambling practices). We do not have to decide whether in a case where the accounts understate the value of the company a shareholder who sells shares and suffers loss could claim that loss as damages for breach of statutory duty. I say this because, in so far as the statutory duty *f* is relied on as dispensing with other proof of proximity, it can only do so within its confines.

I appreciate that it can be said that it is not sensible to distinguish between a shareholder buying shares and a shareholder selling shares, but I regard it as more sensible than the alternative. Let me give an example. Two friends each have money to invest. One is a shareholder and receives the report with the certified accounts; having read it he hands *g* it to his friend, who also reads it, and both decide individually to buy shares. I find it very difficult to draw any distinction between these two and as I am satisfied that the friend does not establish the required proximity I conclude nor does the shareholder.

I have considered the statutory duty of auditors to shareholders. I see no reason to impose any wider duty at common law.

For these reasons I conclude that the auditors did not owe any duty to Caparo in their *h* capacity as shareholders. Something more was required to create what I regard as the necessary linkage and it is not present in this case.

For these reasons I would dismiss this appeal but, as Bingham and Taylor LJJ take a different view, the order must be that the appeal be allowed.

Appeal allowed. Leave to appeal to House of Lords granted.   *j*

Solicitors: *Berwin Leighton* (for Caparo); *Freshfields* (for the auditors).

                                      Raina Levy   Barrister.

ERRATUM

The publishers wish to point out that the following form the questions to Exercise 4 Cases 2(i) and should follow on from page 164.

SECTION A

1. (i) What were the dates of the hearing of the case?
    (ii) On what date were the judgments in the case delivered?

2. (i) Who represented Caparo Industries plc at the hearing?
    (ii) Who where their solicitors?

3. What is the full citation for the *Caparo* case?

4. In what court did the case begin?

5. (i) What is a headnote?
    (ii) Is the headnote authoritative?
    (iii) What does authoritative mean in relation to cases?

6. Was this a civil or a criminal case?

7. Were all the defendants represented at the Court of Appeal hearing?

8. What remedy was being claimed?

9. What is meant when it is said that the question as to whether a duty of care was owed in this case was being tried as a preliminary issue?

SECTION B

10. What is meant by the expression "interlocutory appeal" at p. 800 h–j?

11. What is meant by the expression "*Cur adv vult*" at p. 801 g?

12. What did the Queen's Bench Division of the High Court decide in the case?

13. What did the majority of the Court of Appeal decide in the *Caparo* case? Note the reasons which they gave for their decision.

14. What reasons did O'Connor L.J. give for dissenting?

Now read the House of Lords decision which was made in the same case and then answer the questions which follow.

We apologise for the error.

SECTION A

1. (i) What were the dates of the hearing of the cases?
   (ii) On what date were the judgments in the case delivered?

2. (i) Who represented Caparo Industries plc at the hearing?
   (ii) Who where their solicitors?

3. What is the full citation for the Caparo case?

4. In what court did the case begin?

5. (i) What is a headnote?
   (ii) Is the headnote authoritative?
   (iii) What does authoritative mean in relation to cases?

6. Was this a civil or a criminal case?

7. Were all the defendants represented at the Court of Appeal hearing?

8. What remedy was being claimed?

9. What is meant when it is said that the question as to whether a duty of care was owed in this case was being tried as a preliminary issue?

SECTION B

10. What is meant by the expression "interlocutory appeal" at p. 800 h-j?

11. What is meant by the expression "Carady v..." at p. 801 g?

12. What did the Queen's Bench Division of the High Court decide in the case?

13. What did the majority of the Court of Appeal decide in the Caparo case? Note the reasons which they gave for their decision.

14. What reasons did O'Connor LJ give for dissenting.

Now read the House of Lords decision which was made in the same case and then answer the questions which follow.

We apologise for the error.

Cases II(ii)

Caparo Industries plc v Dickman and others   *a*

HOUSE OF LORDS

LORD BRIDGE OF HARWICH, LORD ROSKILL, LORD ACKNER, LORD OLIVER OF AYLMERTON AND
LORD JAUNCEY OF TULLICHETTLE

16, 20, 23, 27, 28 NOVEMBER 1989, 8 FEBRUARY 1990

b

*Negligence – Information or advice – Knowledge that third party might rely on information –
Auditor – Preparation of company's accounts – Duty to shareholder – Duty to potential investor
– Plaintiffs owning shares in public company – Plaintiffs making successful take-over bid for
company in reliance on audited accounts of company – Accounts showing profit instead of loss –
Whether reasonably foreseeable that shareholders and potential investors might rely on auditor's
report when dealing in company's shares – Whether sufficient proximity between auditor and   c
shareholders or potential investors – Whether auditor owing duty of care to shareholders or
potential investors to carry out audit with reasonable care and skill.*

The respondents owned shares in a public company, F plc, whose accounts for the year
ended 31 March 1984 showed profits far short of the predicted figure which resulted in
a dramatic drop in the quoted share price. After receipt of the audited accounts for the   *d*
year ended 31 March 1984 the respondents purchased more shares in F plc and later that
year made a successful take-over bid for the company. Following the take-over, the
respondents brought an action against the auditors of the company, alleging that the
accounts of F plc were inaccurate and misleading in that they showed a pre-tax profit of
some £1·2m for the year ended 31 March 1984 when in fact there had been a loss of over
£400,000, that the auditors had been negligent in auditing the accounts, that the   *e*
respondents had purchased further shares and made their take-over bid in reliance on the
audited accounts, and that the auditors owed them a duty of care either as potential
bidders for F plc because they ought to have foreseen that the 1984 results made F plc
vulnerable to a take-over bid or as an existing shareholder of F plc interested in buying
more shares. On the trial of a preliminary issue whether the auditors owed a duty of care   *f*
to the respondents, the judge held that the auditors did not. The respondents appealed to
the Court of Appeal, which allowed their appeal in part on the ground that the auditors
owed the respondents a duty of care as shareholders but not as potential investors. The
auditors appealed to the House of Lords and the respondents cross-appealed against the
Court of Appeal's decision that they could not claim as potential investors.

Held – (1) The three criteria for the imposition of a duty of care were foreseeability of   *g*
damage, proximity of relationship and the reasonableness or otherwise of imposing a
duty. In determining whether there was a relationship of proximity between the parties
the court, guided by situations in which the existence, scope and limits of a duty of care
had previously been held to exist rather than by a single general principle, would
determine whether the particular damage suffered was the kind of damage which the   *h*
defendant was under a duty to prevent and whether there were circumstances from
which the court could pragmatically conclude that a duty of care existed (see p 573 *h* to
p 574 *c*, p 581 *b c e j* to p 582 *a h*, p 584 *j* to p 585 *a e* to p 586 *a*, p 587 *a b*, p 599 *e* to *g* and
p 602 *a d f* to *h*, post); dictum of Brennan J in *Sutherland Shire Council v Heyman* (1985) 60
ALR 1 at 43–44 adopted.

(2) Where a statement put into more or less general circulation might foreseeably be   *j*
relied on by strangers for any one of a variety of different purposes which the maker of
the statement had no specific reason to anticipate there was no relationship of proximity
between the maker of the statement and any person relying on it unless it was shown
that the maker knew that his statement would be communicated to the person relying
on it, either as an individual or as a member of an identifiable class, specifically in
connection with a particular transaction or a transaction of a particular kind and that that

a person would be very likely to rely on it for the purpose of deciding whether to enter into that transaction (see p 576 *c* to *h*, p 581 *e*, p 582 *f* to *h*, p 587 *f g*, p 589 *e* to *g*, p 592 *j*, p 593 *c d* and p 607 *b c*, post); *Cann v Willson* (1888) 39 Ch D 39, dictum of Denning LJ in *Candler v Crane Christmas & Co* [1951] 1 All ER 426 at 433–436, *Hedley Byrne & Co Ltd v Heller & Partners Ltd* [1963] 2 All ER 575 and *Smith v Eric S Bush (a firm), Harris v Wyre Forest DC* [1989] 2 All ER 514 considered.

b (3) The auditor of a public company's accounts owed no duty of care to a member of the public at large who relied on the accounts to buy shares in the company because the court would not deduce a relationship of proximity between the auditor and a member of the public when to do so would give rise to unlimited liability on the part of the auditor. Furthermore, an auditor owed no duty of care to an individual shareholder in the company who wished to buy more shares in the company, since an individual shareholder was in no better position than a member of the public at large and the *c* auditor's statutory duty to prepare accounts was owed to the body of shareholders as a whole, the purpose for which accounts were prepared and audited being to enable the shareholders as a body to exercise informed control of the company and not to enable individual shareholders to buy shares with a view to profit. It followed that the auditors did not owe a duty of care to the respondents either as shareholders or as potential investors in the company. The appeal would therefore be allowed and the cross-appeal *d* dismissed (see p 578 *b c*, p 579 *b* to *d*, p 580 *d* to *f j* to p 581 *a d e*, p 582 *d e h*, p 598 *c* to *e j*, p 601 *f* to *j* and p 607 *f* to p 608 *a d e*, post); dictum of Richmond P in *Scott Group Ltd v McFarlane* [1978] 1 NZLR 553 at 566–567 adopted; *Al Saudi Banque v Clark Pixley (a firm)* [1989] 3 All ER 361 approved; dictum of Woolf J in *JEB Fasteners Ltd v Marks Bloom & Co (a firm)* [1981] 3 All ER 289 at 296–297 disapproved.

Decision of the Court of Appeal [1989] 1 All ER 798 reversed.

e

Notes

For auditors' duties and auditors' reports, see 7(1) Halsbury's Laws (4th edn) paras 905, 912–914, and for cases on the subject, see 9 Digest (Reissue) 601–607, 3593–3614.

For negligence in relation to statements by professional men, see 34 Halsbury's Laws
f (4th edn) para 53, and for cases on the subject, see 36(1) Digest (Reissue) 49–50, *149–158*.

Cases referred to in opinions

Al Saudi Banque v Clark Pixley (a firm) [1989] 3 All ER 361, [1990] 2 WLR 344.
Anns v Merton London Borough [1977] 2 All ER 492, [1978] AC 728, [1977] 2 WLR 1024, HL.
g *Caltex Oil (Australia) Pty Ltd v Dredge Willemstad* (1976) 136 CLR 529, Aust HC.
Candler v Crane Christmas & Co [1951] 1 All ER 426, [1951] 2 KB 164, CA.
Candlewood Navigation Corp Ltd v Mitsui OSK Lines Ltd, The Mineral Transporter, The Ibaraki Maru [1985] 2 All ER 935, [1986] AC 1, [1985] 3 WLR 381, PC.
Cann v Willson (1888) 39 Ch D 39.
h *Clayton v Woodman & Son (Builders) Ltd* [1962] 2 All ER 33, [1962] 2 QB 533, [1962] 1 WLR 585, CA.
Courteen Seed Co v Hong Kong and Shanghai Banking Corp (1927) 245 NY 377, NY Ct of Apps.
Donoghue (or M'Alister) v Stevenson [1932] AC 562, [1932] All ER Rep 1, HL.
Elliott Steam Tug Co Ltd v Shipping Controller [1922] 1 KB 127, CA.
j *Glanzer v Shepard* (1922) 233 NY 236, NY Ct of Apps.
Grant v Australian Knitting Mills Ltd [1936] AC 85, [1935] All ER Rep 209, PC.
Hedley Byrne & Co Ltd v Heller & Partners Ltd [1963] 2 All ER 575, [1964] AC 465, [1963] 3 WLR 101, HL.
Hill v Chief Constable of West Yorkshire [1988] 2 All ER 238, [1988] 2 WLR 1049, HL.
Home Office v Dorset Yacht Co Ltd [1970] 2 All ER 294, [1970] AC 1004, [1970] 2 WLR 1140, HL.

JEB Fasteners Ltd v Marks Bloom & Co (a firm) [1981] 3 All ER 289; *affd* [1983] 1 All ER 583, CA.

Junior Books Ltd v Veitchi Co Ltd [1982] 3 All ER 201, [1983] 1 AC 520, [1982] 3 WLR 477, HL.

Kingston Cotton Mill Co, Re [1896] 1 Ch 6, CA.

Le Lievre v Gould [1893] 1 QB 491, CA.

Leigh & Sillavan Ltd v Aliakmon Shipping Co Ltd, The Aliakmon [1986] 2 All ER 145, [1986] AC 785, [1986] 2 WLR 902, HL.

McLoughlin v O'Brian [1982] 2 All ER 298, [1983] 1 AC 410, [1982] 2 WLR 982, HL.

Ministry of Housing and Local Government v Sharp [1970] 1 All ER 1009, [1970] 2 QB 223, [1970] 2 WLR 802, CA.

Mutual Life and Citizen's Assurance Co Ltd v Evatt [1971] 1 All ER 150, [1971] AC 793, [1971] 2 WLR 23, PC.

Overseas Tankship (UK) Ltd v Morts Dock and Engineering Co Ltd, The Wagon Mound [1961] 1 All ER 404, [1961] AC 388, [1961] 2 WLR 126, PC.

Peabody Donation Fund (Governors) v Sir Lindsay Parkinson & Co Ltd [1984] 3 All ER 529, [1985] AC 210, [1984] 3 WLR 953, HL.

Perl (P) (Exporters) Ltd v Camden London BC [1983] 3 All ER 161, [1984] QB 342, [1983] 3 WLR 769, CA.

Pfeiffer (John) Pty Ltd v Cannay (1981) 148 CLR 218, Aust HC.

Rondel v Worsley [1967] 3 All ER 993, [1969] 1 AC 191, [1967] 3 WLR 1666, HL.

Ross v Caunters (a firm) [1979] 3 All ER 580, [1980] Ch 297, [1979] 3 WLR 605.

Rowling v Takaro Properties Ltd [1988] 1 All ER 163, [1988] AC 473, [1988] 2 WLR 418, PC.

Scott Group Ltd v McFarlane [1978] 1 NZLR 553, NZ CA; *affg* [1975] 1 NZLR 582, NZ SC.

Smith v Eric S Bush (a firm), Harris v Wyre Forest DC [1989] 2 All ER 514, [1989] 2 WLR 790, HL.

Smith v Littlewoods Organisation Ltd (Chief Constable, Fife Constabulary, third party) [1987] 1 All ER 710, [1987] AC 241, [1987] 2 WLR 480, HL.

Sutherland Shire Council v Heyman (1985) 60 ALR 1, Aust HC.

Twomax Ltd v Dickson McFarlane & Robinson 1982 SC 113, Outer House; *rvsd* by consent 1984 SLT 424, Inner House.

Ultramares Corp v Touche (1931) 255 NY 170, NY Ct of Apps.

Yuen Kun-yeu v A-G of Hong Kong [1987] 2 All ER 705, [1988] AC 175, [1987] 3 WLR 776, PC.

Appeal
The third defendants, Touche Ross & Co (a firm), the auditors of Fidelity plc, appealed with leave of the Court of Appeal against the decision of that court (Bingham and Taylor LJJ, O'Connor LJ dissenting) ([1989] 1 All ER 798, [1989] QB 653) on 29 July 1988 and the order dated 5 August 1988 allowing in part an appeal by the plaintiff, Caparo Industries plc (Caparo), against the order dated 15 December 1987 made by Sir Neil Lawson ([1988] BCLC 387), sitting as a judge of the High Court in the Queen's Bench Division in chambers, whereby, on the hearing of a preliminary issue in an action brought by Caparo against the first and second defendants, Steven Graham Dickman and Robert Anthony Dickman (directors of Fidelity plc), and the auditors, claiming damages against the first and second defendants for fraud and against the auditors for negligence, the judge held that the auditors did not owe a duty of care to Caparo either as potential investors or as shareholders in the company in respect of the audit of the company's accounts for the year ended 31 March 1984. The Court of Appeal held that the auditors owed a duty to Caparo as shareholders but not as potential investors in the company. Caparo cross-appealed against the dismissal by the Court of Appeal of their claim that the

auditors owed them a duty of care as potential investors. The facts are set out in the
a opinion of Lord Bridge.

Peter Goldsmith QC and *Stephen Moriarty* for the auditors.
Viscount Bledisloe QC, Michael Brindle and *Craig Orr* for Caparo.

Their Lordships took time for consideration.

b
8 February. The following opinions were delivered.

LORD BRIDGE OF HARWICH. My Lords, the appellants are a well-known firm of
chartered accountants. At all times material to this appeal, they were the auditors of a
public limited company, Fidelity plc (Fidelity), which carried on business as manufacturers
c and vendors of electrical equipment of various kinds and whose shares were quoted on
the London Stock Exchange. On 22 May 1984 the directors of Fidelity announced the
results for the year ended 31 March 1984. These revealed that profits for the year fell
well short of the figure which had been predicted, and this resulted in a dramatic drop in
the quoted price of the shares which had stood at 143p per share on 1 March 1984 and
which, by the beginning of June 1984, had fallen to 63p. Fidelity's accounts for the year
d to 31 March 1984 had been audited by the appellants and had been approved by the
directors on the day before the results were announced. On 12 June 1984 they were
issued to the shareholders, with notice of the annual general meeting, which took place
on 4 July 1984 and at which the auditors' report was read and the accounts were adopted.
    Following the announcement of the results, the respondents Caparo Industries plc
(Caparo) began to purchase shares of Fidelity in the market. On 8 June 1984 they
e purchased 100,000 shares but they were not registered as members of Fidelity until after
12 June 1984 when the accounts were sent to shareholders although they had been
registered in respect of at least some of the shares which they purchased by the date of
the annual general meeting, which they did not attend. On 12 June 1984 they purchased
a further 50,000 shares, and by 6 July 1984 they had increased their holding in Fidelity
to 29·9% of the issued capital. On 4 September 1984 they made a bid for the remainder
f at 120p per share, that offer being increased to 125p per share on 24 September 1984.
The offer was declared unconditional on 23 October 1984, and two days later Caparo
announced that it had acquired 91·8% of the issued shares and proposed to acquire the
balance compulsorily, which it subsequently did.
    The action in which this appeal arises is one in which Caparo alleges that the purchases
of shares which took place after 12 June 1984 and the subsequent bid were all made in
g reliance on the accounts and that those accounts were inaccurate and misleading in a
number of respects and, in particular, in overvaluing stock and underproviding for after-
sales credits, with the result that an apparent pre-tax profit of some £1·3m should in fact
have been shown as a loss of over £400,000. Had the true facts been known, it is alleged,
Caparo would not have made a bid at the price paid or indeed at all. Caparo accordingly
h commenced proceedings on 24 July 1985 against two of the persons who were directors
at the material time, claiming that the overvaluations were made fraudulently, and
against the appellants (the auditors), claiming that they were negligent in certifying, as
they did, that the accounts showed a true and fair view of Fidelity's position at the date
to which they related. The substance of the allegation against the auditors is contained in
para 16 of the statement of claim which is in the following terms:

j   'Touche Ross, as auditors of Fidelity carrying out their functions as auditors and
    certifiers of the accounts in April and May 1984, owed a duty of care to investors
    and potential investors, and in particular to Caparo, in respect of the audit and
    certification of the accounts. In support of that duty of care Caparo will rely upon
    the following matters:—(1) Touche Ross knew or ought to have known (a) that in

early March 1984 a press release had been issued stating that profits for the financial
year would fall significantly short of £2.2m (b) that Fidelity's share price fell from   *a*
143p per share on 1st March 1984 to 75p per share on 2nd April 1984 (c) that
Fidelity required financial assistance. (2) Touche Ross therefore ought to have
foreseen that Fidelity was vulnerable to a take-over bid and that persons such as
Caparo might well rely on the accounts for the purpose of deciding whether to take
over Fidelity and might well suffer loss if the accounts were inaccurate.'

On 6 July 1987 Sir Neil Lawson, sitting as a judge of the High Court in the Queen's   *b*
Bench Division in chambers, made an order for the trial of a preliminary issue, as follows:

'. . . whether on the facts set out in paragraphs 4 and 6 and in sub-paragraphs (1)
and (2) of paragraph 16 of the Statement of Claim herein, the Third Defendants,
Touche Ross & Co., owed a duty of care to the Plaintiffs, Caparo Industries plc, (a) as
potential investors in Fidelity PlC; or (b) as shareholders in Fidelity PlC from 8 June   *c*
1984 and/or from 12 June 1984; in respect of the audit of the accounts of Fidelity
PlC for the year ended 31 March 1984 published on 12 June 1984.'

Paragraphs 4 and 6 of the statement of claim are those paragraphs in which are set out
the purchases of shares by Caparo to which I have referred and in which it is claimed that
the purchases made after 12 June 1984 were made in reliance on the information   *d*
contained in the accounts. There is, however, one correction to be made. Paragraph 4
alleges that the accounts were issued on 12 June 1984 'to shareholders, including Caparo'
but it is now accepted that at that date Caparo, although a purchaser of shares, had not
been registered as a shareholder in Fidelity's register of members.
On the trial of this preliminary issue Sir Neil Lawson, sitting as a judge of the Queen's
Bench Division, held (i) that the auditors owed no duty at common law to Caparo as   *e*
investors and (ii) that, whilst auditors might owe statutory duties to shareholders as a
class, there was no common law duty to individual shareholders such as would enable an
individual shareholder to recover damages for loss sustained by him in acting in reliance
on the audited accounts (see [1988] BCLC 387).
Caparo appealed to the Court of Appeal, which, by a majority (O'Connor LJ dissenting)
allowed the appeal holding that, whilst there was no relationship between an auditor and   *f*
a potential investor sufficiently proximate to give rise to a duty of care at common law,
there was such a relationship with individual shareholders, so that an individual
shareholder who suffered loss by acting in reliance on negligently prepared accounts,
whether by selling or retaining his shares or by purchasing additional shares, was entitled
to recover in tort (see [1989] 1 All ER 798, [1989] QB 653). From that decision the
auditors now appeal to your Lordships' House with the leave of the Court of Appeal, and   *g*
Caparo cross-appeal against the rejection by the Court of Appeal of their claim that the
auditors owed them a duty of care as potential investors.
In determining the existence and scope of the duty of care which one person may owe
to another in the infinitely varied circumstances of human relationships there has for
long been a tension between two different approaches. Traditionally the law finds the   *h*
existence of the duty in different specific situations each exhibiting its own particular
characteristics. In this way the law has identified a wide variety of duty situations, all
falling within the ambit of the tort of negligence, but sufficiently distinct to require
separate definition of the essential ingredients by which the existence of the duty is to be
recognised. Commenting on the outcome of this traditional approach, Lord Atkin, in his
seminal speech in *Donoghue v Stevenson* [1932] AC 562 at 579–580, [1932] All ER Rep 1   *j*
at 11, observed:

'The result is that the Courts have been engaged upon an elaborate classification
of duties as they exist in respect of property, whether real or personal, with further
divisions as to ownership, occupation or control, and distinctions based on the
particular relations of the one side or the other, whether manufacterer, salesman or

a landlord, customer, tenant, stranger, and so on. In this way it can be ascertained at any time whether the law recognizes a duty, but only where the case can be referred to some particular species which has been examined and classified. And yet the duty which is common to all the cases where liability is established must logically be based upon some element common to the cases where it is found to exist.'

b It is this last sentence which signifies the introduction of the more modern approach of seeking a single general principle which may be applied in all circumstances to determine the existence of a duty of care. Yet Lord Atkin himself sounds the appropriate note of caution by adding:

'To seek a complete logical definition of the general principle is probably to go beyond the function of the judge, for the more general the definition the more likely it is to omit essentials or to introduce non-essentials.'

c Lord Reid gave a large impetus to the modern approach in *Home Office v Dorset Yacht Co Ltd* [1970] 2 All ER 294 at 297, [1970] AC 1004 at 1026–1027, where he said:

'In later years there has been a steady trend towards regarding the law of negligence as depending on principle so that, when a new point emerges, one should ask not whether it is covered by authority but whether recognised principles apply *d* to it. *Donoghue v Stevenson* may be regarded as a milestone, and the well-known passage in Lord Atkin's speech should I think be regarded as a statement of principle. It is not to be treated as if it were a statutory definition. It will require qualification in new circumstances. But I think that the time has come when we can and should say that it ought to apply unless there is some justification or valid explanation for its exclusion.'

e The most comprehensive attempt to articulate a single general principle is reached in the well-known passage from the speech of Lord Wilberforce in *Anns v Merton London Borough* [1977] 2 All ER 492 at 498, [1978] AC 728 at 751–752:

'Through the trilogy of cases in this House, *Donoghue v Stevenson* [1932] AC 562, *f* [1932] All ER Rep 1, *Hedley Byrne & Co Ltd v Heller & Partners Ltd* [1963] 2 All ER 575, [1964] AC 465, and *Home Office v Dorset Yacht Co Ltd* [1970] 2 All ER 294, [1970] AC 1004, the position has now been reached that in order to establish that a duty of care arises in a particular situation, it is not necessary to bring the facts of that situation within those of previous situations in which a duty of care has been held to exist. Rather the question has to be approached in two stages. First one has to ask whether, as between the alleged wrongdoer and the person who has suffered *g* damage there is a sufficient relationship of proximity or neighbourhood such that, in the reasonable contemplation of the former, carelessness on his part may be likely to cause damage to the latter, in which case a prima facie duty of care arises. Secondly, if the first question is answered affirmatively, it is necessary to consider whether there are any considerations which ought to negative, or to reduce or limit *h* the scope of the duty or the class of person to whom it is owed or the damages to which a breach of it may give rise (see the *Dorset Yacht case* [1970] 2 All ER 294 at 297–298, [1970] AC 1004 at 1027 per Lord Reid).'

But since *Anns's* case a series of decisions of the Privy Council and of your Lordships' House, notably in judgments and speeches delivered by Lord Keith, have emphasised the inability of any single general principle to provide a practical test which can be applied *j* to every situation to determine whether a duty of care is owed and, if so, what is its scope: see *Peabody Donation Fund v Sir Lindsay Parkinson & Co Ltd* [1984] 3 All ER 529 at 533–534, [1985] AC 210 at 239–241, *Yuen Kun-yeu v A-G of Hong Kong* [1987] 2 All ER 705 at 709–712, [1988] AC 175 at 190–194, *Rowling v Takaro Properties Ltd* [1988] 1 All ER 163 at 172, [1988] AC 473 at 501 and *Hill v Chief Constable of West Yorkshire* [1988] 2 All ER 238 at 241, [1989] AC 53 at 60. What emerges is that, in addition to the foreseeability of

damage, necessary ingredients in any situation giving rise to a duty of care are that there
should exist between the party owing the duty and the party to whom it is owed a *a*
relationship characterised by the law as one of 'proximity' or 'neighbourhood' and that
the situation should be one in which the court considers it fair, just and reasonable that
the law should impose a duty of a given scope on the one party for the benefit of the
other. But it is implicit in the passages referred to that the concepts of proximity and
fairness embodied in these additional ingredients are not susceptible of any such precise
definition as would be necessary to give them utility as practical tests, but amount in *b*
effect to little more than convenient labels to attach to the features of different specific
situations which, on a detailed examination of all the circumstances, the law recognises
pragmatically as giving rise to a duty of care of a given scope. Whilst recognising, of
course, the importance of the underlying general principles common to the whole field
of negligence, I think the law has now moved in the direction of attaching greater
significance to the more traditional categorisation of distinct and recognisable situations *c*
as guides to the existence, the scope and the limits of the varied duties of care which the
law imposes. We must now, I think, recognise the wisdom of the words of Brennan J in
the High Court of Australia in *Sutherland Shire Council v Heyman* (1985) 60 ALR 1 at 43–
44, where he said:

> 'It is preferable in my view, that the law should develop novel categories of *d*
> negligence incrementally and by analogy with established categories, rather than by
> a massive extension of a prima facie duty of care restrained only by indefinable
> "considerations which ought to negative, or to reduce or limit the scope of the duty
> or the class of person to whom it is owed".'

One of the most important distinctions always to be observed lies in the law's essentially
different approach to the different kinds of damage which one party may have suffered *e*
in consequence of the acts or omissions of another. It is one thing to owe a duty of care
to avoid causing injury to the person or property of others. It is quite another to avoid
causing others to suffer purely economic loss. A graphic illustration of the distinction is
embodied in the proposition that—

> 'In case of a wrong done to a chattel the common law does not recognize a person *f*
> whose only rights are a contractual right to have the use or services of the chattel for
> purposes of making profits or gains without possession of or property in the chattel.
> Such a person cannot claim for injury done to his contractual right . . .'

(See *Elliott Steam Tug Co Ltd v Shipping Controller* [1922] 1 KB 127 at 139 per Scrutton LJ).
The proposition derives from *Cattle v Stockton Waterworks Co* (1875) LR 10 QB 453,
[1874–80] All ER Rep 220. It has recently been reaffirmed in *Candlewood Navigation Corp* *g*
Ltd v Mitsui OSK Lines Ltd, The Mineral Transporter, The Ibaraki Maru [1985] 2 All ER 935,
[1986] AC 1 and *Leigh & Sillavan Ltd v Aliakmon Shipping Co Ltd, The Aliakmon* [1986] 2 All
ER 145, [1986] AC 785. In the former case Lord Fraser, delivering the judgment of the
Privy Council, said ([1985] 2 All ER 935 at 945, [1986] AC 1 at 25):

> 'Their Lordships consider that some limit or control mechanism has to be imposed *h*
> on the liability of a wrongdoer towards those who have suffered economic damage
> in consequence of his negligence. The need for such a limit has been repeatedly
> asserted in the cases, from *Cattle's* case to *Caltex* (see *Caltex Oil (Australia) Pty Ltd v*
> *Dredge Willemstad* (1976) 136 CLR 529), and their Lordships are not aware that a
> view to the contrary has ever been judicially expressed.'

The damage which may be caused by the negligently spoken or written word will *j*
normally be confined to economic loss sustained by those who rely on the accuracy of
the information or advice they receive as a basis for action. The question what, if any,
duty is owed by the maker of a statement to exercise due care to ensure its accuracy arises
typically in relation to statements made by a person in the exercise of his calling or

profession. In advising the client who employs him the professional man owes a duty to
a exercise that standard of skill and care appropriate to his professional status and will be
liable both in contract and in tort for all losses which his client may suffer by reason of
any breach of that duty. But the possibility of any duty of care being owed to third
parties with whom the profesional man was in no contractual relationship was for long
denied because of the wrong turning taken by the law in *Le Lievre v Gould* [1893] 1 QB
491 in overruling *Cann v Willson* (1888) 39 Ch D 39. In *Candler v Crane Christmas & Co*
b [1951] 1 All ER 426, [1951] 2 KB 164 Denning LJ, in his dissenting judgment, made a
valiant attempt to correct the error. But it was not until the decision of this House in
Hedley Byrne & Co Ltd v Heller Partners Ltd [1963] 2 All ER 575, [1964] AC 465 that the
law was once more set on the right path.

Consistently with the traditional approach it is to these authorities and to subsequent
decisions directly relevant to this relatively narrow corner of the field that we should
c look to determine the essential characteristics of a situation giving rise, independently of
any contractual or fiduciary relationship, to a duty of care owed by one party to another
to ensure that the accuracy of any statement which the one party makes and on which
the other party may foreseeably rely to his economic detriment.

In *Cann v Willson* (1888) 39 Ch D 39 mortgagees advanced money in reliance on a
valuation of the mortgaged property supplied to them by a valuer employed by the
d mortgagor. On the mortgagor's default, the property, having been negligently
undervalued, proved insufficient to cover the mortgage loan. The mortgagees recovered
their loss from the valuer. In his judgment Chitty J said (at 42–43):

> 'In this case the document called a valuation was sent by the Defendants direct to
> the agents of the Plaintiff for the purpose of inducing the Plaintiff and his co-trustee
> *e* to lay out the trust money on mortgage. It seems to me that the Defendants
> knowingly had placed themselves in that position, and in point of law incurred a
> duty towards him to use reasonable care in the preparation of the document called a
> valuation.'

In *Candler v Crane Christmas & Co Ltd* [1951] 1 All ER 426, [1951] 2 KB 164 the
f plaintiff invested money in a limited company in reliance on accounts of the company
prepared by the company's accountants at the request of the managing director, which
were shown to the plaintiff and discussed with him by the accountants in the knowledge
that he was interested as a potential investor in the company. The accounts were
inaccurate and misleading and the plaintiff, having invested in the company in reliance
on them, lost his money. Denning LJ, in his dissenting judgment, held the plaintiff
entitled to recover damages for the accountants' negligence.

g In the *Hedley Byrne* case [1963] 2 All ER 575, [1964] AC 465 bankers were asked about
the financial stability of a customer of the bank. They gave a favourable reference, albeit
with a disclaimer of responsibility. The circumstances of the inquiry made it clear to the
bankers that the party on whose behalf the inquiry was made wanted to know if they
could safely extend credit to the bank's customer in a substantial sum. Acting on the
h reference given, the plaintiffs extended credit to the bank's customer who in due course
defaulted. Although the House held that the bankers were protected by the disclaimer
of responsibility, the case provided the opportunity to review the law, which led to the
reinstatement of *Cann v Willson*, the overruling of the majority decision in the *Candler*
case and the approbation of the dissenting judgment of Denning LJ in that case.

The most recent decision of the House, which is very much in point, is that of the two
j appeals heard together of *Smith v Eric S Bush (a firm), Harris v Wyre Forest DC* [1989] 2 All
ER 514, [1989] 2 WLR 790. The plaintiffs in both cases were house purchasers who
purchased in reliance on valuations of the properties made by surveyors acting for and on
the instructions of the mortgagees proposing to advance money to the plaintiffs to
enable them to effect their purchases. In both cases the surveyors' fees were paid by the
plaintiffs and in both cases it turned out that the inspections and valuations had been

negligently carried out and that the property was seriously defective so that the plaintiffs
suffered financial loss. In *Smith's* case the mortgagees were a building society, the   *a*
surveyors who carried out the inspection and valuation were a firm employed by the
building society, and their report was shown to the plaintiff. In *Harris's* case the
mortgagees were the local authority who employed a member of their own staff to carry
out the inspection and valuation. His report was not shown to the plaintiff, but the
plaintiff rightly assumed from the local authority's offer of a mortgage loan that the
property had been professionally valued as worth at least the amount of the loan. In both   *b*
cases the terms agreed between the plaintiff and the mortgagee purported to exclude any
liability on the part of the mortgagee or the surveyor for the accuracy of the mortgage
valuation. The House held that in both cases the surveyor making the inspection and
valuation owed a duty of care to the plaintiff house purchaser and that the contractual
clauses purporting to exclude liability were struck down by ss 2(2) and 11(3) of the Unfair
Contract Terms Act 1977.   *c*
    The salient feature of all these cases is that the defendant giving advice or information
was fully aware of the nature of the transaction which the plaintiff had in contemplation,
knew that the advice or information would be communicated to him directly or
indirectly and knew that it was very likely that the plaintiff would rely on that advice or
information in deciding whether or not to engage in the transaction in contemplation.
In these circumstances the defendant could clearly be expected, subject always to the   *d*
effect of any disclaimer of responsibility, specifically to anticipate that the plaintiff would
rely on the advice or information given by the defendant for the very purpose for which
he did in the event rely on it. So also the plaintiff, subject again to the effect of any
disclaimer, would in that situation reasonably suppose that he was entitled to rely on the
advice or information communicated to him for the very purpose for which he required
it. The situation is entirely different where a statement is put into more or less general   *e*
circulation and may foreseeably be relied on by strangers to the maker of the statement
for any one of a variety of different purposes which the maker of the statement has no
specific reason to anticipate. To hold the maker of the statement to be under a duty of
care in respect of the accuracy of the statement to all and sundry for any purpose for
which they may choose to rely on it is not only to subject him, in the classic words of
Cardozo CJ, to 'liability in an indeterminate amount for an indeterminate time to an   *f*
indeterminate class' (see *Ultramares Corp v Touche* (1931) 255 NY 170 at 179), it is also to
confer on the world at large a quite unwarranted entitlement to appropriate for their
own purposes the benefit of the expert knowledge or professional expertise attributed to
the maker of the statement. Hence, looking only at the circumstances of these decided
cases where a duty of care in respect of negligent statements has been held to exist, I
should expect to find that the 'limit or control mechanism . . . imposed on the liability of   *g*
a wrongdoer towards those who have suffered economic damage in consequence of his
negligence' (see the *Candlewood* case [1985] 2 All ER 935 at 945, [1986] AC 1 at 25) rested
on the necessity to prove, in this category of the tort of negligence, as an essential
ingredient of the 'proximity' between the plaintiff and the defendant, that the defendant
knew that his statement would be communicated to the plaintiff, either as an individual   *h*
or as a member of an identifiable class, specifically in connection with a particular
transaction or transactions of a particular kind (eg in a prospectus inviting investment)
and that the plaintiff would be very likely to rely on it for the purpose of deciding
whether or not to enter on that transaction or on a transaction of that kind.
    I find this expectation fully supported by the dissenting judgment of Denning LJ in
Candler v Crane Christmas & Co [1951] 1 All ER 426 at 433–436, [1951] 2 KB 164 at 179–   *j*
184 in the following passages:

    'Let me now be constructive and suggest the circumstances in which I say that a
    duty to use care in making a statement does exist apart from a contract in that
    behalf. First, what persons are under such duty? My answer is those persons such as

a accountants, surveyors, valuers and analysts, whose profession and occupation it is
   to examine books, accounts, and other things, and to make reports on which other
   people—other than their clients—rely in the ordinary course of business . . .
   Secondly, to whom do these professional people owe this duty? I will take
   accountants, but the same reasoning applies to the others. They owe the duty, of
   course, to their employer or client; and also, I think, to any third person to whom
   they themselves show the accounts, or to whom they know their employer is going
b to show the accounts so as to induce him to invest money or take some other action
   on them. I do not think, however, the duty can be extended still further so as to
   include strangers of whom they have heard nothing and to whom their employer
   without their knowledge may choose to show their accounts. Once the accountants
   have handed their accounts to their employer, they are not, as a rule, responsible for
   what he does with them without their knowledge or consent . . . The test of
c proximity in these cases is: Did the accountants know that the accounts were
   required for submission to the plaintiff and use by him? . . . Thirdly, to what
   transactions does the duty of care extend? It extends, I think, only to those
   transactions for which the accountants knew their accounts were required. For
   instance, in the present case it extends to the original investment of £2,000 which
   the plaintiff made in reliance on the accounts, because [the accountants] knew that
d the accounts were required for his guidance in making that investment; but it does
   not extend to the subsequent £200 which he invested after he had been two months
   with the company. This distinction, that the duty only extends to the very
   transaction in mind at the time, is implicit in the decided cases . . . It will be noticed
   that I have confined the duty to cases where the accountant prepares his accounts
   and makes his report for the guidance of the very person in the very transaction in
e question. That is sufficient for the decision of this case. I can well understand that it
   would be going too far to make an accountant liable to any person in the land who
   chooses to rely on the accounts in matters of business, for that would expose him, in
   the words of Cardozo, C.J., in Ultramares Corpn. v. Touche ((1931) 255 NY 170 at
   179), to "liability in an indeterminate amount for an indeterminate time to an
   indeterminate class." Whether he would be liable if he prepared his accounts for the
f guidance of a specific class of persons in a specific class of transactions, I do not say. I
   should have thought he might be, just as the analyst and lift inspector would be
   liable in the instances I have given earlier. It is, perhaps, worth mentioning that
   Parliament has intervened to make the professional man liable for negligent reports
   given for the purposes of a prospectus: see s. 40 and s. 43 of the Companies Act,
   1948. That is an instance of liability for reports made for the guidance of a specific
g class of persons—investors in a specific class of transactions—applying for shares.
   That enactment does not help one way or the other to show what result the common
   law would have reached in the absence of such provisions, but it does show what
   result it ought to reach. My conclusion is that a duty to use care in statement is
   recognised by English law, and that its recognition does not create any dangerous
h precedent when it is remembered that it is limited in respect of the persons by
   whom and to whom it is owed and the transactions to which it applies.'

   It seems to me that this masterly analysis, if I may say so with respect, requires little, if
   any, amplification or modification in the light of later authority and is particularly apt to
   point the way to the right conclusion in the present appeal.
       Some of the speeches in the Hedley Byrne case derive a duty of care in relation to
j negligent statements from a voluntary assumption of responsibility on the part of the
   maker of the statements. In his speech in Smith v Eric S Bush [1989] 2 All ER 514 at 534,
   [1989] 2 WLR 790 at 813 Lord Griffiths emphatically rejected the view that this was the
   true ground of liability and concluded:

       'The phrase "assumption of responsibility" can only have any real meaning if it is understood as referring to the circumstances in which the law will deem the maker of the statement to have assumed responsibility to the person who acts on the advice.'   *a*

I do not think that in the context of the present appeal anything turns on the difference between these two approaches.

These considerations amply justify the conclusion that auditors of a public company's accounts owe no duty of care to members of the public at large who rely on the accounts in deciding to buy shares in the company. If a duty of care were owed so widely, it is   *b* difficult to see any reason why it should not equally extend to all who rely on the accounts in relation to other dealings with a company as lenders or merchants extending credit to the company. A claim that such a duty was owed by auditors to a bank lending to a company was emphatically and convincingly rejected by Millett J in *Al Saudi Banque v Clark Pixley (a firm)* [1989] 3 All ER 361, [1990] 2 WLR 344. The only support for an   *c* unlimited duty of care owed by auditors for the accuracy of their accounts to all who may foreseeably rely on them is to be found in some jurisdictions in the United States of America, where there are striking differences in the law in different states. In this jurisdiction I have no doubt that the creation of such an unlimited duty would be a legislative step which it would be for Parliament, not the courts, to take.

The main submissions for Caparo are that the necessary nexus of proximity between   *d* it and the auditors giving rise to a duty of care stems from (1) the pleaded circumstances indicating the vulnerability of Fidelity to a take-over bid and from the consequent probability that another company, such as Caparo, would rely on the audited accounts in deciding to launch a take-over bid or (2) the circumstance that Caparo was already a shareholder in Fidelity when it decided to launch its take-over bid in reliance on the accounts. In relation to the first of these two submissions, Caparo applied, in the course   *e* of the hearing, for leave to amend para 16(2) of the statement of claim by adding the words 'or alternatively that it was highly probable that such persons would rely on the accounts for that purpose'.

The case which gives most assistance to Caparo in support of this submission is *Scott Group Ltd v McFarlane* [1978] 1 NZLR 553. The audited consolidated accounts of a New Zealand public company and its subsidiaries overstated the assets of the group because of   *f* an admitted accounting error. Under the relevant New Zealand legislation its accounts were, as in England, accessible to the public. The circumstances of the group's affairs were such as to make it highly probable that it would attract a take-over bid. The plaintiffs made such a bid successfully and when the accounting error was discovered claimed from the auditors in respect of the shortfall in the assets. Quilliam J held that the auditors owed the plaintiffs no duty of care (see [1975] 1 NZLR 582). The majority   *g* of the New Zealand Court of Appeal (Woodhouse and Cooke JJ) held that the duty of care arose from the probability that the company would attract a take-over bid and the bidder would rely on the audited accounts, although Cooke J held that the shortfall in the assets below that erroneously shown in the accounts did not amount to a loss recoverable in tort. Richmond P held that no duty of care was owed. He said ([1978] 1 NZLR 553 at 566):   *h*

'All the speeches in *Hedley Byrne* seem to me to recognise the need for a "special" relationship: a relationship which can properly be treated as giving rise to a special duty to use care in statement. The question in any given case is whether the nature of the relationship is such that one party can fairly be held to have assumed a responsibility to the other as regards the reliability of the advice or information. I   *j* do not think that such a relationship should be found to exist unless, at least, the maker of the statement was, or ought to have been, aware that his advice or information would in fact be made available to and be relied on by a particular person or class of persons for the purposes of a particular transaction or type of

transaction. I would especially emphasise that to my mind it does not seem
a reasonable to attribute an assumption of responsibility unless the maker of the
statement ought in all the circumstances, both in preparing himself for what he said
and in saying it, to have directed his mind, and to have been able to direct his mind,
to some particular and specific purpose for which he was aware that his advice or
information would be relied on. In many situations that purpose will be obvious.
But the annual accounts of a company can be relied on in all sorts of ways and for
b many purposes.'

I agree with this reasoning, which seems to me to be entirely in line with the principles
to be derived from the authorities to which I have earlier referred and not to require
modification in any respect which is relevant for present purposes by reference to
anything said in this House in *Smith v Eric S Bush*. I should in any event be extremely
reluctant to hold that the question whether or not an auditor owes a duty of care to an
c investor buying shares in a public company depends on the degree of probability that
the shares will prove attractive either en bloc to a take-over bidder or piecemeal to
individual investors. It would be equally wrong, in my opinion, to hold an auditor under
a duty of care to anyone who might lend money to a company by reason only that it was
foreseeable as highly probable that the company would borrow money at some time in
d the year following publication of its audited accounts and that lenders might rely on
those accounts in deciding to lend. I am content to assume the high probability of a take-
over bid in reliance on the accounts which the proposed amendment of the statement of
claim would assert but I do not think it assists Caparo's case.

The only other English authority to which I need refer in this context is *JEB Fasteners
Ltd v Marks Bloom & Co (a firm)* [1981] 3 All ER 289, a decision at first instance of Woolf J.
e This was another case where the plaintiffs, who had made a successful take-over bid for a
company in reliance on audited accounts which had been negligently prepared, sued the
accountants for damages. Woolf J held that the auditors owed the plaintiffs a duty of care
in the preparation of the accounts (at 296–297). He relied on both *Anns's case* [1977] 2
All ER 492, [1978] AC 728 and *Scott Group Ltd v McFarlane* [1978] 1 NZLR 553 in
reaching the conclusion that the duty could be derived from foreseeability alone. For the
f reasons already indicated, I do not agree with this. It may well be, however, that the
particular facts in the *JEB* case were sufficient to establish a basis on which the necessary
ingredient of proximity to found a duty of care could be derived from the actual
knowledge on the part of the auditors of the specific purpose for which the plaintiffs
intended to use the accounts.

The position of auditors in relation to the shareholders of a public limited liability
g company arising from the relevant provisions of the Companies Act 1985 is accurately
summarised in the judgment of Bingham LJ in the Court of Appeal ([1989] 1 All ER 798
at 804, [1989] QB 653 at 680–681):

'The members, or shareholders, of the company are its owners. But they are too
numerous, and in most cases too unskilled, to undertake the day-to-day management
h of that which they own. So responsibility for day-to-day management of the
company is delegated to directors. The shareholders, despite their overall powers of
control, are in most companies for most of the time investors and little more. But it
would, of course, be unsatisfactory and open to abuse if the shareholders received no
report on the financial stewardship of their investment save from those to whom
the stewardship had been entrusted. So provision is made for the company in
j general meeting to appoint an auditor (Companies Act 1985, s 384) whose duty is to
investigate and form an opinion on the adequacy of the company's accounting
records and returns and the correspondence between the company's accounting
records and returns and its accounts (s 237). The auditor has then to report to the
company's members (among other things) whether in his opinion the company's

accounts give a true and fair view of the company's financial position (s 236). In carrying out his investigation and in forming his opinion the auditor necessarily *a* works very closely with the directors and officers of the company. He receives his remuneration from the company. He naturally, and rightly, regards the company as his client. But he is employed by the company to exercise his professional skill and judgment for the purpose of giving the shareholders an independent report on the reliability of the company's accounts and thus on their investment. Vaughan Williams J said in *Re Kingston Cotton Mill Co* [1896] 1 Ch 6 at 11: "No doubt he is *b* acting antagonistically to the directors in the sense that he is appointed by the shareholders to be a check upon them." The auditor's report must be read before the company in general meeting and must be open to inspection by any member of the company (s 241). It is attached to and forms part of the company's accounts (ss 238(3) and 239). A copy of the company's accounts (including the auditor's report) must be sent to every member (s 240). Any member of the company, even *c* if not entitled to have a copy of the accounts sent to him, is entitled to be furnished with a copy of the company's last accounts on demand and without charge (s 246).'

No doubt these provisions establish a relationship between the auditors and the shareholders of a company on which the shareholder is entitled to rely for the protection of his interest. But the crucial question concerns the extent of the shareholder's interest *d* which the auditor has a duty to protect. The shareholders of a company have a collective interest in the company's proper management and in so far as a negligent failure of the auditor to report accurately on the state of the company's finances deprives the shareholders of the opportunity to exercise their powers in general meeting to call the directors to book and to ensure that errors in management are corrected, the shareholders ought to be entitled to a remedy. But in practice no problem arises in this regard since *e* the interest of the shareholders in the proper management of the company's affairs is indistinguishable from the interest of the company itself and any loss suffered by the shareholders, eg by the negligent failure of the auditor to discover and expose a misappropriation of funds by a director of the company, will be recouped by a claim against the auditor in the name of the company, not by individual shareholders.

I find it difficult to visualise a situation arising in the real world in which the individual *f* shareholder could claim to have sustained a loss in respect of his existing shareholding referable to the negligence of the auditor which could not be recouped by the company. But on this part of the case your Lordships were much pressed with the argument that such a loss might occur by a negligent undervaluation of the company's assets in the auditor's report relied on by the individual shareholder in deciding to sell his shares at an undervalue. The argument then runs thus. The shareholder, qua shareholder, is entitled *g* to rely on the auditor's report as the basis of his investment decision to sell his existing shareholding. If he sells at an undervalue he is entitled to recover the loss from the auditor. There can be no distinction in law between the shareholder's investment decision to sell the shares he has or to buy additional shares. It follows, therefore, that the scope of the duty of care owed to him by the auditor extends to cover any loss sustained *h* consequent on the purchase of additional shares in reliance on the auditor's negligent report.

I believe this argument to be fallacious. Assuming without deciding that a claim by a shareholder to recover a loss suffered by selling his shares at an undervalue attributable to an undervaluation of the company's assets in the auditor's report could be sustained at all, it would not be by reason of any reliance by the shareholder on the auditor's report in *j* deciding to sell: the loss would be referable to the depreciatory effect of the report on the market value of the shares before ever the decision of the shareholder to sell was taken. A claim to recoup a loss alleged to flow from the purchase of overvalued shares, on the other hand, can only be sustained on the basis of the purchaser's reliance on the report. The specious equation of 'investment decisions' to sell or to buy as giving rise to parallel claims thus appears to me to be untenable. Moreover, the loss in the case of the sale

a would be of a loss of part of the value of the shareholder's existing holding, which, assuming a duty of care owed to individual shareholders, it might sensibly lie within the scope of the auditor's duty to protect. A loss, on the other hand, resulting from the purchase of additional shares would result from a wholly independent transaction having no connection with the existing shareholding.

I believe it is this last distinction which is of critical importance and which demonstrates

b the unsoundness of the conclusion reached by the majority of the Court of Appeal. It is never sufficient to ask simply whether A owes B a duty of care. It is always necessary to determine the scope of the duty by reference to the kind of damage from which A must take care to save B harmless:

> 'The question is always whether the defendant was under a duty to avoid or prevent that damage, but the actual nature of the damage suffered is relevant to the
c existence and extent of any duty to avoid or prevent it.'

(See *Sutherland Shire Council v Heyman* (1985) 60 ALR 1 at 48 per Brennan J.)

Assuming for the purpose of the argument that the relationship between the auditor of a company and individual shareholders is of sufficient proximity to give rise to a duty of care, I do not understand how the scope of that duty can possibly extend beyond the

d protection of any individual shareholder from losses in the value of the shares which he holds. As a purchaser of additional shares in reliance on the auditor's report, he stands in no different position from any other investing member of the public to whom the auditor owes no duty.

I would allow the appeal and dismiss the cross-appeal.

e **LORD ROSKILL.** My Lords, I have had the advantage of reading in draft the speeches prepared by three of your Lordships. I agree with them and would allow the appeal and dismiss the cross-appeal for the reasons there given. I only add some observations of my own out of respect for the two Lords Justices from whom your Lordships are differing and because of the importance of this case in relation to the vexed question of the extent

f of liability of professional men, especially accountants, for putting into circulation allegedly incorrect statements whether oral or in writing which are claimed to have been negligently made or prepared and which have been acted on by a third party to that party's detriment.

That liability for such negligence if established can exist has been made clear ever since the decision of this House in *Hedley Byrne & Co Ltd v Heller & Partners Ltd* [1963] 2 All

g ER 575, [1964] AC 465 in which the well-known dissenting judgment of Denning LJ in *Candler v Crane Christmas & Co* [1951] 1 All ER 426, [1951] 2 KB 164 was held to have stated the law correctly. Thenceforth it was clear that such a duty of care could be owed by a professional man to third parties in cases where there was no contractual relationship between them, a view of the law long denied as the result of a succession of late nineteenth century cases of which this House then took the opportunity of disapproving.

h But subsequent attempts to define both the duty and its scope have created more problems than the decisions have solved. My noble and learned friends have traced the evolution of the decisions from *Anns v Merton London Borough* [1977] 2 All ER 492, [1978] AC 728 until and including the most recent decisions of your Lordships' House in *Smith v Eric S Bush (a firm), Harris v Wyre Forest DC* [1989] 2 All ER 514, [1989] 2 WLR 790. I agree with your Lordships that it has now to be accepted that there is no simple formula

j or touchstone to which recourse can be had in order to provide in every case a ready answer to the questions whether, given certain facts, the law will or will not impose liability for negligence or, in cases where such liability can be shown to exist, determine the extent of that liability. Phrases such as 'foreseeability', 'proximity', 'neighbourhood', 'just and reasonable', 'fairness', 'voluntary acceptance of risk' or 'voluntary assumption of responsibility' will be found used from time to time in the different cases. But, as your

Lordships have said, such phrases are not precise definitions. At best they are but labels or phrases descriptive of the very different factual situations which can exist in particular *a* cases and which must be carefully examined in each case before it can be pragmatically determined whether a duty of care exists and, if so, what is the scope and extent of that duty. If this conclusion involves a return to the traditional categorisation of cases as pointing to the existence and scope of any duty of care, as my noble and learned friend Lord Bridge, suggests, I think this is infinitely preferable to recourse to somewhat wide generalisations which leave their practical application matters of difficulty and *b* uncertainty. This conclusion finds strong support from the judgment of Brennan J in the High Court of Australia in the passage cited by my noble and learned friends (see *Sutherland Shire Council v Heyman* (1985) 60 ALR 1 at 43–44).

My Lords, I confess that like Lord Griffiths in *Smith v Eric S Bush* [1989] 2 All ER 514 at 534, [1989] 2 WLR 790 at 813, I find considerable difficulty in phrases such as 'voluntary assumption of responsibility' unless they are to be explained as meaning no *c* more than the existence of circumstances in which the law will impose a liability on a person making the allegedly negligent statement to the person to whom that statement is made, in which case the phrase does not help to determine in what circumstances the law will impose that liability or, indeed, its scope. The submission that there is a virtually unlimited and unrestricted duty of care in relation to the performance of an auditor's statutory duty to certify a company's accounts, a duty extending to anyone who may use *d* those accounts for any purpose such as investing in the company or lending the company money, seems to me untenable. No doubt it can be said to be foreseeable that those accounts may find their way into the hands of persons who may use them for such purposes or, indeed, other purposes and lose money as a result. But to impose a liability in those circumstances is to hold, contrary to all the recent authorities, that foreseeability alone is sufficient, and to ignore the statutory duty which enjoins the preparation of and *e* certification of those accounts.

I think that before the existence and scope of any liability can be determined, it is necessary first to determine for what purposes and in what circumstances the information in question is to be given. If a would-be investor or predator commissions a report which he will use, and which the maker of the report knows he will use, as a basis for his decision whether or not to invest or whether or not to make a bid, it may not be difficult *f* to conclude that if the report is negligently prepared and as a result a decision is taken in reliance on it and financial losses then follow, a liability will be imposed on the maker of that report. But I venture to echo the caution expressed by my noble and learned friend Lord Oliver that, because different cases may display certain common features, they are necessarily all cases in which the same consequences regarding liability or the scope of liability will follow. Moreover, there may be cases in which the circumstances in which *g* the report was commissioned justify the inclusion of and reliance on a disclaimer such as succeeded in the *Hedley Byrne* case but by reason of subsequent statutory provisions failed in *Smith v Eric S Bush.*

My Lords, it is for these reasons, in addition to those given by my noble and learned friends, that, as already stated, I would allow this appeal and dismiss the cross-appeal. *h*

LORD ACKNER. My Lords, I have had the advantage of reading the speeches of Lord Bridge, Lord Roskill, Lord Oliver and Lord Jauncey and for the reasons they give I, too, would allow this appeal and dismiss the cross-appeal.

LORD OLIVER OF AYLMERTON. My Lords, this appeal, having come to this *j* House on a preliminary point, involves the making of a number of assumptions of fact which might or might not be substantiated at the trial of the action. To begin with, it is to be assumed against the appellants (the auditors) that they showed a lack of reasonable care in certifying that the accounts of Fidelity plc for the year ended 31 March 1984 gave a true and fair view of Fidelity's position. It is also to be assumed that, when they certified

the accounts, the auditors knew or would, if they had thought about it, have known that
a Fidelity was vulnerable to take-over bids, that a potential bidder would be likely to rely
on the accuracy of the accounts in making his bid and that investors in the market
generally, whether or not already members of Fidelity, would also be likely to or might
well rely on the accounts in deciding to purchase shares in that company.

Your Lordships are not, however, either required or entitled to make any assumption
that the purpose of the certification was anything other than that of fulfilling the
b statutory duty of carrying out the annual audit with a view to the circulation of the
accounts to persons who were either registered shareholders or debenture-holders of
Fidelity and the subsequent laying of the accounts before the annual general meeting of
that company.

Thus, if and so far as the purpose for which the audit was carried out is a relevant
consideration in determining the extent of any general duty in tort owed by the auditors
c to persons other than the company which is their immediate employer, that purpose was
simply that of fulfilling the statutory requirements of the Companies Act 1985. That, in
turn, raises the question, and it is one which lies at the threshold of the inquiry on which
your Lordships are invited to embark, of what is the purpose behind the legislative
requirement for the carrying out of an annual audit and the circulation of the accounts.
For whose protection were these provisions enacted and what object were they intended
d to achieve?

My Lords, the primary purpose of the statutory requirement that a company's accounts
shall be audited annually is almost self-evident. The structure of the corporate trading
entity, at least in the case of public companies whose shares are dealt with on an
authorised stock exchange, involves the concept of a more or less widely distributed
holding of shares rendering the personal involvement of each individual shareholder in
e the day-to-day management of the enterprise impracticable, with the result that
management is necessarily separated from ownership. The management is confided to a
board of directors which operates in a fiduciary capacity and is answerable to and
removable by the shareholders who can act, if they act at all, only collectively and only
through the medium of a general meeting. Hence the legislative provisions requiring
f the board annually to give an account of its stewardship to a general meeting of the
shareholders. This is the only occasion in each year on which the general body of
shareholders is given the opportunity to consider, to criticise and to comment on the
conduct by the board of the company's affairs, to vote on the directors' recommendation
as to dividends, to approve or disapprove the directors' remuneration and, if thought
desirable, to remove and replace all or any of the directors. It is the auditors' function to
g ensure, so far as possible, that the financial information as to the company's affairs
prepared by the directors accurately reflects the company's position in order, first, to
protect the company itself from the consequences of undetected errors or, possibly,
wrongdoing (by, for instance, declaring dividends out of capital) and, second, to provide
shareholders with reliable intelligence for the purpose of enabling them to scrutinise the
conduct of the company's affairs and to exercise their collective powers to reward or
h control or remove those to whom that conduct has been confided.

The requirement of the appointment of auditors and annual audit of the accounts,
now contained in ss 235 to 246 of the Companies Act 1985, was first introduced by the
Companies Act 1879 in relation to companies carrying on the business of banking and
was extended to companies generally by the Companies Act 1900. Section 23 of that Act
required the auditors to make a report to the shareholders on the company's balance
j sheet laid before the company in general meeting, stating whether the balance sheet
exhibited a true and correct view of the state of the company's affairs. By the same
section, the report was required to be read before the company in general meeting.
Section 19 of the Companies Act 1907 substituted a new s 23, which, whilst repeating
the requirement that the auditors' report should be read before the company in general
meeting, added a requirement that it should be open to inspection by any shareholder,

who was entitled, on payment of the fee, to be furnished with a copy of the balance sheet
and report. The new section also made it an offence for any officer of the company to be   *a*
party to issuing, circulating or publishing any copy of the balance sheet which did not
either append or contain a reference to the auditors' report. The matter was carried one
stage further by s 130 of the Companies Act 1929 (consolidating provisions contained in
ss 39 and 41 of the Companies Act 1928) which required the annual balance sheet and
auditors' report of a public company to be sent not less than seven days before the date of
the meeting to every member of the company entitled to receive notice of the meeting   *b*
and entitled any member of the company and any debenture holder to be furnished on
demand and without charge with a copy of the last balance sheet and the auditors' report.
Finally, for relevant purposes, s 158 of the Companies Act 1948 required the accounts
and report to be sent to every member of the company and to every debenture holder
not less than 21 days before the the general meeting before which the accounts were to
be laid.   *c*

Thus the history of the legislation is one of an increasing availability of information
regarding the financial affairs of the company to those having an interest in its progress
and stability. It cannot fairly be said that the purpose of making such information
available is solely to assist those interested in attending general meetings of the company
to an informed supervision and appraisal of the stewardship of the company's directors,
for the requirement to supply audited accounts to, for instance preference shareholders   *d*
having no right to vote at general meetings and to debenture holders, cannot easily be
attributed to any such purpose. Nevertheless, I do not, for my part, discern in the
legislation any departure from what appears to me to be the original, central and primary
purpose of these provisions, that is to say the informed exercise by those interested in the
property of the company, whether as proprietors of shares in the company or as the
holders of rights secured by a debenture trust deed, of such powers as are vested in them   *e*
by virtue of their respective proprietary interests.

It is argued on behalf of the respondents (Caparo) that there is to be discerned in the
legislation an additional or wider commercial purpose, namely that of enabling those to
whom the accounts are addressed and circulated to make informed investment decisions,
for instance by determining whether to dispose of their shares in the market or whether   *f*
to apply any funds which they are individually able to command in seeking to purchase
the shares of other shareholders. Of course, the provision of any information about the
business and affairs of a trading company, whether it be contained in annual accounts or
obtained from other sources, is capable of serving such a purpose just as it is capable of
serving as the basis for the giving of financial advice to others, for arriving at a market
price, for determining whether to extend credit to the company, or for the writing of   *g*
financial articles in the press. Indeed, it is readily foreseeable by anyone who gives the
matter any thought that it might well be relied on to a greater or less extent for all or any
of such purposes. It is, of course, equally foreseeable that potential investors having no
proprietary interest in the company, might well avail themselves of the information
contained in a company's accounts published in the newspapers or culled from an
inspection of the documents to be filed annually with the registrar of companies (which   *h*
includes the audited accounts) in determining whether or not to acquire shares in the
company. I find it difficult to believe, however, that the legislature, in enacting provisions
clearly aimed primarily at the protection of the company and its informed control by the
body of its proprietors, can have been inspired also by consideration for the public at
large and investors in the market in particular.

The question is, I think, one of some importance when one comes to consider the   *j*
existence of that essential relationship between the auditors and Caparo to which, in any
discussion of the ingredients of the tort of negligence, there is accorded the description
'proximity', for it is now clear from a series of decisions in this House that, at least so far
as concerns the law of the United Kingdom, the duty of care in tort depends not solely
on the existence of the essential ingredient of the foreseeability of damage to the plaintiff

a   but on its coincidence with a further ingredient to which has been attached the label 'proximity' and which was described by Lord Atkin in the course of his speech in *Donoghue v Stevenson* [1932] AC 562 at 581, [1932] All ER Rep 1 at 12 as—

> 'such close and direct relations that the act complained of directly affects a person whom the person alleged to be bound to take care would know would be directly affected by his careless act.'

b   It must be remembered, however, that Lord Atkin was using these words in the context of loss caused by physical damage where the existence of the nexus between the careless defendant and the injured plaintiff can rarely give rise to any difficulty. To adopt the words of Bingham LJ in the instant case ([1989] 1 All ER 798 at 808, [1989] QB 653 at 686):

c
> 'It is enough that the plaintiff chances to be (out of the whole world) the person with whom the defendant collided or who purchased the offending ginger beer.'

The extension of the concept of negligence since the decision of this House in *Hedley Byrne & Co Ltd v Heller & Partners Ltd* [1963] 2 All ER 575, [1964] AC 465 to cover cases of pure economic loss not resulting from physical damage has given rise to a considerable and as yet unsolved difficulty of definition. The opportunities for the infliction of *d*   pecuniary loss from the imperfect performance of everyday tasks on the proper performance of which people rely for regulating their affairs are illimitable and the effects are far reaching. A defective bottle of ginger beer may injure a single consumer but the damage stops there. A single statement may be repeated endlessly with or without the permission of its author and may be relied on in a different way by many different people. Thus the postulate of a simple duty to avoid any harm that is, with *e*   hindsight, reasonably capable of being foreseen becomes untenable without the imposition of some intelligible limits to keep the law of negligence within the bounds of common sense and practicality. Those limits have been found by the requirement of what has been called a 'relationship of proximity' between plaintiff and defendant and by the imposition of a further requirement that the attachment of liability for harm which *f*   has occurred be 'just and reasonable'. But, although the cases in which the courts have imposed or withheld liability are capable of an approximate categorisation, one looks in vain for some common denominator by which the existence of the essential relationship can be tested. Indeed, it is difficult to resist a conclusion that what have been treated as three separate requirements are, at least in most cases, in fact merely facets of the same thing, for in some cases the degree of foreseeability is such that it is from that alone that *g*   the requisite proximity can be deduced, whilst in others the absence of that essential relationship can most rationally be attributed simply to the court's view that it would not be fair and reasonable to hold the defendant responsible. 'Proximity' is, no doubt, a convenient expression so long as it is realised that it is no more than a label which embraces not a definable concept but merely a description of circumstances from which, pragmatically, the courts conclude that a duty of care exists.

h   There are, of course, cases where, in any ordinary meaning of the words, a relationship of proximity (in the literal sense of 'closeness') exists but where the law, whilst recognising the fact of the relationship, nevertheless denies a remedy to the injured party on the ground of public policy. *Rondel v Worsley* [1967] 3 All ER 993, [1969] 1 AC 191 was such a case, as was *Hill v Chief Constable of West Yorkshire* [1988] 2 All ER 238, [1989] AC 53, so far as concerns the alternative ground of that decision. But such cases do nothing to assist *j*   in the identification of those features from which the law will deduce the essential relationship on which liability depends and, for my part, I think that it has to be recognised that to search for any single formula which will serve as a general test of liability is to pursue a will-o'-the wisp. The fact is that once one discards, as it is now clear that one must, the concept of foreseeability of harm as the single exclusive test, even a prima facie test, of the existence of the duty of care, the attempt to state some general

principle which will determine liability in an infinite variety of circumstances serves not
to clarify the law but merely to bedevil its development in a way which corresponds with *a*
practicality and common sense. In *Sutherland Shire Council v Heyman* (1985) 60 ALR 1 at
43–44 Brennan J, in the course of a penetrating analysis, observed:

> · 'Of course, if foreseeability of injury to another were the exhaustive criterion of a
> prima facie duty to act to prevent the occurrence of that injury, it would be essential
> to introduce some kind of restrictive qualification—perhaps a qualification of the
> kind stated in the second stage of the general proposition in *Anns*. I am unable to *b*
> accept that approach. It is preferable, in my view, that the law should develop novel
> categories of negligence incrementally and by analogy with established categories,
> rather than by a massive extension of a prima facie duty of care restrained only by
> indefinable "considerations which ought to negative, or to reduce or limit the scope
> of the duty or the class of person to whom it is owed".'
>   *c*

The same approach is, I think, reflected in that passage in the speech of Lord Devlin in
the *Hedley Byrne* case [1963] 2 All ER 575 at 607–608, [1964] AC 465 at 524–525 in
which he considered the impact of *Donoghue v Stevenson* on the facts of that case and in
which he analysed and described the method by which the law develops:

> 'In his celebrated speech in that case LORD ATKIN did two things. He stated what *d*
> · he described as a general conception ([1932] AC 562 at 580, [1932] All ER Rep 1 at
> 11) and from that conception he formulated a specific proposition of law ([1932]
> AC 562 at 599, [1932] All ER Rep 1 at 20). In between he gave a warning ([1932]
> AC 562 at 584, [1932] All ER Rep 1 at 13) "against the danger of stating propositions
> of law in wider terms than is necessary, lest essential factors be omitted in a wider
> survey and the inherent adaptability of English law be unduly restricted." What *e*
> LORD ATKIN called a "general conception of relations giving rise to a duty of care" is
> now often referred to as the principle of proximity. You must take reasonable care
> to avoid acts or omissions which you can reasonably foresee would be likely to injure
> your neighbour. In the eyes of the law your neighbour is a person who is so closely
> and directly affected by your act that you ought reasonably to have him in
> contemplation as being so affected when you are directing your mind to the acts or *f*
> omissions which are called in question . . . Now it is not in my opinion a sensible
> application of what LORD ATKIN was saying for a judge to be invited on the facts of
> any particular case to say whether or not there was "proximity" between the plaintiff
> and the defendant. That would be a misuse of a general conception and it is not the
> way in which English law develops. What LORD ATKIN did was to use his general
> conception to open up a category of cases giving rise to a special duty. It was already *g*
> clear that the law recognised the existence of such a duty in the category of articles
> that were dangerous in themselves. What *Donoghue* v. *Stevenson* did may be described
> either as the widening of an old category or as the creation of a new and similar one.
> The general conception can be used to produce other categories in the same way.
> An existing category grows as instances of its application multiply, until the time
> comes when the cell divides . . . In my opinion the appellants in their argument *h*
> tried to press *Donoghue* v. *Stevenson* too hard. They asked whether the principle of
> proximity should not apply as well to words as to deeds. I think that it should, but
> as it is only a general conception it does not get them very far. Then they take the
> specific proposition laid down by *Donoghue* v. *Stevenson* and try to apply it literally to
> a certificate or a banker's reference. That will not do, for a general conception cannot
> be applied to pieces of paper in the same way as to articles of commerce, or to writers *j*
> in the same way as to manufacturers. An inquiry into the possibilities of intermediate
> examination of a certificate will not be fruitful. The real value of *Donoghue* v.
> *Stevenson* to the argument in this case is that it shows how the law can be developed
> to solve particular problems. Is the relationship between the parties in this case such

a that it can be brought within a category giving rise to a special duty? As always in English law the first step in such an inquiry is to see how far the authorities have gone, for new categories in the law do not spring into existence overnight.'

Perhaps, therefore, the most that can be attempted is a broad categorisation of the decided cases according to the type of situation in which liability has been established in the past in order to found an argument by analogy. Thus, for instance, cases can be classified according to whether what is complained of is the failure to prevent the
b infliction of damage by the act of the third party (such as *Home Office v Dorset Yacht Co Ltd* [1970] 2 All ER 294, [1970] AC 1004, *P Perl (Exporters) Ltd v Camden London BC* [1983] 3 All ER 161, [1984] QB 342, *Smith v Littlewoods Organisation Ltd (Chief Constable, Fife Constabulary, third party)* [1987] 1 All ER 710, [1987] AC 241 and, indeed, *Anns v Merton London Borough* [1977] 2 All ER 492, [1978] AC 728 itself), in failure to perform properly a statutory duty claimed to have been imposed for the protection of the plaintiff either as
c a member of a class or as a member of the public (such as *Anns's* case, *Ministry of Housing and Local Government v Sharp* [1970] 1 All ER 1009, [1970] 2 QB 233, *Yuen Kun-yeu v A-G of Hong Kong* [1987] 2 All ER 705, [1988] AC 175) or in the making by the defendant of some statement or advice which has been communicated, directly or indirectly, to the plaintiff and on which he has relied. Such categories are not, of course, exhaustive.
d Sometimes they overlap as in the *Anns* case, and there are cases which do not readily fit into easily definable categories (such as *Ross v Caunters (a firm)* [1979] 3 All ER 580, [1980] Ch 297). Nevertheless, it is, I think, permissible to regard negligent statements or advice as a separate category displaying common features from which it is possible to find at least guidelines by which a test for the existence of the relationship which is essential to ground liability can be deduced.

e The damage which may be occasioned by the spoken or written word is not inherent. It lies always in the reliance by somebody on the accuracy of that which the word communicates and the loss or damage consequential on that person having adopted a course of action on the faith of it. In general, it may be said that when any serious statement, whether it takes the form of a statement of fact or of advice, is published or communicated, it is foreseeable that the person who reads or receives it is likely to accept
f it as accurate and to act accordingly. It is equally foreseeable that if it is inaccurate in a material particular the recipient who acts on it may suffer a detriment which, if the statement had been accurate, he would not have undergone. But it is now clear that mere foreseeability is not of itself sufficient to ground liability unless by reason of the circumstances it itself constitutes also the element of proximity (as in the case of direct physical damage) or unless it is accompanied by other circumstances from which that
g element may be deduced. One must, however, be careful about seeking to find any general principle which will serve as a touchstone for all cases, for even within the limited category of what, for the sake of convenience, I may refer to as 'the negligent statement cases', circumstances may differ infinitely and, in a swiftly developing field of law, there can be no necessary assumption that those features which have served in one case to create the relationship between the plaintiff and the defendant on which liability
h depends will necessarily be determinative of liability in the different circumstances of another case. There are, for instance, at least four and possibly more situations in which damage or loss may arise from reliance on the spoken or written word and it must not be assumed that because they display common features of reliance and foreseeability they are necessarily in all respects analogous. To begin with, reliance on a careless statement may give rise to direct physical injury which may be caused either to the person who acts
j on the faith of the statement or to a third person. One has only to consider, for instance, the chemist's assistant who mislabels a dangerous medicine, a medical man who gives negligent telephonic advice to a parent with regard to the treatment of a sick child or an architect who negligently instructs a bricklayer to remove the keystone of an archway (as in *Clayton v Woodman & Son (Builders) Ltd* [1962] 2 All ER 33, [1962] 2 QB 533). In such

cases it is not easy to divorce foreseeability simpliciter and the proximity which flows
from the virtual inevitability of damage if the advice is followed. Again, economic loss *a*
may be inflicted on a third party as a result of the act of the recipient of the advice or
information carried out in reliance on it (as, for instance, the testator in *Ross v Caunters (a
firm)* [1979] 3 All ER 580, [1980] Ch 297 or the purchaser in *Ministry of Housing and Local
Government v Sharp* [1970] 1 All ER 1009, [1970] 2 QB 223, both cases which give rise to
certain difficulties of analysis). For present purposes, however, it is necessary to consider
only those cases of economic damage suffered directly by a recipient of the statement or *b*
advice as a result of his personally having acted in reliance on it.

In his dissenting judgment in *Candler v Crane Christmas & Co* [1951] 1 All ER 426 at
433–435, [1951] 2 KB 164 at 179–182 Denning LJ suggested three conditions for the
creation of a duty of care in tort in such cases. First, the advice must be given by one
whose profession it is to give advice on which others rely in the ordinary course of
business, such as accountants, surveyors, valuers and the like. Second, it must be known *c*
to the adviser that the advice would be communicated to the plaintiff in order to induce
him to adopt a particular course of action. Third, the advice must be relied on for the
purpose of the particular transaction for which it was known to the adviser that the
advice was required. It is plain, however, from other passages in his judgment, that
Denning LJ did not consider these conditions as necessarily exhaustive criteria of the
existence of a duty and the speeches in this House in the *Hedley Byrne* case [1963] 2 All *d*
ER 575, [1964] AC 465, where his judgment was approved, indicate a number of
directions in which such criteria are to be extended. To begin with, Lord Reid would not
have confined liability to statements made or advice given in the exercise of a profession
involving the giving of such advice but would have extended it to—

> 'all those relationships where it is plain that the party seeking information or *e*
> advice was trusting the other to exercise such a degree of care as the circumstances
> required, where it was reasonable for him to do that, and where the other gave the
> information or advice when he knew or ought to have known that the inquirer was
> relying on him.'

(See [1963] 2 All ER 575 at 583, [1964] AC 465 at 486.)   *f*

Lord Morris, with whom Lord Hodson agreed, whilst initially referring to persons
'possessed of a special skill' nevertheless went on to state the conditions in which a duty
of care might arise in very much wider terms ([1963] 2 All ER 575 at 594, [1964] AC
465 at 502–503):

> 'Furthermore, if in a sphere in which a person is so placed that others could
> reasonably rely on his judgment or his skill or on his ability to make careful inquiry, *g*
> a person takes it on himself to give information or advice to, or allows his
> information or advice to be passed on to, another person who, as he knows or should
> know, will place reliance on it, then a duty of care will arise.'

None the less, the subsequent decision of the Privy Council in *Mutual Life and Citizens'
Assurance Co Ltd v Evatt* [1971] 1 All ER 150, [1971] AC 793, from which Lord Reid and *h*
Lord Morris dissented, would have confined the duty of care to where the advice relied
on was given in the course of a business or profession involving the giving of advice of
the kind in question. For present purposes, it is unnecessary to attempt a resolution of
the difference of opinion arising from the *Mutual Life* case, since there is no question here
but that the certifying of the accounts was something done in the course of the ordinary
business of the auditors.   *j*

Leaving this on one side, however, it is not easy to cull from the speeches in the *Hedley
Byrne* case any clear attempt to define or classify the circumstances which give rise to the
relationship of proximity on which the action depends and, indeed, Lord Hodson
expressly stated (and I respectfully agree) that he did not think it possible to catalogue the
special features which must be found to exist before the duty of care will arise in the

given case (see [1963] 2 All ER 575 at 601, [1964] AC 465 at 514). Lord Devlin is to the
a same effect (see [1963] 2 All ER 575 at 611, [1964] AC 465 at 530). The nearest that one
gets to the establishment of a criterion for the creation of a duty in the case of a negligent
statement is the emphasis to be found in all the speeches on 'the voluntary assumption of
responsibility' by the defendant. This is a convenient phrase but it is clear that it was not
intended to be a test for the existence of the duty for, on analysis, it means no more than
that the act of the defendant in making the statement or tendering the advice was
b voluntary and that the law attributes to it an assumption of responsibility if the statement
or advice is inaccurate and is acted on. It tells us nothing about the circumstances from
which such attribution arises.
     The point that is, as it seems to me, significant in the present context, is the unanimous
approval in this House of the judgment of Denning LJ in *Candler's case* [1951] 1 All ER
426 at 434, [1951] 2 KB 164 at 181, in which he expressed the test of proximity in these
c words: 'Did the accountants know that the accounts were required for submission to the
plaintiff and use by him?' In so far as this might be said to imply that the plaintiff must
be specifically identified as the ultimate recipient and that the precise purpose for which
the accounts were required must be known to the defendant before the necessary
relationship can be created, Denning LJ's formulation was expanded in the *Hedley Byrne*
case, where it is clear that, but for an effective disclaimer, liability would have attached.
d The respondents there were not aware of the actual identity of the advertising firm for
which the credit reference was required nor of its precise purpose, save that it was
required in anticipation of the placing of advertising contracts. Furthermore, it is clear
that 'knowledge' on the part of the respondents embraced not only actual knowledge but
such knowledge as would be attributed to a reasonable person placed as the respondents
were placed. What can be deduced from the *Hedley Byrne* case, therefore, is that the
e necessary relationship between the maker of a statement or giver of advice (the adviser)
and the recipient who acts in reliance on it (the advisee) may typically be held to exist
where (1) the advice is required for a purpose, whether particularly specified or generally
described, which is made known, either actually or inferentially, to the adviser at the
time when the advice is given, (2) the adviser knows, either actually or inferentially, that
f his advice will be communicated to the advisee, either specifically or as a member of an
ascertainable class, in order that it should be used by the advisee for that purpose, (3) it is
known, either actually or inferentially, that the advice so communicated is likely to be
acted on by the advisee for that purpose without independent inquiry and (4) it is so
acted on by the advisee to his detriment. That is not, of course, to suggest that these
conditions are either conclusive or exclusive, but merely that the actual decision in the
g case does not warrant any broader propositions.
     Those propositions are, I think, in accord with the two United States authorities which
were referred to in the course of the speeches in the *Hedley Byrne* decision. In *Glanzer v
Shepard* (1922) 233 NY 236, where a public weigher negligently certified an overweight
so that the purchaser of the goods paid too much for them, the identity of the recipient
of the certificate was known, the purpose of the certificate was known, and the certificate
h was issued for the very purpose of enabling the price of the goods to be ascertained and
with the knowledge that it would be acted on by the recipient for that purpose. In
Ultramares Corp v Touche (1931) 255 NY 170, on the other hand, a case much nearer to
the present, the action failed. There auditors, although aware generally that the certified
accounts of the company would be shown to others by the company as the basis of
financial dealings generally 'according to the needs of the occasion', were unaware of the
j company's specific purpose of obtaining financial help from the plaintiff.
     The most recent authority on negligent misstatement in this House, the two appeals
in *Smith v Eric S Bush (a firm)* and *Harris v Wyre Forest DC* [1989] 2 All ER 514, [1989] 2
WLR 790 which were heard together, do not, I think, justify any broader proposition
than that already set out, save that they make it clear that the absence of a positive
intention that the advice shall be acted on by anyone other than the immediate recipient,

indeed an expressed intention that it should not be acted on by anyone else, cannot prevail against actual or presumed knowledge that it is in fact likely to be relied on in a *a* particular transaction without independent verification. Both appeals were concerned with surveyors' certificates issued to mortgagees in connection with the proposed purchases for which the mortgagees were contemplating making advances. In each case there was an express disclaimer of responsibility, but in each case it was known to the surveyor that the substance of the report (in the sense of what was important to a purchaser), that is to say whether or not any repairs to the property were considered *b* essential, would be made known by the mortgagee to the purchaser, the plaintiff in the action, and would be likely to be acted on by him in entering into a contract to purchase the property. In so far as the case was concerned with the effects of the disclaimer, it does not require consideration in the present context, but there are important passages in the speeches in this House bearing on the questions which arise on this appeal and indicative of the features which, in that case, led their Lordships to conclude that the necessary *c* relationship of proximity existed between the surveyors and the purchasers of the respective properties. Lord Templeman deduced the relationship from a combination of factors. He said ([1989] 2 All ER 514 at 522–523, [1989] 2 WLR 790 at 799–800):

> 'I agree that, by obtaining and disclosing a valuation, a mortgagee does not assume responsibility to the purchaser for that valuation. But in my opinion the valuer *d* assumes responsibility to both mortgagee and purchaser by agreeing to carry out a valuation for mortgage purposes knowing that the valuation fee has been paid by the purchaser and knowing that the valuation will probably be relied on by the purchaser in order to decide whether or not to enter into a contract to purchase the house ... In general, I am of the opinion that in the absence of a disclaimer of liability the valuer who values a house for the purpose of a mortgage, knowing that *e* the mortgagee will rely and the mortgagor will probably rely on the valuation, knowing that the purchaser mortgagor has in effect paid for the valuation, is under a duty to exercise reasonable skill and care and that duty is owed to both parties to the mortgage for which the valuation is made.'

Lord Griffiths rejected the 'voluntary assumption of responsibility' as a helpful formula *f* for testing the existence of a duty of care, observing that the phrase—

> 'can only have any real meaning if it is understood as referring to the circumstances in which the law will deem the maker of the statement to have assumed responsibility to the person who acts on the advice.'

(See [1989] 2 All ER 514 at 534, [1989] 2 WLR 790 at 813.)
He continued ([1989] 2 All ER 514 at 534, 536, [1989] 2 WLR 790 at 813–816): *g*

> 'The essential distinction between the present case and the situation being considered in the *Hedley Byrne* case and in the two earlier cases is that in those cases the advice was being given with the intention of persuading the recipient to act on it. In the present case the purpose of providing the report is to advise the mortgagee but it is given in circumstances in which it is highly probable that the purchaser *h* will in fact act on its contents, although that was not the primary purpose of the report. I have had considerable doubts whether it is wise to increase the scope of the duty for negligent advice beyond the person directly intended by the giver of the advice to act on it to those whom he knows may do so ... I therefore return to the question in what circumstances should the law deem those who give advice to have assumed responsibility to the person who acts on the advice or, in other words, in *j* what circumstances should a duty of care be owed by the adviser to those who act on his advice? I would answer: only if it is foreseeable that if the advice is negligent the recipient is likely to suffer damage, that there is a sufficiently proximate relationship between the parties and that it is just and reasonable to impose the

liability. In the case of a surveyor valuing a small house for a building society or local authority, the application of these three criteria leads to the conclusion that he owes a duty of care to the purchaser. If the valuation is negligent and is relied on damage in the form of economic loss to the purchaser is obviously foreseeable. The necessary proximity arises from the surveyor's knowledge that the overwhelming probability is that the purchaser will rely on his valuation, the evidence was that surveyors knew that approximately 90% of purchasers did so, and the fact that the surveyor only obtains the work because the purchaser is willing to pay his fee. It is just and reasonable that the duty should be imposed for the advice is given in a professional as opposed to a social context and liability for breach of the duty will be limited both as to its extent and amount. The extent of the liability is limited to the purchaser of the house: I would not extend it to subsequent purchasers. The amount of the liability cannot be very great because it relates to a modest house. There is no question here of creating a liability of indeterminate amount to an indeterminate class. I would certainly wish to stress, that in cases where the advice has not been given for the specific purpose of the recipient acting on it, it should only be in cases when the adviser knows that there is a high degree of probability that some other identifiable person will act on the advice that a duty of care should be imposed. It would impose an intolerable burden on those who give advice in a professional or commercial context if they were to owe a duty not only to those to whom they give the advice but to any other person who might choose to act on it.'

Finally, in relation to the *Smith* appeal, Lord Jauncey observed ([1989] 2 All ER 514 at 541–542, [1989] 2 WLR 790 at 822):

'The four critical facts are that the surveyors knew from the outset (1) that the report would be shown to Mrs Smith, (2) that Mrs Smith would probably rely on the valuation contained therein in deciding whether to buy the house without obtaining an independent valuation, (3) that if, in these circumstances, the valuation was, having regard to the actual condition of the house, excessive Mrs Smith would be likely to suffer loss and (4) that she had paid to the building society a sum to defray the surveyors' fee. In the light of this knowledge the surveyors could have declined to act for the building society, but they chose to proceed. In these circumstances they must be taken not only to have assumed contractual obligations towards the building society but delictual obligations towards Mrs Smith, whereby they became under a duty towards her to carry out their work with reasonable care and skill. It is critical to this conclusion that the surveyors knew that Mrs Smith would be likely to rely on the valuation without obtaining independent advice. In both *Candler v Crane Christmas & Co* [1951] 1 All ER 426, [1951] 2 KB 164 and *Hedley Byrne & Co Ltd v Heller & Partners Ltd* [1963] 2 All ER 575, [1964] AC 465 the provider of the information was the obvious and most easily available, if not the only available, source of that information. It would not be difficult therefore to conclude that the person who sought such information was likely to rely on it. In the case of an intending mortgagor the position is very different since, financial considerations apart, there is likely to be available to him a wide choice of sources of information, to wit independent valuers to whom he can resort, in addition to the valuer acting for the mortgagee. I would not therefore conclude that the mere fact that a mortgagee's valuer knows that his valuation will be shown to an intending mortgagor of itself imposes on him a duty of care to the mortgagor. Knowledge, actual or implied, of the mortgagor's likely reliance on the valuation must be brought home to him. Such knowledge may be fairly readily implied in relation to a potential mortgagor seeking to enter the lower end of the housing market but non constat that such ready implication would arise in the case of a purchase of an expensive property whether residential or commercial.'

Thus *Smith v Eric S Bush*, although establishing beyond doubt that the law may attribute an assumption of responsibility quite regardless of the expressed intentions of the adviser, provides no support for the proposition that the relationship of proximity is to be extended beyond circumstances in which advice is tendered for the purpose of the particular transaction or type of transaction and the adviser knows or ought to know that it will be relied on by a particular person or class of persons in connection with that transaction. The judgment of Millett J in the recent case of *Al Saudi Banque v Clark Pixley (a firm)* [1989] 3 All ER 361, [1990] 2 WLR 344 (decided after the decision of the Court of Appeal in the instant case) contains an analysis of the decision of this House in *Smith v Eric S Bush* and concludes (and I agree) that it established a more stringent test of the requirements for proximity than that which had been applied by the Court of Appeal in the instant case. Millett J gives what I find a helpful analysis of that case and of the features which distinguished it from the *Hedley Byrne* case and from the instant case (at 370):

> 'In each of the cases considered by the House of Lords, therefore, there was a tripartite transaction in which the valuation could realistically be regarded as provided by the valuer to the purchaser. In each of the cases the valuation was given to the mortgagee with the intention of being acted on by him in a specific transaction known to the valuer, viz the making of a mortgage offer in connection with a specific transaction of house purchase, and in the knowledge that the valuation or the gist of the valuation would be communicated to the purchaser and would in all probability be relied on by him in deciding whether to go ahead with the very transaction for which the mortgage offer was sought. This was a much more restricted context in which to found a duty of care than was present in the *Caparo* case, for there was in contemplation not only a particular and identified recipient of the information to whom the defendant knew that it would be communicated, but a particular and known purpose for which he could foresee that it would be relied on. In *Hedley Byrne* and the cases which followed it, the statement was made directly to the plaintiff with the intention that the plaintiff should act on it. The *JEB Fasteners* case (*JEB Fasteners Ltd v Marks Bloom & Co (a firm)* [1981] 3 All ER 289) can be supported only on the basis that the statement was impliedly confirmed directly to the plaintiff without any such intention, but with a particular transaction in contemplation, and it was foreseeable that the plaintiff would rely on it in that transaction. In *Caparo* it was made to the plaintiff without any such intention and without any particular transaction in contemplation, but it was foreseeable that the plaintiff might rely on it in some unknown future transaction. In *Smith v Eric S Bush* it was made to a third party with the intention that he should act on it in a known and contemplated transaction, but in the knowledge that it would be communicated to the plaintiff and would almost certainly be relied on by him in connection with a transaction without which the transaction of the third party could not proceed.'

My Lords, no decision of this House has gone further than *Smith v Eric S Bush*, but your Lordships are asked by Caparo to widen the area of responsibility even beyond the limits to which it was extended by the Court of Appeal in this case and to find a relationship of proximity between the adviser and third parties to whose attention the advice may come in circumstances in which the reliance said to have given rise to the loss is strictly unrelated either to the intended recipient or to the purpose for which the advice was required. My Lords, I discern no pressing reason of policy which would require such an extension and there seems to me to be powerful reasons against it. As Lord Reid observed in the course of his speech in the *Hedley Byrne* case [1963] 2 All ER 575 at 581, [1964] AC 465 at 483, words can be broadcast with or without the consent or foresight of the speaker or writer; and in his speech in the same case Lord Pearce drew attention to the necessity for the imposition of some discernible limits to liability in such cases. He said ([1963] 2 All ER 575 at 613–614, [1964] AC 465 at 534):

a   'The reason for some divergence between the law of negligence in word and that
of negligence in act is clear. Negligence in word creates problems different from
those of negligence in act. Words are more volatile than deeds. They travel fast and
far afield. They are used without being expended and take effect in combination
with innumerable facts and other words. Yet they are dangerous and can cause vast
financial damage. How far they are relied on unchecked ... must in many cases be
a matter of doubt and difficulty. If the mere hearing or reading of words were held
b   to create proximity, there might be no limit to the persons to whom the speaker or
writer could be liable.'

As I have already mentioned, it is almost always foreseeable that someone, somewhere
and in some circumstances, may choose to alter his position on the faith of the accuracy
of a statement or report which comes to his attention and it is always foreseeable that a
c   report, even a confidential report, may come to be communicated to persons other than
the original or intended recipient. To apply as a test of liability only the foreseeability of
possible damage without some further control would be to create a liability wholly
indefinite in area, duration and amount and would open up a limitless vista of uninsurable
risk for the professional man.
      On the basis of the pleaded case, as amended, it has to be assumed that the auditors, as
d   experienced accountants, were aware or should have been aware that Fidelity's results
made it vulnerable to take-over bids and that they knew or ought to have known that a
potential bidder might well rely on the published accounts in determining whether to
acquire shares in the market and to make a bid. It is not, however, suggested that the
auditors, in certifying the accounts, or Parliament, in providing for such certification,
did so for the purpose of assisting those who might be minded to profit from dealings in
e   the company's shares. Caparo, whilst accepting that it is no part of the purpose of the
preparation, certification and publication of the accounts of a public company to provide
information for the guidance of predators in the market, nevertheless argue that the
auditors' knowledge that predators might well rely on the accounts for this purpose
sufficiently establishes between them and potential bidders that relationship of 'proximity'
which founds liability. On the face of it, this submission appears to equate 'proximity'
f   with mere foreseeability and to rely on the very misinterpretation of the effect of the
decision of this House in *Anns's* case [1977] 2 All ER 492, [1978] AC 728 which was
decisively rejected in *Peabody Donation Fund v Sir Lindsay Parkinson & Co Ltd* [1984] 3 All
ER 529, [1985] AC 210 and in *Yuen Kun-yeu v A-G of Hong Kong* [1987] 2 All ER 705,
[1988] AC 175. Your Lordships have been referred, however, to three authorities, one
from New Zealand and two from the United Kingdom, which do undoubtedly support
g   Caparo's contention.
      In *Scott Group Ltd v McFarlane* [1978] 1 NZLR 553 the defendants were the auditors of
a company which had been successfully taken over in reliance on certified consolidated
accounts in which, as a result of double-counting, the assets were overstated. It was
admitted that the failure of the defendants to discover the discrepancy was due to
h   negligence. In the Supreme Court of New Zealand Quilliam J dismissed the plaintiffs'
claim on the ground that the defendants, though careless, owed them no duty of care (see
[1975] 1 NZLR 582). An appeal to the Court of Appeal failed but the court was divided
as to the reasons. Richmond P held that the appeal failed for the same reason as that
stated by the trial judge. Woodhouse J would have allowed the appeal. Cooke J, on the
other hand, whilst concurring with Woodhouse J that the defendants did in fact owe a
j   duty of care to the plaintiffs, held that the appeal failed because the plaintiffs had failed
to show any recoverable loss.
      The more restrictive view was expressed by Richmond P in the following terms
([1978] 1 NZLR 553 at 566–567):

      'The question in any given case is whether the nature of the relationship is such that one party can fairly be held to have assumed a responsibility to the other as regards the reliability of the advice or information. I do not think that such a *a* relationship should be found to exist unless, at least, the maker of the statement was, or ought to have been, aware that his advice or information would in fact be made available to and be relied on by a particular person or class of persons for the purposes of a particular transaction or type of transaction. I would especially emphasise that to my mind it does not seem reasonable to attribute an assumption of responsibility unless the maker of the statement ought in all the circumstances, *b* both in preparing himself for what he said and in saying it, to have directed his mind, and to have been able to direct his mind, to some particular and specific purpose for which he was aware that his advice or information would be relied on. In many situations that purpose will be obvious. But the annual accounts of a company can be relied on in all sorts of ways and for many purposes. It would be going too far to treat accountants as assuming a responsibility towards all persons *c* dealing with the company or its members, in reliance to some greater or lesser degree on the accuracy of the accounts, merely because it was reasonably foreseeable, in a general way, that a transaction of the kind in which the plaintiff happened to become involved might indeed take place. The relationship between the parties would, I think, be too general and not sufficiently "special" to come within the principles underlying the decision in *Hedley Byrne*. As I have said, I believe it to be *d* essential to the existence of a "special relationship" that the maker of the statement was or should have been aware that his advice was required for use in a specific type of contemplated transaction. This requirement has not always required emphasis in the course of judicial discussion as to the nature of a special relationship. Probably this is because in most cases the purpose for which the information was required was, on the facts, quite obvious. But certainly this particular point was made very *e* clear indeed in Lord Denning's judgment in *Candler v Crane, Christmas & Co*. I would think that it must almost inevitably follow, once the maker of the statement is aware of a specific purpose for which his information will be used, that he will also have in direct contemplation a specific person or class of persons, even though unidentified by name.'   *f*

The New Zealand Companies Act 1955 contained provisions relating to the auditor's report which is similar in substance to those contained in the United Kingdom legislation but with this variation, that the 'true and fair view' which group accounts are certified to give are qualified by the words 'so far as concerns members of the company'. In relation to these provisions, Richmond P observed (at 568):

'The provisions of the Act to which I have just referred are aimed essentially at *g* the protection of the members of the company and of course the auditors, whose contract of employment is with the company itself, are under a contractual duty of care to the company. These provisions do not encourage me to take the view that there is any reason why the auditors of a public company should thereby come under a common law duty of care to third persons dealing with the company or its members on the faith of their audit certificate, such liability being in some way *h* based on a much wider principle than would apply, for example, in the case of auditors certifying the accounts of a private company. Like Quilliam J, I can also see no reason to differentiate between auditors as such and a firm of chartered accountants employed to prepare the accounts of the company. The only point which has given me some concern, so far as the statutory provisions are concerned, *j* is the requirement of s 133(1) whereby a copy of the balance sheet and auditor's report is required to be annexed to the annual return and thus becomes available to the public under s 9(1) of the Act. But on reflection, this only means that the auditor of the accounts of a public company knows that the accounts and his report will become available to the public generally and, consequently, may be relied on by one a or more members of the public, to some greater or lesser degree, as the basis of some business transaction. It is not suggested, however, that the Companies Act imposes any statutory duty of care as between auditors and members of the public who rely on the accounts. In the case of a company whose shares are listed on the stock exchange the auditor will also know that under the stock exchange rules a copy of the accounts must be made available. He knows, too, that shareholders will receive copies of the accounts and that the company itself may well make copies available

b to business institutions and individuals for various purposes. In the end all these matters merely add up to the fact that the auditor of a public company will necessarily have in his contemplation the possibility that the accounts may be relied on in all sorts of ways by persons other than the company and its members. This, as I have said, is not sufficient to bring about a "special relationship".'

c   Both Woodhouse and Cooke JJ, who favoured a wider view of responsibility, based themselves on an interpretation of the speech of Lord Wilberforce in *Anns's* case [1977] 2 All ER 492 at 498, [1978] AC 728 at 751–752 which required, as the first stage of the two-stage inquiry to which he there referred, no more than a consideration of whether harm was foreseeable, thus equating the 'proximate relationship' as comprehending foresight and nothing more. This is made quite clear from the following passage in the

d judgment of Woodhouse J (at 574):

'In this regard it will be noticed that although the first part of the inquiry outlined by Lord Wilberforce is to ask whether "there is a sufficient relationship of proximity" in order to decide whether there is a prima facie duty of care, he would test the sufficiency of proximity simply by the reasonable contemplation of likely harm. And, with respect, I do not think there is any need for or any sound reason in favour

e of a more restrictive approach. The issue has been made increasingly complex by the successive and varying formulas that have been used in an effort to confine the general area of responsibility, in particular for negligent words or in respect of purely economic losses. At this initial stage at least it should be possible to remove some degree of uncertainty—in my opinion it is done by the comprehensible and

f straightforward test of foreseeability.'

Woodhouse J again emphasised foreseeability as the relevant test for the creation of the relationship of proximity where he said (at 575):

'Although an audit is undertaken on behalf of the members of a public company it must be within the reasonable contemplation of any auditor that confidence in its

g ability to handle its commercial arrangements would depend upon the authenticity of its accounts—a confidence that would disappear if reliance could not be put upon the audit report. So I think that when auditors deliberately undertake to provide their formal report upon the accounts of a public company they must be taken to have accepted not merely a direct responsibility to the shareholders but a further duty to those persons whom they can reasonably foresee will need to use and rely

h upon them when dealing with the company or its members in significant matters affecting the company assets and business. An example, no doubt, would be the banker asked to make substantial advances on the security of the company undertaking. On the other hand, there would seem to be formidable difficulties for a plaintiff who attempted to prove that an auditor should have foreseen the plaintiff's likely reliance upon some newspaper or a stock exchange reference to a

j company's accounts. However, it is sufficient for present purposes to restrict consideration to a takeover offer related, as so frequently is the position, to the value of shareholders' funds. In such a situation the need to rely upon audited accounts is, I think, quite obvious. As a matter of commercial reality I think the auditor and offeror are in a relationship of close proximity.'

194   *Cases II(ii)*

Cooke J was to the same effect. He adopted (at 583), as the first step of Lord
Wilberforce's two-stage approach, the formulation which equates the relationship of   *a*
proximity with foreseeability, although at an earlier stage of his judgment he seemed to
be disposed to regard the essential relationship as arising not simply from the foreseeability
that a member of the public might rely on the accounts as a basis of some transaction
but, for a reason which I confess I do not fully understand, from the foreseeability that
some member of the public might rely on the accounts for the making of a take-over
bid. He said (at 581):   *b*

'The learned judge in the Supreme Court was disposed to regard the requirement
of filing audited accounts, which are available for public inspection, as not imposed
by Parliament for the purpose of enabling people to deal confidently in reliance on
the accuracy of the accounts. He thought it much more likely that the purpose was
to enable a proper supervision to be exercised over the activities of companies, and   *c*
to enable those concerned to ensure that the companies were not trading illegally or
dishonestly. With respect, I am unable to agree with him on that point. The
statutory requirements regarding the filing of financial information stem, I think,
from the view that those *dealing with* or *investing in* a limited liability company have
a legitimate interest in being afforded reasonable access to relevant information; and
that this interest has to be balanced against the wish for confidentiality naturally   *d*
entertained by family companies and the like which do not appeal to the public for
funds ... I would agree, though, that the provisions are probably not aimed, or at
least not primarily, at protecting purchasers of shares in the market.' (Cooke J's
emphasis.)

Thus the majority of the Court of Appeal favoured a more extensive view of the
circumstances from which the essential relationship between plaintiff and defendant   *e*
may be inferred in a negligent statement case than had yet emerged from any decision
in the United Kingdom.

Now, of course, any decision of the Court of Appeal of New Zealand is entitled to the
very greatest respect, but it has to be observed that the majority view was based on an
interpretation of Lord Wilberforce's observations in *Anns's* case which has since been   *f*
severely qualified by subsequent decisions of this House.

The *Scott Group* case has, however, since been referred to and accepted in two cases
decided in the United Kingdom. In *JEB Fasteners Ltd v Marks Bloom & Co (a firm)* [1981]
3 All ER 289 the plaintiffs, who had acquired the shares of the company as a result of a
take-over, claimed damages against the company's auditors who, it was claimed, had
been negligent in certifying the accounts. Woolf J dismissed the claim on the ground
that the plaintiffs failed to show the causative connection between reliance on the   *g*
erroneous accounts and the take-over and his decision was subsequently affirmed by the
Court of Appeal (see [1983] 1 All ER 583). In the course of his judgment, however,
Woolf J made the following observations with regard to the auditors' liability ([1981] 3
All ER 289 at 296–297):

'Without laying down any principle which is intended to be of general application,   *h*
on the basis of the authorities which I have cited, the appropriate test for establishing
whether a duty of care exists appears in this case to be whether the defendants knew
or reasonably should have foreseen at the time the accounts were audited that a
person might rely on those accounts for the purpose of deciding whether or not to
take over the company and therefore could suffer loss if the accounts were inaccurate.
Such an approach does place a limitation on those entitled to contend that there has   *i*
been a breach of duty owed to them. First of all, they must have relied on the
accounts and, second, they must have done so in circumstances where the auditors
either knew that they would or ought to have known that they might. If the
situation is one where it would not be reasonable for the accounts to be relied on,

a
then, in the absence of express knowledge, the auditor would be under no duty. This places a limit on the circumstances in which the audited accounts can be relied on and the period for which they can be relied on. The longer the period which elapses prior to the accounts being relied on, from the date on which the auditor gave his certificate, the more difficult it will be to establish that the auditor ought to have foreseen that his certificate would, in those circumstances, be relied on.'

b
Now although he disclaimed any intention of laying down a general principle, it is clear that Woolf J, like Woodhouse and Cooke JJ, was interpreting Lord Wilberforce's two-stage approach in the *Anns* case as establishing a test of proximity which depended on the foreseeability of harm alone and that he regarded the limits of liability as being set not by the need for any relationship other than such as might be inferred from such foreseeability but by the factual difficulties likely to be encountered in establishing
c
foreseeability in cases in which the reliance essential to the cause of action was separated in time from the statement or advice relied on. In the light, therefore, of the observations of Lord Keith in the *Peabody* case [1984] 3 All ER 529 at 533–534, [1985] AC 210 at 239–241 and in the *Yuen Kun-yeu* case [1987] 2 All ER 705 at 709–712, [1988] AC 175 at 190–194, this case provides no very convincing authority for Caparo's proposition, although, as Bingham LJ observed in the instant case, the facts were such as to justify a finding of a
d
relationship of proximity without any extension of the criteria suggested by Denning LJ in his judgment in *Candler's* case [1951] 1 All ER 426, [1951] 2 KB 164.

The third case on which Caparo rely is the decision of the Outer House of the Court of Session in *Twomax Ltd v Dickson McFarlane & Robinson* 1982 SC 113, the facts of which have a broad similarity to those in the *JEB Fasteners* case and in the instant case. The court was concerned with three separate claims from investors (one of whom was a company
e
and two of whom were individuals) who had acquired shares in a private company which, shortly after the investments were made, went into receivership and was subsequently wound up. All three investors claimed that their respective investments were made on the faith of the company's audited accounts which had been negligently prepared and certified by the defenders, the company's auditors, in the course of their statutory audit. The Lord Ordinary (Stewart), having contrasted the limitations appearing
f
from the speeches of Lord Morris and Lord Hodson in the *Hedley Byrne* case with the broader formulation of general principle in the speech of Lord Wilberforce in the *Anns* case, accepted the latter as governing the proper approach to the question of whether or not the essential relationship between pursuers and defenders was established in a negligent statement case and followed the guidance of the majority judgments of the New Zealand Court of Appeal in the *Scott Group* case, save that he could not draw any
g
sensible distinction between the case of the corporate pursuer, which had acquired the controlling interest, and that of the individual minority investors. He thus, by implication, rejected the suggestion that a potential bidder in the market is in some special position as compared with other investors such as to create between him and the auditors carrying out their statutory duties, a special relationship which does not arise in the case of an investor concerned to acquire only a minority interest. And this, with
h
respect, must be correct, for there can be no logical distinction according to whether an investor is likely to acquire many shares or only a few. Such distinction as there is lies only in the scale of the potential loss which may be little or great according to the magnitude of the investment. Indeed, as he pointed out, it could legitimately be said that the smaller the investment the greater the likelihood of the investor accepting the audited accounts as the basis for his action without making any independent investigation.
j
In the result, the Lord Ordinary held that the knowledge to be imputed to the defenders that there would or might well be potential investors in the market who would be interested in purchasing existing shares or subscribing for new shares and who might be influenced by the accounts was sufficient to create between them and such investors the relationship of proximity which gave rise to an enforceable duty of care.

This case, therefore, falls into the same category as the other two cases. All three were based on the view of Lord Wilberforce's exposition in the *Anns* case which would result   *a* in foreseeability and proximity being treated as synonymous, a view which this House (and, indeed, Lord Wilberforce himself in *McLoughlin v O'Brian* [1982] 2 All ER 298, [1983] 1 AC 410) has now decisively rejected. That, of course, does not conclude the question, for it would still be open to your Lordships to find in the circumstances of this case that a special relationship existed between the auditor conducting an annual audit in pursuance of his statutory duty and every potential investor in the market or, indeed,   *b* any other person who might do business with the company without relying solely on the foreseeability of potential damage to such person. Just as, for instance, in *Smith v Eric S Bush* [1989] 2 All ER 514, [1989] 2 WLR 790 one of the factors giving rise to the relationship in that case was the circumstance that the plaintiff was the person who paid for the report on which the reliance was placed, so here it might be said that a special relationship was to be found in the nature and extent of the statutory duties which the   *c* auditor is called on to fulfil.

For my part, however, I can see nothing in the statutory duties of a company's auditor to suggest that they were intended by Parliament to protect the interests of investors in the market and I see no reason in policy or in principle why it should be either desirable or appropriate that the ambit of the special relationship required to give rise to liability in cases such as the present should be extended beyond those limits which are deducible   *d* from the *Hedley Byrne* case and *Smith v Eric S Bush*. Those limits appear to me to be correctly and admirably stated in the passages from the judgment of Richmond P in the *Scott Group* case to which I have already referred. In particular, I see no reason why any special relationship should be held to arise simply from the circumstance that the affairs of the company are such as to render it susceptible to the attention of predators in the market who may be interested in acquiring all or the majority of the shares rather than   *e* merely a parcel of shares by way of addition to a portfolio. It follows that I would dismiss Caparo's cross-appeal.

I turn, therefore, to the question raised by the auditors' appeal. The Court of Appeal, whilst rejecting unanimously Caparo's contention that the auditors owed them a duty of care simply as potential investors in the market, nevertheless by a majority allowed their   *f* claim that a similar duty was owed to them in their capacity as shareholders from the date when they first became registered in respect of shares which they had purchased. Now it cannot be nor is it claimed that this event created for the auditors any new or greater risk of harm in relation to a certification which had already taken place; nor can it be claimed that it brought about some change in the quality or extent of Caparo's reliance on the (ex hypothesi) inaccurate information which they had previously received and digested. The only difference in their position before registration and their position   *g* afterwards was that, as registered shareholders, they now had the statutory right to receive the accounts on which they had already relied in acquiring their original shares and to receive notice of and attend the annual general meeting of Fidelity at which the accounts were to be read and, if thought fit, approved and passed. This change of position seems, on the face of it, less than momentous and in fact they did not trouble to appoint   *h* a representative to attend the meeting on their behalf. If a distinction is to be found at all, therefore, it can only be that the nature and purpose of the statutory provisions governing the appointment and duties of auditors and the certification and publication to shareholders and others of the accounts have the effect of creating, between the auditors and individual shareholders, as potential investors in that capacity, that special relationship of proximity which is required to give rise to the duty of care and which   *j* does not exist between the auditors and the investing public generally.

Now if it be right, as, for my part, I believe that it is and as the Court of Appeal has held, that no relationship of proximity and thus no duty of care exists between auditors and the investing public generally in relation to the statutory audit (I say nothing, of course, about a case where accounts are audited specifically for the purpose of submission *a* to a potential investor), the attribution of such a duty arising from the receipt of exactly the same information by a person who happens to be the registered holder of a share in the company whose accounts are in question produces entirely capricious results. O'Connor LJ, in his dissenting judgment ([1989] 1 All ER 798 at 830, [1989] QB 653 at 715), instanced the case of a shareholder who, having purchased further shares at an overvalue on the basis of the accounts, shows the accounts to a friend who has no existing shareholding but proceeds to make a similar purchase. Each receives exactly the same

b information; each relies on it in exactly the same way and for the same purpose; and the loss sustained in both cases is identical and is equally foreseeable. Yet liability is said to exist in the one case but not in the other. One has indeed only to consider the circumstances of the instant case which must ultimately result in drawing a distinction between the loss sustained as a result of the initial purchase of shares (irrecoverable) and that sustained as a result of purchases made after the first registration (recoverable)

c although all purchases were made in reliance on exactly the same information.

So unreasonable a distinction must call in question the analysis which leads to it. The majority in the Court of Appeal deduced the relationship from what Bingham LJ described as 'the degree of closeness between the parties' (see [1989] 1 All ER 798 at 807, [1989] QB 653 at 684). It was pointed out that although the auditors are appointed and paid by the company that is the result of the vote of the shareholders in general meeting

d and their remuneration is paid out of funds which might otherwise be available for distribution to shareholders by way of dividend. Their duty is to report to the shareholders whether the accounts give a true and fair view of the company's financial position and their report is sent to each shareholder as an identifiable individual. Thus, it was said, the relationship, although not a contractual one, was very close to being contractual and was moreover one in which a lack of care would be likely directly to affect the very person

e whose interest the auditor is engaged to protect, should that person choose to rely on the accounts for the purpose of making or disposing of an investment. My Lords, of course I see the force of this, but, as I have already suggested, 'proximity' in cases such as this is an expression used not necessarily as indicating literally 'closeness' in a physical or metaphorical sense but merely as a convenient label to describe circumstances from which the law will attribute a duty of care. It has to be borne in mind that the duty of

f care is inseparable from the damage which the plaintiff claims to have suffered from its breach. It is not a duty to take care in the abstract but a duty to avoid causing to the particular plaintiff damage of the particular kind which he has in fact sustained. I cannot improve on the analysis which is to be found in the judgment of Brennan J in the High Court of Australia in *Sutherland Shire Council v Heyman* (1985) 60 ALR 1, to which I have already referred. After citing the speech of Viscount Simonds in *Overseas Tankship (UK)*

g *Ltd v Morts Dock and Engineering Co Ltd, The Wagon Mound* [1961] 1 All ER 404 at 414–415, [1961] AC 388 at 425, where he observed that it was vain to isolate the liability from its context and to say that B is or is not liable and then to ask for what damage he is liable, Brennan J continued (at 48):

h   'The corollary is that a postulated duty of care must be stated in reference to the kind of damage that a plaintiff has suffered and in reference to the plaintiff or a class of which the plaintiff is a member. I venture to repeat what I said in *John Pfeiffer Pty Ltd v Cannay* ((1981) 148 CLR 218 at 241–242): "His duty of care is a thing written on the wind unless damage is caused by the breach of that duty; there is no actionable negligence unless duty, breach and consequential damage coincide . . . .

j   For the purposes of determining liability in a given case, each element can be defined only in terms of the others." It is impermissible to postulate a duty of care to avoid one kind of damage—say, personal injury—and, finding the defendant guilty of failing to discharge that duty, to hold him liable for the damage actually suffered that is of another and independent kind—say, economic loss. Not only may the respective duties differ in what is required to discharge them; the duties may be

owed to different persons or classes of persons. That is not to say that a plaintiff who
suffers damage of some kind will succeed or fail in an action to recover damages a
according to his classification of the damage he suffered. The question is always
whether the defendant was under a duty to avoid or prevent that damage, but the
actual nature of the damage suffered is relevant to the existence and extent of any
duty to avoid or prevent it.'

In seeking to ascertain whether there should be imposed on the adviser a duty to avoid b
the occurrence of the kind of damage which the advisee claims to have suffered it is not,
I think, sufficient to ask simply whether there existed a 'closeness' between them in the
sense that the advisee had a legal entitlement to receive the information on the basis of
which he has acted or in the sense that the information was intended to serve his interest
or to protect him. One must, I think, go further and ask, in what capacity was his interest
to be served and from what was he intended to be protected? A company's annual c
accounts are capable of being utilised for a number of purposes and if one thinks about it
it is entirely foreseeable that they may be so employed. But many of such purposes have
absolutely no connection with the recipient's status or capacity, whether as a shareholder,
voting or non-voting, or as a debenture-holder. Before it can be concluded that the duty
is imposed to protect the recipient against harm which he suffers by reason of the
particular use that he chooses to make of the information which he receives, one must, I d
think, first ascertain the purpose for which the information is required to be given.
Indeed, the paradigmatic *Donoghue v Stevenson* case of a manufactured article requires, as
an essential ingredient of liability, that the article has been used by the consumer in the
manner in which it was intended to be used (see *Grant v Australian Knitting Mills Ltd*
[1936] AC 85 at 104, [1935] All ER Rep 209 at 217 and *Junior Books Ltd v Veitchi Co Ltd*
[1982] 3 All ER 201 at 216, 218, [1983] 1 AC 520 at 549, 552). I entirely follow that if e
the conclusion is reached that the very purpose of providing the information is to serve
as the basis for making investment decisions or giving investment advice, it is not
difficult then to conclude also that the duty imposed on the adviser extends to protecting
the recipient against loss occasioned by an unfortunate investment decision which is
based on carelessly inaccurate information. Bingham LJ did, indeed, conclude that the
provision of guidance for the making of investment decisions was one of the purposes to f
be discerned in the statutory provisions. He observed ([1989] 1 All ER 798 at 805, [1989]
QB 653 at 681–682):

'. . . I think these provisions also reflect a wider and more commercial intention.
The growth and development of limited liability companies over a relatively very
short period have been phenomenal. Their proliferation and expansion have
depended on their acceptance by the investing public as an advantageous and (on g
the whole) reliable medium of investment. The statutory requirements that
companies account to their members and that auditors express an independent
opinion to shareholders on the truth and accuracy of company accounts are in my
view designed (in part at least) to fortify confidence in the holding of shares as a
medium of investment by enabling shareholders to make informed investment h
decisions. These are obvious reasons, both economic and social, why this end should
be regarded as desirable.'

How far he regarded this as an essential feature of the relationship of proximity which
he held to exist between the auditors and Caparo as shareholders is not, however, entirely
clear, for he attributed the same intention to the legislature in relation to investors
generally. He said: j

'The publication of accounts must limit, if it cannot eliminate, the scope for
rumour-inspired speculation and thus promote an informed and orderly market. It
enables prospective investors, like shareholders, to make informed decisions. For
such prospective investors the independent opinion of the auditor has the same
significance as for existing shareholders.'

a As I have already indicated, I am not, for my part, able to share this view of the intention of the legislature. I do not believe and I see no grounds for believing that, in enacting the statutory provisions, Parliament had in mind the provision of information for the assistance of purchasers of shares or debentures in the market, whether they be already the holders of shares or other securities or persons having no previous proprietary interest in the company. It is unnecessary to decide the point on this appeal, but I can see more force in the contention that one purpose of providing the statutory information *b* might be to enable the recipient to exercise whatever rights he has in relation to his proprietary interest by virtue of which he receives it, by way, for instance, of disposing of that interest. I can, however, see no ground for supposing that the legislature was intending to foster a market for the existing holders of shares or debentures by providing information for the purpose of enabling them to acquire such securities from other holders who might be minded to sell.

c   For my part, I think that the position as regards the auditor's statutory duty was correctly summarised by O'Connor LJ in his dissenting judgment when he said ([1989] 1 All ER 798 at 830, [1989] QB 653 at 714):

'The statutory duty owed by auditors to shareholders is, I think, a duty owed to them as a body. I appreciate that it is difficult to see how the overstatement of the *d* accounts can cause damage to the shareholders as a body: it will be the underlying reasons for the overstatement which cause damage, for example fraudulent abstraction of assets by directors or servants, but such loss is recoverable by the company. I am anxious to limit the present case to deciding whether the statutory duty operates to protect the individual shareholder as a potential buyer of further shares. If I am wrong in thinking that under the [Companies Act 1985] no duty is *e* owed to shareholders as individuals, then I think that the duty must be confined to transactions in which the shareholder can only participate because he is a shareholder. The statute imposes a duty to shareholders as a class and the duty should not extend to an individual save as a member of the class in respect of some class activity. Buying shares in a company is not such an activity.'

f   In my judgment, accordingly, the purpose for which the auditors' certificate is made and published is that of providing those entitled to receive the report with information to enable them to exercise in conjunction those powers which their respective proprietary interests confer on them and not for the purposes of individual speculation with a view to profit. The same considerations as limit the existence of a duty of care also, in my judgment, limit the scope of the duty and I agree with O'Connor LJ that the duty of care is one owed to the shareholders as a body and not to individual shareholders.

g   To widen the scope of the duty to include loss caused to an individual by reliance on the accounts for a purpose for which they were not supplied and were not intended would be to extend it beyond the limits which are so far deducible from the decisions of this House. It is not, as I think, an extension which either logic requires or policy dictates and I, for my part, am not prepared to follow the majority of the Court of Appeal in *h* making it. In relation to the purchase of shares of other shareholders in a company, whether in the open market or as a result of an offer made to all or a majority of the existing shareholders, I can see no sensible distinction, so far as a duty of care is concerned, between a potential purchaser who is, vis-à-vis the company, a total outsider and one who is already the holder of one or more shares. I accordingly agree with what has already fallen from my noble and learned friend Lord Bridge, and I, too, would allow the appeal *j* and dismiss the cross-appeal.

LORD JAUNCEY OF TULLICHETTLE. My Lords, it no longer requires a detailed citation of authority to vouch the well-established proposition that a negligent statement may, in certain circumstances, render the maker thereof liable for economic loss occasioned thereby to another. It is sufficient to mention *Cann v Willson* (1888) 39 Ch D 39, the dissenting judgment of Denning LJ in *Candler v Crane Christmas & Co* [1951] 1

All ER 426, [1951] 2 KB 164 and two cases in this House, *Hedley Byrne & Co Ltd v Heller & Partners Ltd* [1963] 2 All ER 575, [1964] AC 465 and *Smith v Eric S Bush (a firm), Harris v Wyre Forest DC* [1989] 2 All ER 514, [1989] 2 WLR 790. Whether liability exists in any particular case will depend on whether the maker of the statement owes a duty of care to the person who has suffered loss. In this connection I cannot do better than quote the words of Lord Keith in *Peabody Donation Fund v Sir Lindsay Parkinson & Co Ltd* [1984] 3 All ER 529 at 534, [1985] AC 210 at 240–241:

> 'The true question in each case is whether the particular defendant owed to the particular plaintiff a duty of care having the scope which is contended for, and whether he was in breach of that duty with consequent loss to the plaintiff. A relationship of proximity in Lord Atkin's sense must exist before any duty of care can arise, but the scope of the duty must depend on all the circumstances of the case ... So in determining whether or not a duty of care of particular scope was incumbent on a defendant it is material to take into consideration whether it is just and reasonable that it should be so.'

The relationship of proximity to which Lord Keith referred is not one which is created solely by the foreseeability of harm resulting from carelessness in the statement, but is one in which some further ingredient importing proximity is present. Thus in *Hill v Chief Constable of West Yorkshire* [1988] 2 All ER 238 at 241, [1989] AC 53 at 60 Lord Keith said:

> 'It has been said almost too frequently to require repetition that foreseeability of likely harm is not in itself a sufficient test of liability in negligence. Some further ingredient is invariably needed to establish the requisite proximity of relationship between the plaintiff and defendant, and all the circumstances of the case must be carefully considered and analysed in order to ascertain whether such an ingredient is present.'

Once foreseeability of likely harm from a careless statement has been established, it becomes necessary to examine the circumstances in and the purposes for which the statement was made in order to determine whether there are also present the further ingredients necessary to establish the requisite proximity of relationship between the maker of the statement and the person who has acted on it. As Bingham LJ observed in the present case, the concept of proximity is somewhat elusive, extending as it does beyond mere physical proximity (see [1989] 1 All ER 798 at 802, [1989] QB 653 at 678). It might be described as the circumstances in which the law considers it proper that a duty of care should be imposed on one person towards another. If in any given circumstances a relationship of proximity is found to exist, consideration must still be given to the scope of the duty which arises therefrom. In the case of physical proximity, few problems will arise, but where there exists a duty of care in relation to the making of statements, written or oral, problems may arise if those statements are capable of being used for more than one purpose. It is not disputed in the present case that economic loss to the plaintiff as a shareholder was foreseeable by the auditors as a result of any failure on their part to exercise reasonable care in the conduct of the audit. What is disputed is whether the auditors owed any duty to individual shareholders, and if so, what was the scope of that duty.

Before examining the circumstances in this case which may be relevant to the existence of a relationship of proximity, it is helpful to look in a little more detail at the four cases dealing with negligent statements to which I have already referred. In *Cann v Willson* (1888) 39 Ch D 39 valuers instructed by an intending mortgagor sent the valuation to solicitors acting for an intending mortgagee knowing that it was hoped thereby to induce the mortgagee to make a loan. Chitty J held that in the circumstances the valuers owed a duty of care to the mortgagee. In *Candler v Crane Christmas & Co* [1951] 1 All ER 426, [1951] 2 KB 164 the accountants were aware that the accounts were to be shown by their

employer to the plaintiff who was a potential investor, and indeed their clerk discussed
a those accounts with him. Denning LJ in suggesting the circumstances in which a duty
to use care in a statement by professional persons would exist apart from contract, posed
three questions. First, what persons are under such duty? Second, to whom do those
professional people owe this duty? And third, to what transactions does the duty of care
extend? In relation to the second question, he said ([1951] 1 All ER 426 at 434, [1951] 2
KB 164 at 180–181):

b   'I will take accountants, but the same reasoning applies to the others. They owe
the duty, of course, to their employer or client, and also, I think, to any third person
to whom they themselves show the accounts, or to whom they know their employer
is going to show the accounts so as to induce him to invest money or take some
other action on them. I do not think, however, the duty can be extended still further
c   so as to include strangers of whom they have heard nothing and to whom their
employer without their knowledge may choose to show their accounts. Once the
accountants have handed their accounts to their employer, they are not, as a rule,
responsible for what he does with them without their knowledge or consent . . .
Excluding such cases as those, however, there are some cases—of which the present
is one—where the accountants know all the time, even before they present their
d   accounts, that their employer requires the accounts to show to a third person so as
to induce him to act on them, and then they themselves, or their employers, present
the accounts to him for the purpose. In such cases I am of opinion that the
accountants owe a duty of care to the third person. The test of proximity in these
cases is: Did the accountants know that the accounts were required for submission
to the plaintiff and use by him?'

e In relation to the third question, he said ([1951] 1 All ER 426 at 435, [1951] 2 KB 164 at
182–184):

'[The duty of care] extends, I think, only to those transactions for which the
accountants knew their accounts were required. For instance, in the present case it
extends to the original investment of £2,000 which the plaintiff made in reliance
f   on the accounts, because the defendants knew that the accounts were required for
his guidance in making that investment, but it does not extend to the subsequent
£200 which he invested after he had been two months with the company. This
distinction, that the duty only extends to the very transaction in mind at the time,
is implicit in the decided cases . . . It will be noticed that I have confined the duty to
cases where the accountant prepares his accounts and makes his report for the
g   guidance of the very person in the very transaction in question. That is sufficient
for the decision of this case. I can well understand that it would be going too far to
make an accountant liable to any person in the land who chooses to rely on the
accounts in matters of business, for that would expose him, in the words of CARDOZO,
C.J., in *Ultramares Corpn. v. Touche* (1931) 255 NY 170, to ". . . liability in an
indeterminate amount for an indeterminate time to an indeterminate class."
h   Whether he would be liable if he prepared his accounts for the guidance of a specific
class of persons in a specific class of transactions, I do not say.'

Denning LJ clearly considered that the scope of any duty of care was limited to the
precise transaction for which the accountants knew that the accounts were to be used. In
the *Hedley Byrne* case [1963] 2 All ER 575, [1964] AC 465 a company's bankers were
j asked by the plaintiffs' bankers whether the company 'would be good for an advertising
contract of £8,000 to £9,000'. The company's bankers answered the question in the
affirmative but, 'without responsibility on the part of the bank'. When the company
failed, the plaintiffs sought to recover damages from the bankers for negligence in
making the statement. The action failed because of the express disclaimer of responsibility,
but this House, after detailed review of authority, held that a negligent statement, oral or

written, could give rise to an action for damages for economic loss apart from any
contractual or fiduciary relationship subsisting between the parties. In the context of this   *a*
case, *Hedley Byrne* is perhaps most important for its approval of the dissenting judgment
of Denning LJ in *Candler v Crane Christmas & Co*. After setting out the facts in *Candler's*
case, Lord Reid said ([1963] 2 All ER 575 at 583, [1964] AC 465 at 487):

> 'This seems to me to be a typical case of agreeing to assume a responsibility: [the
> accountants] knew why the plaintiff wanted to see the accounts and why their   *b*
> employers, the company, wanted them to be shown to him, and agreed to show
> them to him without even a suggestion that he should not rely on them.'

Lord Reid is again there emphasising the fact that the maker of the statement was
aware of the purpose for which the accounts were required to be seen. Finally, in *Smith v
Eric S Bush* [1989] 2 All ER 514, [1989] 2 WLR 790 the plaintiff applied for a mortgage
to a building society which in pursuance of its statutory duty under the Building Societies   *c*
Act 1962 instructed independent surveyors to prepare a written report as to the value of
the house in question. The plaintiff paid to the building society a fee in respect of this
report, and subsequently a copy thereof was provided to her. Without obtaining an
independent valuation, the plaintiff bought the house which later turned out to be
structurally defective. The surveyor was found to have been negligent in failing to
discover the defect. This House held that, notwithstanding the presence of an exclusion   *d*
clause in his report, he was thereby in breach of a duty of care owed to the plaintiff. It is
clear from the speeches which were delivered that the facts which created the proximate
relationship between the surveyor and the plaintiff were that the former knew that the
valuation had been paid for by the plaintiff and would be shown to and probably relied
on by her in deciding whether or not to buy the house. Thus, Lord Templeman said
([1989] 2 All ER 514 at 522–523, [1989] 2 WLR 790 at 799):   *e*

> 'I agree that, by obtaining and disclosing a valuation, a mortgagee does not assume
> responsibility to the purchaser for that valuation. But in my opinion the valuer
> assumes responsibility to both mortgagee and purchaser by agreeing to carry out a
> valuation for mortgage purposes knowing that the valuation fee has been paid by
> the purchaser and knowing that the valuation will probably be relied on by the   *f*
> purchaser in order to decide whether or not to enter into a contract to purchase the
> house.'

Lord Templeman undoubtedly considered that one of the necessary ingredients of the
relationship of proximity was the fact that the valuer knew of the particular transaction
for the purposes of which reliance would probably be placed on his report.   *g*

Lord Griffiths, after setting out three criteria for the imposition of a duty of care on an
adviser, namely foreseeability of damage, proximity of relationship and reasonableness,
continued ([1989] 2 All ER 514 at 536, [1989] 2 WLR 790 at 816):

> 'The necessary proximity arises from the surveyor's knowledge that the
> overwhelming probability is that the purchaser will rely on his valuation, the   *h*
> evidence was that surveyors knew that approximately 90% of purchasers did so, and
> the fact that the surveyor only obtains the work because the purchaser is willing to
> pay his fee. It is just and reasonable that the duty should be imposed for the advice
> is given in a professional as opposed to a social context and liability for breach of the
> duty will be limited both as to its extent and amount. The extent of the liability is
> limited to the purchaser of the house: I would not extend it to subsequent   *j*
> purchasers.'

Here Lord Griffiths is limiting the existence and scope of the duty of care to the very
person and the very transaction which were in the contemplation of the surveyor at the
material time.

a My Lords, in each of these cases where a duty of care has been held to exist, the statement in question has, to the knowledge of its maker, been made available to the plaintiff for a particular purpose on which he has relied. In the present case, the auditors, by accepting office, came under a statutory duty to make their report to the members of the company. The crucial issue is the purpose for which the report was made. To quote the words of Denning LJ in *Candler's case* [1951] 1 All ER 426 at 435, [1951] 2 KB 164 at 183, what was the 'very transaction' for which it was provided? To answer this question
b it is necessary to look at the relevant provisions of Pt VII of the Companies Act 1985.

Section 221 requires every company to cause accounting records to be kept which should be sufficient to show and explain the company's transactions, and should be such as (a) to disclose with reasonable accuracy the financial position of the company at the time, and (b) to enable the directors to ensure that any profit and loss account complies with the requirements of the Act. If a company's business involves dealing in goods, the
c accounting records are required to contain statements of stock at the end of each financial year and all statements of stocktaking from which such statements of stock derive. Section 227 requires that the directors, by sub-s (1), prepare a profit and loss account for the financial year in respect of each accounting reference period of the company and, by sub-s (3), prepare a balance sheet as at the last day of the financial year. Section 228(2) is in the following terms:
d

'The balance sheet shall give a true and fair view of the state of affairs of the company as at the end of the financial year; and the profit and loss account shall give a true and fair view of the profit or loss of the company for the financial year.'

In terms of s 235(1)(a) the directors are required to prepare a report 'containing a fair review of the development of the business of the company and its subsidiaries during the
e financial year and of their position at the end of it', and giving particulars of, inter alia, changes in asset values, directors' shareholdings and other interests and contributions for political and charitable purposes. Section 236 makes provision for an auditors' report, inter alia, in the following terms:

f '(1) A company's auditors shall make a report to its members on the accounts examined by them, and on every balance sheet and profit and loss account, and on all group accounts, copies of which are to be laid before the company in general meeting during the auditors' tenure of office.
(2) The auditors' report shall state—(a) whether in the auditors' opinion the balance sheet and profit and loss account and (if it is a holding company submitting group accounts) the group accounts have been properly prepared in accordance with
g this Act; and (b) without prejudice to the foregoing, whether in their opinion a true and fair view is given—(i) in the balance sheet, of the state of the company's affairs at the end of the financial year, (ii) in the profit and loss account (if not framed as a consolidated account), of the company's profit or loss for the financial year . . .'

Section 237(1) defines auditors' duties as follows:

h 'It is the duty of the company's auditors, in preparing their report, to carry out such investigations as will enable them to form an opinion as to the following matters—(a) whether proper accounting records have been kept by the company and proper returns adequate for their audit have been received from branches not visited by them, (b) whether the company's balance sheet and (if not consolidated) its profit and loss account are in agreement with the accounting records and returns.'
j
Section 241 provides, inter alia:

'(1) In respect of each financial year of a company the directors shall lay before the company in general meeting copies of the accounts of the company for that year.

(2) The auditors' report shall be read before the company in general meeting, and be open to the inspection of any member of the company.

(3) In respect of each financial year the directors—(a) shall deliver to the registrar of companies a copy of the accounts for the year . . .'

The accounts of a company are defined by s 239 to include, inter alia, the company's profit and loss account and balance sheet, and the directors' and auditors' reports. In terms of s 240, a copy of the company's accounts must be sent to every member not less than 21 days before the date of the meeting referred to in s 241(1). Finally, s 245 imposes penalties on directors whose defective accounts are laid before the company or delivered to the registrar of companies.

Three matters emerge from the statutory provisions, namely: (1) that the responsibility for the preparation of accounts giving a true and fair view of the company's financial state is placed fairly and squarely on the shoulders of the directors; (2) that the role of the auditors is to provide an independent report to the members on the proper preparation of the balance sheet and profit and loss account, and as to whether those documents give a true and fair view respectively of the state of the company's affairs at the end of the financial year and of the company's profit and loss for that year. Their role is thus purely investigative rather than creative; (3) that the company's accounts, including the auditors' report, will be furnished to all members of the company as well as to debenture holders and any other persons entitled to receive notice of general meeting. The accounts will, of course, also be available to any member of the public who chooses to examine the company file in the office of the registrar of companies.

So much for the circumstances in which company accounts reach the members, circumstances which render it inevitable that auditors will be aware that their reports will be seen and relied on by the members. However, that does not answer the fundamental question of the purpose, and hence the very transactions, for which the annual accounts of a company are prepared and distributed to its members. Counsel for the auditors submitted that the principal purpose was to provide an account of the stewardship of the directors to the shareholders as a body, and not to provide individual investors, whether shareholders or members of the public, with comparative information. Counsel for Caparo, on the other hand, argued that the purpose was to enable shareholders to make such individual decisions as they wished in relation to the company, including decisions as to investment, they already being investors, and decisions as to voting in general meetings.

In the Court of Appeal Bingham LJ concluded that the auditors had voluntarily assumed direct responsibility to individual shareholders to whom they owed a duty to exercise reasonable care in carrying out their audit (see [1989] 1 All ER 798 at 807–811, [1989] QB 653 at 685–690). He further concluded that such duty was owed to a shareholder in respect of any loss sustained by him in selling, retaining, or buying shares in the company. Bingham LJ referred to the approval by Cardozo CJ in *Ultramares Corp v Touche* (1931) 255 NY 170 at 185 of an earlier statement (of Pound J in *Courteen Seed Co v Hong Kong and Shanghai Banking Corp* (1927) 245 NY 377 at 381) that—

'negligent words are not actionable unless they are uttered directly, with knowledge or notice that they will be acted on, to one to whom the speaker is bound by some relation of duty, arising out of public calling, contract or otherwise, to act with care if he acts at all.'

He then said:

'This formulation would not exclude the finding of a sufficiently proximate relationship in the present case if the words "will be acted on" are replaced, as in English law I think they should be, by "may be acted on".'

Taylor LJ said ([1989] 1 All ER 798 at 821, [1989] QB 653 at 703):

a   '. . . once proximity to the shareholder is established, the auditor ought prima facie to be liable for any loss suffered in foreseeable reliance on the report . . .'

In my view these observations go too far. Possibility of reliance on a statement for an unspecified purpose will not impose a duty of care on the maker to the addressee. More is required. In *Smith v Eric S Bush* it was probable, if not highly probable, that the potential purchaser would rely on the valuer's report. This probable reliance was an essential

b   ingredient in establishing proximity. Had it merely been a possibility that the purchaser would rely on the report I very much doubt whether this House would have decided that the valuer owed a duty of care to the purchaser. Furthermore, reliance, even if probable, thereby establishing proximity, does not establish a duty of care of unlimited scope. Regard must be had to the transaction or transactions for the purpose of which the statement was made. It is loss arising from such transaction or transactions rather than

c   'any loss' to which the duty of care extends.

I do not understand that either Bingham LJ or Taylor LJ, in reaching their conclusions, relied to any material extent on the purpose for which accounts of a company, including the auditors' report, are provided to members or consequentially on the transactions for which the members were expected to use them. O'Connor LJ, in a dissenting judgment, considered that the statutory duty owed by auditors to shareholders was owed to them as

d   a body and not as individuals.

My Lords, Pt VII of the Companies Act 1985 provides that the accounts of a company for each financial year shall be laid before the company's general meeting, that is to say before the members in general meeting. Copies of the accounts must be sent to the members at least 21 days in advance, and it is obvious that the reason for this is to enable the members to prepare themselves for attendance at and participation in the meeting.

e   The annual general meeting provides the opportunity for members to question the stewardship of the company during the preceding year, to vote for or against election or re-election of directors, to approve or disapprove the appointment or reappointment of auditors and to take other decisions affecting the company as a whole or themselves as members of a particular class of shareholders. There is nothing in Pt VII which suggests that the accounts are prepared and sent to members for any purpose other than to enable

f   them to exercise class rights in general meeting. I therefore conclude that the purpose of annual accounts, so far as members are concerned, is to enable them to question the past management of the company, to exercise their voting rights, if so advised, and to influence future policy and management. Advice to individual shareholders in relation to present or future investment in the company is no part of the statutory purpose of the preparation and distribution of the accounts. It follows that I am in agreement with the

g   views of O'Connor LJ as to the nature of the statutory duty owed by auditors to shareholders.

If the statutory accounts are prepared and distributed for certain limited purposes, can there nevertheless be imposed on auditors an additional common law duty to individual shareholders who choose to use them for another purpose without the prior knowledge of the auditors? The answer must be No. Use for that other purpose would no longer be

h   use for the 'very transaction' which Denning LJ in *Candler's* case [1951] 1 All ER 426 at 435, [1951] 2 KB 164 at 183 regarded as determinative of the scope of any duty of care. Only where the auditor was aware that the individual shareholder was likely to rely on the accounts for a particular purpose such as his present or future investment in or lending to the company would a duty of care arise. Such a situation does not obtain in the present case.

j   The Court of Appeal unanimously rejected a submission by Caparo that an auditor owed a duty to a potential investor who held no shares. In this House it was argued that the relationship of the unwelcome bidder in a potential takeover situation was nearly as proximate to the auditor as was the relationship of a shareholder to whom the report was directed. Since I have concluded that the auditor owed no duty to an individual shareholder, it follows that this argument must also fail. The fact that a company may at a time when the auditor is preparing his report be vulnerable to a take-over bid cannot *a* per se create a relationship of proximity between the auditor and the ultimate successful bidder. Not only is the auditor under no statutory duty to such a bidder but he will have reason at the material time to know neither of his identity nor of the terms of his bid. In this context the recent case of *Al Saudi Banque v Clark Pixley (a firm)* [1989] 3 All ER 361, [1990] 2 WLR 344 is in point. There Millett J held that the auditors of a company owed no duty of care to a bank which lent money to the company, regardless of whether the *b* bank was an existing creditor or a potential one, because no sufficient proximity of relationship existed in either case between the auditor and the bank. I have no doubt that this case was correctly decided and I would only add that that I am in entire agreement with the careful process of reasoning whereby the judge reached his decision.

It only remains to mention *Twomax Ltd v Dickson McFarlane & Robinson* 1982 SC 113, to which your Lordships were referred. The Lord Ordinary (Stewart) held that auditors *c* owed a duty of care to potential investors who were not shareholders by applying the test of whether the defenders knew or reasonably should have foreseen at the time the accounts were audited that a person might rely on those accounts for the purpose of deciding whether or not to take over the company, and therefore would suffer loss if the accounts were inaccurate. There were in that case no such findings in fact as would support the existence of a relationship of proximity between the auditor and the *d* unknown potential investor. I therefore consider that the reasoning of the Lord Ordinary was unsound and that the decision cannot be supported.

For the foregoing reasons, I would allow the appeal and dismiss the cross-appeal.

Appeal allowed ; cross-appeal dismissed.
e
Solicitors: *Freshfields* (for the auditors); *Berwin Leighton* (for Caparo).

Mary Rose Plummer   Barrister.

SECTION A

1. Who were counsel for Caparo in the House of Lords?

2. How many cases were referred to in the opinions delivered by the judges in the House of Lords?

3. Why does Lord Roskill say he has decided to comment on the case rather than simply agreeing with his fellow judges in the House of Lords?

4. Why does Lord Oliver think that it is impossible to provide a general formula for the relationship of proximity which must exist in cases of economic loss through negligence? If Lord Oliver is correct can you think of any problems which might result?

5. Why does Lord Oliver think that the majority view of the Court of Appeal regarding the duty of care owed to Caparo by the auditors of Fidelity plc is wrong?

SECTION B

6. What is a cross-appeal?

7. Where in the report does it tell you where you would find out more about the law relating to auditors?

8. According to Lord Roskill, what liability for negligence for professional people was established in *Hedley Bryne & Co. Ltd. v. Hellers & Partners Ltd.*?

9. A dissenting judgment is one which, by definition, is not in the majority view the correct analysis of the law. Nevertheless you will be expected to read dissenting judgments. There is an example of a dissenting judgment discussed by the Law Lords in *Caparo* which indicates why it is sometimes necessary to read dissenting judgments. What example is this and why is it necessary to read it?

10. Why does Lord Bridge think that it is wrong "[t]o hold the maker of [a] statement to be under a duty of care in respect of the accuracy of the statement to all and sundry for any purpose for which they may choose to rely on it"? Do you agree with him?

11. Since Lord Ackner did not give judgment in *Caparo* what purpose, if any, was there in having him sitting on the case?

12. Do you think that Bingham L.J. and Taylor L.J, who gave the majority judgments in *Caparo* in the Court of Appeal, would, in the light of the House of Lords decision, agree that their own reasoning was incorrect? Do you think there are any arguments they might be able to think of to rebut the criticism of their approach made by the Law Lords?

EXERCISE 5

Reading research materials

Reading and understanding research materials does not just involve seeing what conclusion the author has reached. Understanding the evidence the author has for the conclusion drawn is as important as understanding the conclusion itself. This section is intended to improve your critical awareness of the materials that you are reading. Reading something critically means reading it to see what weaknesses there are in it. The fewer the weaknesses, the stronger the conclusion.

Start by reading "Remands in Custody: Problems and Prospects" by Rod Morgan, the article extracted below. When you have read the article once go back and read it again making detailed notes. When doing this, concentrate on trying to identify the strand of argument which Morgan is trying to develop, paying close attention to the evidence that he presents for the various points that he makes. When you have made your notes try to answer the questions in Section A below. After you have finished compare your answers with those which we give. As with the other exercises, Section B below contains questions for use as part of a course or for discussion with others studying law. We have not included our answers to these questions.

Remands in Custody: Problems and Prospects

By Rod Morgan

Centre for Criminal Justice, University of Bath

In spite of the largest prison building programme since the middle of the nineteenth century prison overcrowding continues with no officially predicted end in sight. The growth in the prison population is only to a small extent the result of a rising number of sentenced prisoners. It is largely attributable to an explosion in the number of custodial remands. Since the Government has adopted most of the measures which critics have suggested might arrest the trend, has there been some analytical failure regarding the causes of the increase? Or has it rather been a failure to implement reforms with sufficient vigour? In this article I examine both questions and consider what further might be done to reverse a trend which, if allowed to continue, will set at naught Government efforts to eliminate prison crowding by the mid-1990s.

The changing composition of the prison population

In Table 1 are set out, by legal category of prisoner, the number of receptions into prison. In order to access the impact of the Bail Act 1976, 1975 has been selected as the starting point.[1]

Table 1—Prison receptions by legal category

	Untried	Convicted unsentenced	Sentenced	Civil	Total
1975	52967	24936	64313	5423	147639
1976	46561	22882	68479	5900	143822
1977	44988	22106	69898	6198	143190
1978	40087	20894	72311	5882	139174
1979	41782	22083	74079	5275	143219
1980	40315	21480	75896	4743	142434
1981	47246	23413	88110	4753	163504
1982	48517	22538	94377	4715	170147
1983	47496	19585	93414	4050	164545
1984	51940	18156	92810	3683	166589
1985	54789	18055	96189	3444	172477
1986	55469	16128	86153	3665	161415
1987	59468	15481	86358	3354	164661

1976–77 saw a significant fall in the number of untried prisoner receptions; not until 1985 did the number climb above the 1975 level. By contrast the number of convicted but unsentenced receptions initially exhibited a modest fall, but has since followed a more substantial decline which continues. The receptions data show that untried and sentenced prisoners have contributed equally to the 14 per cent. overall rise in prison receptions since 1976 with increases of 28 and 26 per cent. respectively. By contrast

[1] Though the Bail Act 1976 was not implemented until 1978, it was preceded by a Home Office Circular issued in 1975.

the number of convicted but unsentenced prisoner receptions has fallen by one third.

A different story emerges from the daily average population data. Table 2 shows what whereas the total number of prisoners has risen by 11 per cent. since 1976, the number of sentenced prisoners has remained fairly constant. The rise in the prison population of recent years is largely attributable to growth in the number of untried prisoners. Only in 1977 was there a fall in their number. Their average number has risen from 3,303 in 1976 to 9,074 in 1987, an increase of 175 per cent.

Table 2—Average daily prison population by legal category

	Untried	Convicted unsentenced	Sentenced	Civil	Total
1975	3573	2036	33733	478	39820
1976	3303	1787	35838	515	41443
1977	3539	1742	35659	630	41570
1978	3849	1782	35561	604	41796
1979	4019	2113	35591	497	42220
1980	3921	1872	35891	490	42264
1981	4804	2101	36022	384	43311
1982	5362	2023	35928	394	43707
1983	6003	1649	35487	323	43462
1984	7173	1514	34321	288	43296
1985	8132	1565	36305	231	46233
1986	8530	1432	36571	238	46770
1987	9074	1551	37531	270	48426

The proportion of the prison population comprising untried prisoners rose from 8 per cent. in 1976 to 19 per cent. in 1987. Together with convicted but unsentenced prisoners, whose number after reaching a peak in 1981 has since declined, remand and trial prisoners together make up 22 per cent. of the prison population.

The disjunction between the reception and average population data is explained by the changing duration of custody. Whereas untried male prisoners spent on average 25 days in custody in 1975, this had increased to 56 days by 1987. The figures for untried female prisoners show an even greater increase, albeit from a lower base—a rise from 15 days in 1975 to 45 days in 1987. There has been no comparable increase in the duration of custody for the declining number of convicted but unsentenced prisoners.

The criminal justice statistics

The prisons data suggest, therefore, that the growth in the remand population is only to a small extent explained by the courts refusing bail to an increased number of accused persons. It would appear that court waiting periods are getting longer. In fact the explanation is not so straightforward.

The proportion of defendants dealt with summarily who have their cases remanded and are refused bail has declined from 16 per cent. in 1978 to 13 per cent. in 1987. Because the number of cases coming before the courts has increased very little—993,000 cases (excluding motoring offences) in 1987 compared to 890,000 in 1978—the number of cases remanded in custody has declined over the same period.

Not so with committals to the Crown Court for trial. Here both the number and proportion of defendants committed for trial, and the number and proportion refused bail, has increased. This is in spite of the Bail Act 1976 and the Criminal Law Act 1977 (which reduced the number of offences triable on indictment). Both statutes temporarily reduced the committal and the committal in custody rates but the effects were short-lived. In 1975, before the Bail Circular and Act, some 20 per cent. of committals were refused bail. That proportion fell to 17 per cent., but by 1987 had climbed to 22 per cent. This increased committal in custody rate was superimposed on a rising committal rate. In 1978–9 the number of committals declined but thereafter began to rise again. Between 1979 and 1986 the number of either-way cases committed—these constitute approximately 85 per cent. of all committals—increased from 55,000 to 81,000, a rise of 48 per cent. This represented an increase from 15 to 21 per cent. of all defendants proceeded against for either-way offences.

This is the upward trend which largely accounts for the rise in the prison remand population. An increasing number of defendants are committed from magistrates' courts for trial at the Crown Court and an increasing proportion of the committals are in custody. It is principally because of this shift in their mode of trial that prisoners are waiting longer for their cases to be heard. The result has been an explosion in the average daily prison remand population.

The factors contributing to these aggregate figures have been carefully analysed using data for the period 1980–4.[2] The rising propor-

---

[2] Pearce R. (1987) *Waiting for Crown Court trial: the remand population*, Home Office Research and Planning Unit Paper No. 40, London: Home Office.

tion of cases committed by magistrates' courts for trial to the Crown Court is only to a small extent explained by the fact that the lower courts are now receiving more defendants being proceeded against for the sort of offences more likely to be committed. Rather, there appears to be a real increase in committal rates for offences such as burglary, theft and handling, more likely to involve a remand in custody. Moreover, there has been an increase in the rate at which bail is being refused during committal in certain types of cases, particularly burglary and drugs. What is unclear is whether the rising committal and committal in custody rates are a consequence of more serious examples of offences coming before the courts, or changes in prosecution recommendations, or changes in magisterial willingness to take cases, or the fact that more defendants are electing trial by jury. It could be the combined consequence of all these factors.

From work recently completed by the Home Office[3] it is apparent that there are large variations in committal rates from one part of the country to another. The study sampled cases in four court areas and found that the proportions of either-way cases committed ranged from 21 to 64 per cent. A large proportion of committals, possibly a majority, involve triable-either-way cases where magistrates decline jurisdiction as opposed to defendants opting for trial by jury. Moreover, in the vast majority of cases, 93 per cent., the magistrates' decision was in line with the recommendation of the Crown Prosecution Service.[4]

Clearly this is an area on which a good deal of research needs to be done. Since approximately two fifths of defendants committed for trial would have consented to have their cases dealt with summarily had they been given the option,[5] and since almost half of all cases committed subsequently received sentences within the range that could have been passed in the magistrates' court, there is considerable scope for reducing the committal rate.

As far as the average daily remand population is concerned the picture is clear. The increase in the average duration of custodial remands is largely explained by the fact that an increasing proportion of untried prisoners are awaiting Crown Court trials rather than further proceedings in magistrates' courts. The fact that more prisoners are awaiting trial by jury has led to greater delays at some Crown Court centres. But this is not the principal explana-

[3] Riley D. and Vennard J. (1988) *Triable-Either-Way Cases: Crown Court or Magistrates' Court?*, Home Office Research and Planning Unit Study No. 98, London: HMSO.
[4] *Ibid.*, p. 11.
[5] *Ibid.*, p. 22.

tion for the overall increase in the average duration of custody. It is the committal rate which is central.

Guiding principles and prison conditions

Before considering what it means to be remanded in custody and whether there is evidence of its avoidable use, there is need to agree the principles which should govern this area of decision making. I submit that there are three principles to guide our analysis. First, unconvicted persons must be presumed to be innocent and treated accordingly. Secondly, and countervailing the first, the course of justice must proceed unhindered by the activities of those against whom there is reasonable cause to believe that they will seek to subvert it. Thirdly, justice delayed is justice denied.

The first and second principles are embodied in the right to bail of the Bail Act 1976 and the conditions which must be satisfied to deny bail. Though the terms of the Act are capable of wide interpretation the underlying doctrine is clear: unnecessary resort to custody is as legally wrong as it is morally offensive. Regrettably the principle has yet to be extended to the statutory framework governing the administration of imprisonment. There are degrees of custody.[6] It should follow, therefore, that no defendant should suffer greater loss of liberty, both in duration or degree, than is necessary to secure the course of justice. The extension of the Bail Act doctrine is officially admitted to be breached in prisons almost as a matter of routine.

Almost 40 years ago a chairman of the Prison Commission wrote that conditions for unconvicted prisoners were more depressing than those for the convicted yet had "never excited public comment."[7] That statement is truer today than at any time since 1945. Regimes for untried prisoners are typically more impoverished than those for unsentenced and sentenced prisoners.[8] They are for the most part held in local prisons, the oldest part of the prisons estate. These are also the most overcrowded prisons. Indeed, as a matter of policy overcrowding has always, to the greatest possible

---

[6] Further, if the Government's proposals to contract out remand facilities or develop "more secure" or "more structured" bail hostels come to fruition then the degree of custody seems likely to be extended: *Private Sector Involvement in the Remand System*, Cm 434 (1988), London: HMSO.

[7] Fox L.W., *The English Prison and Borstal System* (1952), London: Routledge, p. 286.

[8] See King R.D. and Morgan R.E. (1976) *A taste of prison: custodial conditions for trials and remand prisoners*. London: Routledge, and King R.D. and McDermot C., "British prisons 1970–1987: the ever deepening crisis" (1989) *British Journal of Criminology*, Spring.

extent, been concentrated in remand institutions. The appalling conditions for the majority of remand prisoners—confined two or three to a cell for upwards of twenty three hours a day, the squalor and indignities of slopping out, few recreational facilities apart from the basic statutory exercise periods, and little or no work available for those willing to undertake it—are well known and need no recapitulation.[9]

The reason why the dictates of moral as well as legal logic have been inverted by the Prison Department—untried prisoners get the worst conditions while sentenced, generally longer term, prisoners get the best—stems from the organisational goals and managerial convenience of the prison system.

The prison system is geared to the achievement of Prison Rule 1, the "training and treatment of convicted prisoners . . . to encourage and assist them to lead a good and useful life."[10] In terms of resources allocation, staff training, new buildings and regime planning this has meant an emphasis on those prisoners legally eligible to be worked upon and who stay long enough to undertake some programme in the "training prisons" to which they are allocated.[11] The local prisons and remand centres have become the clearing houses where prisoners are merely held. Regime planning for untried prisoners has been virtually non-existent. This phenomenon is well illustrated in the Green Paper canvassing the possibility of contracted out remand facilities.[12] Contracts will have to incorporate "clear and enforceable standards."[13] For this to be done the Home Office will have to undertake preparatory work because "in the present prison system there is no existing composite document which lays out comprehensively and in detail the requirements for a remand centre regime."[14] Even this formulation involves sleight of hand. It implies that the requirements could be collated from various documents. This is not so. There are no Prison Department standards for the regime of untried prisoners and, contrary to the spirit of the Criminal Justice Act 1948, s.48(6) and the Prison Act 1952, s.47, there has never been a separate set of rules for remand centres.

---

[9] *Report of Chief Inspector of Prisons for 1984*, London: HMSO, 1985, paras. 2.11–2.13; Chief Inspector of Prisons (1989) *Prison Sanitation*, Home Office: London.

[10] Prison Rules 1964 (S.I. 388).

[11] For a fuller analysis of this logic and its repercussions see King R.D. and Morgan R., *The future of the prison system* (1980), Farnborough: Gower.

[12] *Private Sector Involvement in the Remand System*, London: HMSO, 1988.

[13] *Ibid.*, para. 69.

[14] *Ibid.*, para. 69.

Secondly, unconvicted prisoners are vulnerable to the management imperatives of a prison system operating under pressure. Remand prisoners are relatively easy to manage as a group. It is true that because they are new arrivals they are generally unknown quantities. It is also true that their individual response to custody is often problematic; for example, their risk of suicide is the highest of any prisoner group.[15] Nevertheless, remand prisoners are largely oriented to the outside world. They are primarily concerned with their prospects of bail, conviction and sentence rather than the physical conditions in which they are held. They are a relatively transitory population and lack the motivation, group consciousness and opportunity effectively to protest against those conditions. Were sentenced prisoners subject to the same regime they would almost certainly rebel.

In the absence of legally enforceable standards and the courts' unwillingness to interfere with custodial conditions—conditions clearly more oppressive than is necessary to safeguard the process of justice—there is little to stop further deterioration in regimes as the population continues to rise. For the past eight years remand prisoners have almost continuously been held in what are officially admitted to be inadequate police cells,[16] and a recent amendment to the Prison Rules has removed one of the few longstanding privileges—to have food and drink supplied from outside—that those few untried prisoners with friends and material support were able to enjoy.[17] Both of these changes have been challenged unsuccessfully in the courts.[18]

There are two basic solutions to the management problem posed by remand prisoners: the reductionist approach—granting a higher proportion of defendants bail and/or reducing the duration of committals in custody—or the expansionist approach—adding to the total stock of prison accommodation and/or making more of the existing plant available to remand prisoners, that is by spreading the population overload more equitably between institutions and/ or categories of prisoners. The solutions are not mutually exclusive. Indeed arguably it would be irresponsible to pursue one course to the exclusion of the other.

[15] Chief Inspector of Prisons (1984) *Suicides in Prisons*, London: Home Office.

[16] Following the Imprisonment (Temporary) Provisions Act 1980; for a review see Kemp C. and Morgan R., *Behind the Front Counter: lay visitors to police stations* (1989) Bristol and Bath Centre for Criminal Justice, University of Bath.

[17] Prison (Amendment) Rules 1988 (S.I. 89); see also Prison Department Circular Instruction 10/1988, February 18, 1988.

[18] *R. v. Commissioner of Police of the Metropolis ex parte Nahar* 1983, *The Times*, May 28, 1983; *R. v. Secretary of State for Home Department, ex parte Simmons* 1988, Unreported.

The Government is pursuing a vigorous expansionist course. Of the 26 new prisons in the current building programme 11 are local prisons, providing 6714 extra places. Further, the number of prisons receiving remand prisoners has been increased. The Government has also taken several reductionist initiatives. Before reviewing these measures we need to pose the general question as to whether there is evidence of avoidable resort to custodial remands.

Too many remands in custody?

There is as much variation in opinion as to what warrants a remand in custody as there is argument about the appropriateness of custodial sentences.[19] Indeed more so because bail decisions have often to be made with little information. Nevertheless there is evidence that many remands in custody might with agreement be avoided.

First it is clear that many untried prisoners are in custody for too long. The delay in bringing prisoners to trial at some Crown Court centres is now a major problem. There was a 175 per cent. increase in the overall remand population between 1976 and 1987: the number of prisoners in custody for more than six months increased by 300 per cent. These figures speak for themselves.

Secondly, many prisoners are clearly being avoidably refused bail. This question must be approached with caution because the bail-remand data have sometimes been treated cavalierly. Let us begin with the frequently cited relationship between bail refusals and subsequent conviction rates and sentencing decisions.

Approximately 5 per cent. of all persons refused bail are subsequently not proceeded against or found not guilty. This proportion has not altered greatly during the last 10 years. The difficulties which persons found to be innocent currently face in securing compensation for periods in custody is a matter for concern: but the acquittal rate does not of itself appear to suggest a problem. Not so, it is often argued, with the non-custodial sentence rate. The proportion of persons refused bail at some stage before trial or sentence, found guilty and subsequently given a non-custodial sentence—36 per cent. of males and 55 per cent. of females found guilty—has marginally decreased in recent years. But does this constitute progress?

Bail and sentencing decisions are different. The high proportionate use of non-custodial sentences for offenders refused bail certainly raises a question about the necessity of their custodial

[19] See editorial at [1987] Crim.L.R. 437.

remands, but a non-custodial sentence does not establish that a prior remand in custody was unwarranted. Indeed were all persons refused bail subsequently to be given custodial sentences that might equally be a cause for concern. Commentators in other jurisdictions have observed that sentencers feel obliged to pass custodial sentences at least as long as periods already spent in custody.[20] I know of no evidence that such a relationship exists in Britain but to the extent that it does then remands in custody have a doubly adverse impact on the prison population. The bail-sentence relationship is complex. The decision to grant bail has often to be decided on the basis of limited information and persons accused of offences which if proved would not warrant a custodial sentence may nevertheless not surrender to bail. Conversely, the fact that a person has been held in custody prior to sentence may persuade a sentencer that enough is enough and a non-custodial penalty should now be imposed. Alternatively, the experience of presentence detention undermines—through loss of employment, accommodation, family and other community ties—offenders' capacity to present themselves in a light favourable to receiving a non-custodial sentence.[21]

For these reasons it is difficult to decide unequivocally whether the declining proportion of offenders refused bail receiving non-custodial sentences represents an advance. My feeling is that the trend is in the right direction but judgments should probably by reserved on this question until we have more information about the relationship between pre-trial custody and subsequent sentencing decisions.

Bail decisions

Contrary to what might be expected, between one half and three quarters of decisions to remand in custody at first appearance are uncontested.[22] Cynics argue this is because a high proportion of defendants know they are guilty and accurately judge they are destined for a custodial sentence: they prefer to spend a high proportion of their sentence as a privileged remand prisoner. Some defendants undoubtedly do calculate on these lines. Remand prisoners are still mostly held in places close to home with the possi-

---

[20] Faugeron C., "Prisons in France" (1988) and Heinz W., "The problems of imprisonment in West Germany" (1988) both papers presented to the *European Colloquium on Research on Crime and Criminal Policy in Europe*, University of Oxford, July.
[21] King M., *Bail or Custody*, (1971) London: Cobden Trust.
[22] Brink B. and Stone C., "Defendants who do not ask for bail" [1988] Crim.L.R. 152.

bility of frequent, albeit brief, visits. However, given the squalid conditions in which most are held, the erosion of their few privileges and the widespread use of dispersed police accommodation, one would have to be an ill-informed defendant to see the lot of the untried as preferable to that of sentenced prisoners. To the extent that prisoners do not seek bail it is more plausible to suggest that they know the evil day is coming and want to get it over with as soon as possible. Whatever the thought processes involved, the calculating eager prisoner is almost certainly an exception. A recent bail experiment found that only 10 per cent. of the target remand population said they did not want to apply for bail.[23]

Since 1980 many remands in custody have not initially been contested because, following the *Nottingham Justices* decision,[24] solicitors often judged it to be an unwise move. Court practices limiting the number of bail applications gave rise to solicitors' uncertainty as to whether, if their first shot was unsuccessful, a subsequent hearing would be allowed.[25] Further, inconsistencies between and within benches as to what constituted a "change of circumstances" permitting a fresh application made solicitors cautious about pursuing a bail application which might not succeed if they thought a better case might be made later. Somewhat belatedly the Government recognised the need to repair the damage resulting from the *Nottingham Justices* decision. The Criminal Justice Act 1988 provides for restoration of the procedure which ironically the Nottingham justices had originally been pursuing. Henceforth at the first hearing after a defendant has been refused bail any argument as to fact or law may used whether or not it has been used previously. Thereafter "the court need not hear arguments as to fact or law which it has heard previously" (s.154(3)).

Though welcome, this provision will not of itself eliminate remands in custody due either to solicitors' tardiness about gathering information in support of an early bail application, or magistrates' preparedness to remand defendants by default—allowing cases to proceed when little or no information is presented and which could with a little imagination be gathered in the course of a day's court proceedings. Magistrates also remand by default when they hear but do not listen to facts presented at second or subsequent bail hearings because they believe that either they or their colleagues have heard those facts before. The enormous disparities in the rates at which different benches refuse bail, as much as

---

[23] Mair G., *Bail and Probation Work: the ILPS bail action project* (1988) Research and Planning Unit Paper No. 46, London: Home Office.

[24] *R. v. Nottingham Justices, ex parte Davies* 1980.

[25] Brink and Stone, *op. cit.*

ten times, are not explained by differences in the types of cases coming before them.[26] These disparities have recently been the subject of calls from the Government for greater consistency.[27]

The extent to which bail is being avoidably refused for want of early information is well illustrated by the results of the recent Vera Institute Probation Bail Information Project[28] and a Home Office-monitored Probation Bail Project.[29] The Probation Service often possesses information about defendants which could be relevant to the CPS assessment of whether or not to oppose bail. The Vera Project involved an initiative by eight Probation Services to provide information to the CPS in cases where the police had indicated an objection to bail. The eight schemes differed, as did the quality and extent of the information they provided. The initiatives typically involved the verification of defendants' addresses, medical condition, employment record and status and probation supervision history. In some cases extra efforts were made to secure hostel accommodation or make referrals to drink or drug abuse centres or to employment schemes.[30] Many defendants were well known to the Probation Services.

The Vera Institute has wisely been cautious about the results. The number of cases in each project was small. Nevertheless in all three areas where data on police and CPS recommendations were systematically collected before and after the project began, there was a significant decline in the proportion of cases for which the police recommended and the CPS sought a custodial remand. Further, in two of the three areas the correspondence between CPS and police recommendations for remands in custody were even lower in those cases for which the Probation Service supplied information. The Vera Institute points out that the declining correspondence did not mean that the police view was necessarily overruled: as a result of getting extra information from the Probation Service the police as well as the CPS were often persuaded that a remand in custody was not necessary. Significantly the Vera Institute was able to say that "none of the police representatives

---

[26] Winfield M. (1984) *Lacking Conviction: the remand system in England and Wales*, London: Prison Reform Trust.

[27] Home Office Circular 25/1988, *Bail*, May 11; see also the Home Secretary's speech to the West Midlands Branch of the Magistrates' Association, November 1987.

[28] Stone C. (1988) *Bail Information for the Crown Prosecution Service*, London: Vera Institute of Justice.

[29] Mair G. (1988) *Bail and Probation Work: the ILPS bail action project*, Research and Planning Unit Paper No. 40, London: Home Office.

[30] Stone, *op. cit.*, p. 13.

on the local advisory groups (set up to oversee the initiatives locally) reported complaints from within their forces about CPS decisions not to seek custody as a result of information provided by the schemes, nor did prosecutors reported receiving such complaints.[31]

The Home Office-monitored bail project was conducted on two sites, at H.M. Prison Wormwood Scrubs and Inner London Probation Headquarters for a team serving the community at large. A similarly positive outcome was reported, though once again the number of cases involved was small. In this and the Vera project even the most pessimistic estimates showed that the costs of seconding or recruiting extra personnel to gather bail information were substantially outweighed by the immediate savings resulting from the removal of persons from custody.[32]

These two projects demonstrate that large numbers of defendants are being avoidably remanded in custody. The best estimates of the Vera evaluators suggest that as a result of supplying information in 1,367 cases during the pilot projects, 391 persons were bailed who would otherwise have been remanded in custody.[33] Further, there was no evidence that granting bail led to increased failure to respond to bail. For the three pilot project courts where full information was available, Vera found that the proportions of defendants who breached their bail was almost identical in those cases bailed following additional information as those bailed without it. This was true whether the test was arrest for a new offence, or for breach of bail conditions, or failure to answer bail.[34]

As far as bail failure generally is concerned there are not data adequate to say whether compliance levels have declined. Data on failure to answer to bail have been collected and published annually only since the late '70s. They do not show a deterioration. Approximately 4 per cent. of all persons bailed by the police and by magistrates' courts fail, for whatever reason, to appear in court on the due date: in neither case has the proportion changed substantially since 1979. Moreover many defendants fail to appear for valid and excusable reasons. Of course these breach data tell only part of the story. It is possible that higher proportions of defendants now commit offences on bail or breach bail conditions. There

[31] *Ibid.*, p. 31.
[32] *Ibid.*, pp. 62–66; Mair, *op. cit.*, pp. 28–30.
[33] Stone, *op. cit.*, Table 1.
[34] *Ibid.*, Figure 6.

are no recent studies to shed light on the proportion of defendants granted conditional bail and breaching their conditions.[35]

The bail projects suggest there is a powerful case for drawing up guidelines nationally between the Probation Services and the CPS for the provision of bail information and setting up full-time Probation bail information schemes throughout the country. Were this done the evidence indicates that the number of remands in custody would be reduced significantly. There may nevertheless be resistance to this recommendation on resource grounds. Some critics maintain that the bail schemes demonstrate the poor performance of solicitors: that the information collected by the Probation Service could and should be collected by solicitors. This may to some extent be true. But there are two counter-arguments. Some of the information available to the Probation Service is not readily available to solicitors. Second, it is doubtful if the same information would be so influential in the hands of solicitors.[36]

Time limits and further alternatives to custody

There are three further policy initiatives currently being pursued which might have impact on the size of the remand population: time limits; the provision of more bail hostels; and the use of electronic surveillance as a condition of bail.

Following experiments in four counties time limits are now in force in 13 English counties and throughout Wales for cases awaiting both summary and jury trials.[37] The implementation of general time limits has so far been shelved in order to give priority to custody cases in an attempt to reduce the pressure on the prison population. These experiments are obviously welcome. However, the new limits are unlikely to have great impact on the duration of remands in custody. To date they have been set at levels encompassing the careers of the vast majority of current cases: they reflect, in effect, the status quo. Moreover the only analysis so far conducted of files for cases currently exceeding the experimental time limits leads to doubts as to whether courts could or would reject applications for time extensions.[38] The second initiative concerns bail hostels. The Government has announced funding for

---

[35] King M. ((1971) *Bail or Custody*, London: Cobden Trust) and the Home Office (1984) *Remands in Custody*, London: HMSO) found that 15 and 20 per cent. of defendants respectively were subject to bail conditions. It is generally supposed that bail is now more often conditional.

[36] Stone, *op. cit.*, p. 33, provides some evidence for this contention.

[37] Under provisions introduced by the Prosecution of Offenders Act 1985.

[38] Corbett C. and Korn Y., "Custody Time Limits in Serious and Complex Cases: Will they work in Practice?" (1987) Crim.L.R. 737.

a further 200 bail hostels places during 1988/9, thereby raising the number of places in bail-only and probation/bail hostels to over 2,000. Bail hostels generally have high occupancy levels. However, whereas past assessments suggested that hostel occupants were generally at high risk of custody,[39] recent research sheds doubt on this proposition; in many cases, it appears, "those remanded to hostels would not—or, perhaps, should not—have been remanded in custody."[40] It is not at all clear how this problem would be diminished by the Government suggestion that there be more secure hostels providing curfew enforcement and "more structured" daytime activities and that hostels providing such regimes might be privately managed.[41]

More secure bail hostels, along with the Government experiment electronically to tag persons on bail, is clearly designed to persuade the courts that a high level of security can be achieved without resort to prison. There is not space to discuss this development here. However, in addition to the careful examination of the rights and liberties of the untried which should accompany any introduction of electronic surveillance, we need to know much more about the making of bail, conditional bail and remand in custody decisions at present. Clearly there is not currently the most parsimonious use of custody. It seems probable that were research undertaken the same conclusion would emerge about the use of bail conditions. Until there is evidence to the contrary on that question I doubt we should risk the net-widening potential of additional means of surveillance.

Conclusions

The Government has adopted a twin-track response to the rising number of remand prisoners. It is substantially expanding custodial remand accommodation. It has also taken several initiatives, all of them widely canvassed by the penal pressure groups, to encourage the courts to make more use of bail: case time limits are being introduced; the *Nottingham Justices* decision has been amended by statute; more bail hostels are coming on stream; probation bail information schemes are being encouraged; a possible new condition of bail, electronic tagging, is being investigated; and by drawing attention to bail decision-making disparities between courts, the Government is exhorting magistrates to be more parsi-

[39] White K. and Brody S., "The use of bail hostels" [1980] Crim.L.R. 420.
[40] Lewis H. and Mair G., *Bail and Probation Work II: the use of London probation/bail hostels for bailees* (1989) Research and Planning Unit Paper 50, London: Home Office.
[41] Cm. 434, *op. cit.* para. 6.

monious in their use of custody. All of these reductionist initiatives are welcome and each should serve marginally to reduce the number of remands in custody. Given Home Office impetus the introduction of probation bail information schemes might have a significant impact on the number of remands in custody.

None of the current initiatives, however, serves directly to address the principal engine behind the growth in the remand population. None deals with the rising committal rate. It is not at all clear why there are such wide disparities between magistrates' courts in the proportion of cases in which they decline jurisdiction. It seems probable that liaison judges or clerks to justices offer different advice as to which cases should be committed, and that these differences are now being reproduced in the local representations by the CPS.[42] Whatever the cause the differences require urgent investigation. Central guidelines encouraging magistrates to accept a higher proportion of the cases coming before them is potentially the most powerful weapon for turning back the custodial remand tide which threatens to overwhelm the Government's prison building programme.

SECTION A

1. What problem is Morgan trying to solve?

2. Can you suggest any way in which the manner in which he formulates his problem might be criticised?

3. What information does Morgan derive from a comparison of Table 1 and Table 2?

4. One possible explanation for untried prisoners spending longer in prison is an overall growth in court waiting lists. Is this the explanation that Morgan accepts?

5. What principles guide Morgan's analysis of the decision to remand a defendant in prison?

6. Can you suggest any possible defects in the way Morgan's principles are put forward or any difficulties in applying them to a factual situation?

SECTION B

7. Why are magistrates remanding more cases to the Crown Court without granting bail?

8. If you read Morgan's article only can you be sure of the

---

[42] See Riley and Vennard, *supra*, note 3.

accuracy of his statement about the reasons why magistrates remand cases to the Crown Court?

9. In Morgan's view why do untried prisoners get the worst treatment of all legal categories of prisoner in the prison system?

10. Why, according to Morgan, might a solicitor believe that contesting an application to remand a prisoner in custody is an unwise move?

11. Are there any defects, technical or otherwise, in the way that Morgan presents his evidence for his views on this matter?

12. Why does Morgan use the word 'illustrated' when he discusses the Vera Probation Bail Information Project and the Probation Bail Project at p. 219?

13. What does Morgan suggest is the best way of reversing the increase in the number of custodial remand prisoners?

14. What research would you need to do to test whether Morgan is correct or not? List the difficulties you think you would encounter in doing such research.

EXERCISE 6

Study Skills Exercise

ESSAY AND PROBLEM EVALUATION

This exercise has a different format to those which have preceded it.

In this exercise you are asked to evaluate written work. There are two titles. One is an "essay" question and the other is a "problem" question. For each title, two student answers are reproduced for you to assess. *The exercise is best done with another student*, although you can also do it on your own.

Instructions

1. Take the answers to the essay title. Read the two answers *on your own*, as if you were the tutor. Decide which one is better, and why. For each answer, write down any comments which you may have on good or bad features.
2. Now compare your assessment and comments with those of your fellow student. It is unlikely that both of you will have made the same comments. You may not agree which is "best." Discuss whether you are using similar criteria to judge the answers, and account for differences. Consider whether the students giving the two answers were trying to do the same thing.
3. Together, draw up a list of criteria for judging the essay. Read the two answers again and decide whether the two students have performed well or badly on *each* item on your list.
4. Now take the "problem" answers and go through steps 1 and 2. Think again about your criteria, add to them or amend them if necessary, and once again re-evaluate the answers by working through each item on the list.

5. Imagine that you are the tutor handing the answers back to the four students. What was good about the answers? How could they be improved? Be constructive.
6. Is there any similarity between any of these answers and your own, in terms of style, approach and faults? Imagine that you are the student who has written the answer. How do you feel about the comments of the "tutor"? What are you going to do about them?

ESSAY EVALUATION

Essay title:

"The House of Commons has been described as 'male, middle-aged and middle-class.' Discuss the extent to which M.P.s are unrepresentative of the electorate and assess the significance of this."

Answer 1

In socio-economic terms the most unrepresentative characteristic of the House of Commons is the presence of so few women M.P.s: women have never comprised more than 5 per cent. of all M.P.s. In terms of class and occupation, analysis of M.P.s elected in 1983, reveals that only 1 per cent. of Conservative M.P.s and 29 per cent. of Labour M.P.s manual workers, whereas over 75 per cent. of Conservative M.P.s and 50 per cent. of Labour M.P.s were engaged in the professions or business.

More than 70 per cent. of all Conservative and Labour M.P.s elected between 1945 and 1983 were university graduates.

The area in which the closest socio-economic correspondence between M.P.s and their constituents is that of age, but even here there are big differences. Nearly three-fifths of all M.P.s elected between 1970 and 1974 were aged between 40 and 49, approximately a sixth were under 40 and nearly a quarter (25 per cent.) were over 60. The two middle-aged groups (40–49, 50–59) were represented in the Commons in twice the proportion found in the adult population. The youngest age-group (under 30), which accounts for 21 per cent. of the adult population, accounted for less than 2 per cent. of M.P.s and the elderly were also considerably under-represented.

Thus it can be seen that the House of Commons is a male, middle-class and middle-aged elite. This is bound to influence the way in which the M.P.s scrutinise legislation and government action.

They cannot represent the interests of women, racial minorities or working-class people effectively if they do not understand or share the experiences of such people. The situation also leads to a loss of confidence in Parliament by voters. On the other hand many people believe that it would create more problems to try to remedy the situation than to leave it as it is. People with a good education and experience are more likely to understand the problems of the nation than a typical cross-section of the electorate.

Answer 2

It is well-known and well documented that the House of Commons is disproportionate to the rest of the population in terms of sex, age, race, education and occupational background. Neither does the House accurately reflect the voting support of the political parties, with votes in marginal seats counting for more than in safe seats, and the "first-past-the-post system" favouring the two big parties and penalising Liberal/S.D.P. voters, as well as the Green Party. Proportional representation and the supply of socially representative lists would seem to be the only way to improve matters, although it would go too far if random selection by computer became the order of the day.

It is not surprising that Conservative M.P.s are overwhelmingly drawn from public schools, Oxbridge, business, professions and the aristocracy. However, great changes have also been seen in Labour M.P.s, who have become more middle-class (though this may be changing). Many constituency Labour parties find it difficult to resist selecting well-educated and often highly articulate middle-class individuals over people from lower down the social scale. Both parties think that women and blacks lose votes (only 45 out of 650 M.P.s in 1987 were women) but because so few candidates of this kind are selected it must be difficult to know if this is true. Not many women or black people put themselves forward, probably because they know they won't be selected.

The trouble about getting younger M.P.s is that they may not have the experience to run the country. And no one wants senile geriatrics to decide the deployment of nuclear missiles. So I think that middle-aged M.P.s are not necessarily bad.

At the end of the day does it matter that the House is unrepresentative? Most M.P.s vote on party lines, due to strict discipline by the whips. The issue is constructive criticism and the purpose of Parliament. Would Parliament (or the nation) be better served by a House of Commons which was a microcosm of the population? There is no evidence on whether there is a causal link between the socio-economic characteristics of M.P.s and their attitudes and voting behaviour, or Parliamentary business. But maybe if we had a wider pool of background, sex and knowledge, M.P.s would have more useful experience to criticise the Government or pass better Acts. Other people say M.P.s should have more research facilities to help them and spend more time in the constituencies understanding ordinary peoples' problems. Basically, the system is wrong and there have been some improvements, *e.g.* select committees but without P.R. not much change is likely.

PROBLEM

George was wandering around the Colditz Student Hall of Residence in a drunken state. Rosemary, as a joke, bundled him into a spare bedroom and locks the door. George, who was unaware he was locked in, fell asleep. The door was unlocked next morning by the cleaner, who did not disturb George. Later, when George had emerged from the room, he was told of the prank.

Advise George as to whether he has any action against Rosemary.

Answer A

In *Herring* v. *Boyle* (1834) 1 Cr.M. & R. 377, a mother wanted to remove her son from his school but the headmaster refused to let the boy go until the fees were paid. However, the court said this was not false imprisonment because the court did not know the feelings of the son. They did not know if he was willing to stay, or whether he was aware of any restraint, or whether the headmaster had laid a hand on him. A police officer can arrest someone without laying a hand upon him, but there is no imprisonment in the absence of the party supposed to be imprisoned. The boy did not appear in court. In the absence of evidence to show the boy knew he was being restrained, the court unanimously held there was no false imprisonment.

In *Meering* v. *Graham-White Aviation Co. Ltd.* (1920) 122 L.T. 44, the Court of Appeal also discussed false imprisonment. Here the plaintiff lived in a bedroom of Rose Cottage, which he shared with a friend, Lamb. They both worked for the same company. The cottage was searched by Askew and Burgess, two Metropolitan police officers, and they arrested Lamb on suspicion of stealing goods from the company. A sergeant of the works police, Prudence, was told that the plaintiff was wanted for questioning at the company's offices, and he instructed two of the works police to inform the plaintiff of this. The plaintiff, accompanied by these two men, went to the offices and was taken or invited to go to the waiting room. He said if he was not told what he was there for and why he was wanted, he would go away, but was informed that he was wanted for the purpose of inquiries as things had been stolen and he was wanted to give evidence. Having been told this he stayed. Three members of the works police remained on duty in the neighbourhood of the waiting room until the Metropolitan Police arrived, and arrested Meering. The court held, by a majority of two to one, that he had been falsely imprisoned. Duke L.J. (dissenting) said there was no evidence that the plaintiff did not have the liberty to leave if he wanted to. Warrington L.J. said that the evidence showed the plaintiff was detained. Atkin L.J. agreed, and said that a man could be imprisoned without knowing it.

In *Murray* v. *Ministry of Defence* [1981] 1 W.L.R. 692 a woman was detained in her house by the Army in Northern Ireland. She was told to dress. As she left her house she was told she was being arrested. Lord Griffiths held that she must have known from the moment that she was detained by the army that she was under arrest and that it was reasonable in the circumstances to delay giving the words of arrest until the house in which the woman had been detained had been searched. He therefore refused to uphold her claim for false imprisonment. He also said *Herring* v. *Boyle* was an extraordinary decision and that he did not think it would be similarly decided today.

Depending on which authority is followed, George may have an action for false imprisonment against Rosemary. He will probably fail. Atkin L.J. was the only judge in *Meering* to hold that knowledge of imprisonment was irrelevant and he did not cite *Herring* v. *Boyle*. *Meering* in fact turned on a discussion of whether, in the circumstances, the presence of the works officers outside the room prevented the plaintiff's exercise of his liberty. The older, unanimous decision of *Herring* v. *Boyle* is to be preferred. On the other hand, it might be felt it should not apply any more, and *Meering*, as a modern authority, more closely reflects the thinking of today and that *Murray* indicates that that is what the court should do.

Answer B

George may have an action for false imprisonment against Rosemary. False imprisonment is a trespass which may be defined as an act of the defendant which directly or indirectly or intentionally or negligently causes the confinement of the plaintiff within an area delimited by the defendant (*Street on Torts*). The problem seems to be about the question of whether George knew he was imprisoned, and whether this matters. However, we must first establish whether he was really imprisoned, and whether Rosemary intended it. I think she did, and the act of turning the key seems to indicate he was imprisoned for several hours, though we are not told whether there was an alternative exit, such as a window and if there was, whether he could have escaped (for example, the room might have been on the fourth floor).

However, let us assume there was no escape. Then we must ask, can a man be imprisoned without knowing it? In *Meering* v. *Graham-White Aviation*, Atkin L.J. said: "I think a man can be imprisoned while he is asleep, while he is in a state of drunkenness, while he is unconscious and while he is a lunatic. Those are cases where it seems to me that the person might properly complain if he were imprisoned, though the imprisonment began and ceased while he was in that state."

We do not know whether George is a lunatic or whether, on the facts, he was unconscious, but he does appear to fit into Atkin L.J.'s definition because he was both drunk and asleep. However, in the older case of *Herring* v. *Boyle*, Bolland B. said a schoolboy was not falsely imprisoned when a teacher refused to allow his mother to take him away, saying: "We cannot construe the refusal to the mother in the boy's absence, and without his being cognizant of any restraint, to be imprisonment of him against his will." This case has been disapproved of in *Murray* v. *Ministry of Defence*.

The difference between *Herring* and *Murray* is that there was no evidence that the boy was locked up, whereas there was a finding, by a majority, that the jury was justified in finding that Meering was imprisoned. Since George was definitely locked in the room, the Court of Appeal decision (which is more recent) should apply, and his action for false imprisonment should succeed.

George should also consider an action in trespass or assault or battery against Rosemary, which will probably succeed.

Part 4

CHAPTER 8

Where next?

This chapter introduces students to questions they should consider when applying to read law as a degree subject and outlines the career options open to students wishing to qualify as lawyers.

LAW COURSES

Law may be studied at degree level either at University, Polytechnic or College of Higher Education. It may be studied as a single subject, or in combination with another discipline, such as economics, politics or a foreign language. Thus, a student wishing to study law has two different decisions to make, "Do I want to study law on its own" and "Do I want to study at University or Polytechnic"?

Before making these decisions, it is wise to obtain a wide selection of prospectuses. Looking at these it will quickly become clear that law courses differ radically from institution to institution. There is a wide variety of legal subjects which can be studied, different balances of optional to compulsory subjects, and varying views about the purpose of studying for a law degree.

Begin by asking:

—why do I want to study law as a degree subject? Is there a strong vocational intention or is the subject being studied purely for its own sake? Do you just want a professional training (in which case why go to a university which stresses the academic, rather than the professional, study of law) or do you just want a liberal education (in which case what is your specific reason for studying law?)

—do I want to combine the study of law with the study of some other subject? What other subjects are you interested in? Would a combination of any of them with law suit your interests?

—what useful information and guidance can I obtain from my school, teachers, family or friends?

Bearing in mind the answers to these questions, read the prospectuses you have obtained and ask:

—what reputation has the course, law school and institution got? Why does it have that reputation and is it one which I find attractive?

—how much choice does the course offer me and is the law school of sufficent size to offer a wide variety of optional subjects? (be suspicious of small law schools who claim to offer a wide variety of subjects. Only a few may actually be on offer in any one year.)

—what connections has the law school got with the outside world and what are the career opportunities it considers open to its students?

—what guidance does it offer to students on optional choices and careers? Does it offer help in selecting courses best suited for my intended career?

—how much flexibility does the course give me if my motivations or interests change during my three years?

—what type of teaching methods are used and what is the mode of assessment?

Eventually, you will have to decide which institution to apply to. If you are applying to university, you can only apply to five universities. You must apply through the Universities Central Council for Admissions (U.C.C.A.). The address for this is *U.C.C.A., P.O. Box 28, Cheltenham, Gloucestershire. GL50 1HY.* As with U.C.C.A., you can apply to five institutions in any one year. Your choices must be listed in alphabetical order. A similiar scheme is operated by the polytechnics. The polytechnic scheme is called the Polytechnics Central Admission Scheme (P.C.A.S.). Its address is *P.C.A.S., P.O. Box 67, Cheltenham, Gloucestershire, GL50 3AP.* You can apply through both schemes at the same time. In deciding where to apply you should bear in mind the examination grades which the institution may expect you to get if you are given an offer of a place (can you realistically hope to get the required grades?). Do not judge an institution by the grades it offers. Somewhere that expects prospective students to achieve very high grades may have a lot of applicants and may attract only the very best students. On the other hand, very few law schools, if any, have any difficulty finding students. Some deliberately ask for lower grades than they could because they believe that, at the margins, "A" levels are poor indicators of degree potential. Somewhere asking for high "A" level grades may simply be trying to make its admissions task easier by putting off students.

Many law schools will want to interview candidates before deciding whether or not to give them a place. An interview is not only a chance for the law school to find out about the candidate. It is also a chance for the candidate to find out about the law school. Be prepared to ask questions about the aims of the law degree, the range and nature of the optional subjects available, and the research interests of the staff. However, never ask a question that can be answered by reference to material that has already been sent to you or which you should already have obtained. Do not, for example, ask what subjects are taught if this in a faculty brochure you have been given. Do ask, if the brochure does not tell you, whether a particular course is a "blackletter law" course, a sociolegal course, etc. Asking no questions at all shows that you have not prepared for the interview and perhaps have little interest in the institution. Asking questions that can be answered from available literature shows the same thing. Use the literature that you have been sent as a basis for asking further, more detailed questions.

In many degree courses contract, tort, criminal law, land law, equity and constitutional and administrative law will be studied as compulsory subjects, in either the first or second year. One reason for this is that many academics see these subjects as being basic to the study of English law. Either they contain principles or concepts that are of importance in a wide range of legal subjects or they are about matters which are themselves of general significance. There is also a pragmatic justification for making these subjects compulsory. Students wishing to qualify as barristers or solicitors must study these subjects at degree level in order to be exempt from having to take them in professional examinations. The subjects are sometimes referred to as *core subjects*.

In addition to the six subjects above, a normal law degree would involve a student in studying another seven or eight courses. A list of typical course might include:

English Legal System, EEC Law, Labour Law, Commercial

Law, Public International Law, Family Law, Jurispudence, Sociology of Law, Revenue Law and Company Law.

There may be scope for a student to write a disseration (an extended essay) under the supervision of a member of staff. Prospectuses should be read so as to get an idea of the context of the courses and the different individual emphases and approaches adopted. Some of these course may also be compulsory. Some will certainly be options selected by the individual student. Choice of these options is dictated by many factors. The student's own interests, career intentions, the way in which the subject is taught and the folk-lore surrounding it within the institution a student is studying all play their part. Subjects vary both in content and the style in which they are taught. For example, international law in one institution may involve different material and be taught in a different way from another course labelled international law in a different institution.

Many optional subjects, with the notable exceptions of subjects such as the sociology of law and philosophy of law, have as their starting points principles, concepts and techniques which are acquired in studying the core subjects. The core subjects studied tend to place an emphasis on common law at the expense of statute law, on private law at the expense of public law and on applying legal principles without considering their origins and social effects. Some law degree courses seek to redress this balance as there is an argument that the core subjects, with their emphasis on individuals' property and other private rights perpetuate a vision of English law which is outmoded.

No law school can guarantee that it will still be offering the same subjects in its syllabus three years hence. Lecturers may leave, or may lose interest in something which they have taught. Thus, be wary of deciding to go to a particular institution just because of one course, particularly if it is unusual, and particularly if it is taught in the third year. It may not be there when you reach the third year.

LAW AS A PROFESSION

When looking and deciding your future career, it is vital to make a realistic assessment of the range of opportunities open to you. This means deciding what are your own aptitudes and interests, as well as what are the actual jobs on offer. Vacation or other temporary work experience of any sort can be a very useful way in which to test out your prejudices and instincts about different types of work and to help you make an informed choice about them. Such experience will also help you in job applications and interviews for other, more permanent, jobs. Never be afraid to ask teachers and friends about their jobs and career decisions. Use every opportunity to take advantage of careers advice that is available in your school, college or university. Consider whther participating in a placement scheme would help. When you have made a tentative decision and apply for a job, take time in preparing your letter of application, application form and/or curriculum vitae (resumé of career to date). Get friends and your tutor to read through your applications and ensure that you present yourself in as interesting and as favourable a light as possible. *Never hesitate to take advice. Never be diffident about applying for a particular job.*

There is a wide variety of jobs with some legal content. The level and kind of prior legal knowledge which they demand (if any) varies from job to job. You will find an extensive list of such jobs, together with addresses to write for more information about them, in the first appendix to this book. In the remainder of this chapter we will concentrate on the legal profession; by this we mean solicitors and barristers.

SOLICITORS AND BARRISTERS

The legal profession in England and Wales is divided into two branches (solicitors and barristers) which have their own entry and training schemes. The majority of lawyers are solicitors. There are nearly 50,000 practising solicitors in England and Wales. Firms of solicitors exist in all large towns, although there is a high concentration in the South East, particularly in London. It has been said that solicitors are generalists. They advise clients from all walks of life on a wide variety of legal matters, with a traditional emphasis on conveyancing and property-related matters. The majority of solicitors work in private practice, in partnerships employing less than 50 people, many of whom have no formal qualifications. There are, however, around 9,000 solicitors employed in commerce and industry, local government, law centres and other occupations.

The vast majority of barristers work in central London. They have restricted access to clients. They can normally only represent a client when instructed by a solicitor. They have an exclusive right to act as paid advocates in the High Court, Court of Appeal and House of Lords. Barristers work as individual fee-earners on their own account, sharing overheads with other barristers who are members of a set of chambers. They have few of the protections which are afforded to employees and partners in firms of solicitors. Their success or failure is linked directly to their own ability, flair and preparedness to work. There are just over 5,000 practising barristers, and in common with solicitors a high proportion of the profession is aged under 40.

Sometimes comparisons have been drawn between the legal and medical professions. Solicitors, in common with general practitioners, are generalists. Barristers, in common with consultants, are specialists. This comparison still has some validity, although it does overlook the specialist work undertaken by many firms of solicitors, particularly in London, covering such areas as commercial, company and tax law. It also is the case that a considerable number of solicitors act as advocates before tribunals, magistrates' courts and county courts. Many barristers spend much of their time out of court, advising solicitors and their clients on points of law and drafting pleadings during the initial stages of litigation. It is only a small proportion of barristers who are able to specialise in the area of law in which they work. The majority are involved in general advocacy.

Those primarily interested in advocacy working (in courts) should normally consider going to the Bar. Court work done by solicitors tends to involve less important cases, even for those solicitors who specialise in the area. In making this decision, however, some thought should be given to the relative career opportunities at the Bar and in practice as a solicitor. Practice as a solicitor, in the early stages of a person's career, has the attraction of providing some element of predictability and financial security. It is often the case, at the Bar, that it is only the extremely able who have the opportunity to specialise. Newly qualified barristers must be prepared to put up with fairly modest incomes in their first years of practice, compared with newly qualified solicitors, particularly in City of London practices.

Choosing between the two branches of the profession is extremely difficult, especially at the present time, when the legal profession is in a state of transition. Changing attitudes towards the function and conduct of the legal profession, the advent of professional advertising, the demise of the conveyancing monopoly, and the impact of new technology, will all change the nature of legal practice and career opportunities within it. The debate as to whether or not the legal profession is overstaffed is likely to continue and the effects of the existing age profile of the profession have yet to be evaluated.

EDUCATION AND TRAINING OF SOLICITORS

The Law Society's Training Regulations can be obtained from *The Law Society, The Law Society's Hall, 113 Chancery Lane, London WC2A 1PL.* The purpose of this section is to summarise those regulations as they apply to the majority of entrants to the profession. The regulations make special provision for overseas solicitors, barristers and some other limited groups. This section only covers four basic categories of entrants to the profession:

1. Law graduates (the largest category of entrant).
2. Non-law graduates.
3. Non-graduates over the age of 25.
4. Non-graduates under the age of 25.

Entrants to the profession undergo an *academic stage*, a *vocational stage* of education and training and a practical stage by serving two years in articles of clerkship.

The academic stage

The academic stage of training for law graduates will normally be covered in their degree course, provided that they study the six "core subjects." Non-law graduates have to pass a Common Professional Examination, the syllabus for which covers the six core subjects, together with two other legal subjects which must be approved by the Law Society. Non-graduates under the age of 25 take the Solicitors' First Examination, instead of a Common Professional Examination. This covers the same subjects as the Common Professional Examination in a way that is more appropriate for school leavers. Most non-graduates choose to qualify using the examinations and qualifications of the Institute of Legal Executives.

The vocational stage

The solicitors' final course and examination is designed to ensure that every prospective solicitor has "a common knowledge of the areas of substantive law which are of the greatest practical importance and to integrate this substantive law into practical instruction." Those attending the course and sitting the examinations must have been accepted for membership by the Law Society.

The subject division of the course is:

(1) Conveyancing.
(2) Business Organisations and Insolvency.

(3) Wills, Probate and Administration.
(4) Civil and Criminal Litigation.
(5) Family Law and Practice.
(6) Consumer Protection and Employment Law.
(7) Accounts.

Revenue Law and Professional Ethics are covered within the teaching and examination of each subject.

The course can be studied at the College of Law in either Guildford, London, Chester or York (for details write to *The Registrar, College of Law, Braboeuf Manor, St. Catherines, Guildford, Surrey. GU3 1HA*) or at a number of polytechnics (Manchester, Trent, Bristol, City of London, Newcastle, Leeds, Birmingham, Wolverhampton, Leicester).

The final examination is normally followed by a two-year period of articles with an experienced solicitor. Trainee solicitors are in essence solicitor apprentices. The terms of their contracts, with the solicitor to whom they are articled, are regulated by the Training Regulations. The quality and range of work undertaken by trainee solicitors varies from law practice to law practice. Provisions exist, which are monitored by the Law Society, to try to ensure that trainee solicitors receive work experience in an appropriate spectrum of legal topics germane to professional practice. Recommendations exist as to the minimum pay of trainee solicitors.

Summary of basic training requirements for each category of entrant

The Law Graduate

(i)	Law degree
(ii)	Final course
(iii)	Final examination
(iv)	Two years' service under articles

In cases of financial or domestic hardship, full-time attendance at a Common Professional Examination course may be excused.

The Non-Law Graduate

(i)	Non-law degree
(ii)	One year course for C.P.E. in six core subjects.

(iii)	Final course
(iv)	Final examination
(v)	Two years' service under articles

Non-Graduate Over 25

(A) *Mature Student*

(i)	Two year course for C.P.E. in 8 subjects.
(ii)	Final course.
(iii)	Final examination.
(iv)	Two years' service under articles.

(B) *Fellow of the Institute of Legal Executives*

(i)	Obtain exemption from the six C.P.E. core subjects.
(ii)	Either attend Final Course or serve two years service under articles of clerkship.
(iii)	Final examination.

Non-Graduate Under 25

(i) Attain required standard of general education.

> This entails –
> (a) Passing in five subjects in GCE or GCSE of which two are at 'A' level.
> (b) One pass at either 'A' or GCSE level must be in English, English Language or English Literature.
> (c) Obtaining minimum 'A' level grades.
>
> The following table is used to calculate the grades required.
>
> Grade A – 10 points
> Grade B – 8 points
> Grade C – 6 points
> Grade D – 4 points
> Grade E – 1 point
>
> The minimum requirements are:
> 14 points from 2 subjects taken at one sitting, or

18 from 3 subjects taken at one sitting, or 20
points from 3 subjects taken at not more than 2
sittings.

(ii) Attend an approved polytechnic for one year to take the
first four of the core subjects in the Solicitors' First Examination.
(iii) After passing four subjects in the Solicitors' First Examination, enter into articles for a minimum period of five years,
one of which will be spent on the Final course.
(iv) Take the remaining four subjects in the Solicitors' First
Examination during the first two years of articles by part-time
study at a polytechnic or correspondence course. If the last
four subjects are not passed during the first two years of
articles, the period of articles may be extended by one year, to
permit further attempts.
(v) After passing eight subjects in the Solicitors' First Examination and after a minimum of two years' service, attend Final
Course.
(vi) Final Examination.
(vii) Minimum of 18 months' service under articles after passing the Final Examinations.

N.B. Students who obtain the minimum "A" level grades should
carefully review their options and see if they would gain admit-
tance to read for a law degree at a university or polytechnic.

Types of articles

(a) *Private practice*

Most articles are served with private firms of solicitors. Firms vary
considerably in size and type of work; therefore the trainee solicitor's range of experience and salary may also vary considerably.
Before making an application you need to think of the sort of
articles you are seeking.

(i) In rural areas, firms will tend to consist of five or six
partners at most, with total staffs often not exceeding 15
people. Most such firms will be "general practitioners," which
means that they will mostly do conveyancing, landlord and
tenant, trusts, wills and probate, small-scale commercial and
company work, family law, civil and criminal litigation.
(ii) In large cities most firms will also do the kinds of work
listed above though there will tend to be some degree of spe-

cialisation, (*e.g.* towards property work and conveyancing, or crime). The larger firms do more commercial work. Some of these firms may have around 20 partners (with some specialising in certain types of work) and staffs of 100 or more. Generally, the poorer the district in which a firm is situated, the higher the percentage of work done on Legal Aid and the greater the emphasis on welfare law, (*e.g.* family, employment, social security and housing law).

(iii) In London, there is the greatest degree of specialisation, with the large firms in the City concentrating very heavily on company, financial and commercial work; shipping is another City area of specialisation. The biggest City firms are very large with over 100 partners, and staffs of 750 or more. Several smaller firms near the Inns of Court act for prosperous private clients, which involves work in trusts, tax, and property law. Other firms have distinct specialisations, (*e.g.* entertainment law or labour law).

(b) *Local government*

Legal work in local government covers many aspects of conveyancing and planning, and commercial work. Local authorities do a certain amount of prosecuting work both in those areas where they have special law enforcement reponsibilities, (*e.g.* weights and measures or public health legislation) and also, sometimes, on behalf of the public. Some local authorities are involved in child care law.

(c) *Industry and commerce*

A few large organisations, both in the private and the public sectors have their own legal departments, with qualified solicitors who occasionally take on articled clerks. While the work tends to be specialised, large commercial organisations can offer valuable experience in property and commmercial work and in areas such as employment, insurance and pension law. Considerable opportunities exist to work in commerce once a person has qualified as a solicitor, especially where experience has been gained with a large City of London firm.

(d) *Law centres*

In the inner areas of many cities there are Law Centres, offering occasional opportunities for articled clerks seeking to specialise in welfare law. There are opportunities for young solicitors to work for Law Centres and similiar agencies, especially where they have had an all-round experience of litigation during articles.

EDUCATION AND TRAINING OF BARRISTERS

In contrast to the solicitors' branch of the profession, the Bar, in essence, stipulates that all its entrants must be graduates. Full details of the entrance requirements can be obtained from *The Council of Legal Education, 4 Gray's Inn Road, London WC1R 5DX*. The Council also publishes a calendar which contains the Consolidated Regulations of the four Inns of Court. Further information can also be obtained from *The Senate of the Inns of Court, 11 South Square, Gray's Inn, London, W.C.1.*

The academic stage

The academic stage for law graduates will normally be covered in their degree course, provided that they study the six core subjects. Non-law graduates must obtain a *certificate of eligibility* which establishes that they have obtained a certain standard of education at degree and "O" and "A" level. They must then normally attend a one-year course, in the six core subjects, at the City University, London or the Polytechnic of Central London and pass the Diploma in Law examinations. Special provisions exist for mature students over the age of 25 who are not graduates but have shown exceptional ability in other fields.

The vocational stage

Intending barristers must be admitted to one of the four Inns of Court (Lincoln's Inn, *The Under-Treasurer, Lincoln's Inn, London, W.C. 2.* Inner Temple, *The Sub-Treasurer, Inner Temple, London. E.C. 4.* Middle Temple, *The Under-Treasurer, Middle Temple, London. E.C. 4.* Gray's Inn, *The Under-Treasurer, Gray's Inn, London. W.C. 1.*). They must comply with certain requirements of the Inn. The most noteworthy of these is the need, prior to qualification, to "keep term," which means eating a certain number of dinners in the Inn Court during set periods. This requirement is said to enable judges, barristers and intending barristers to meet and get to know each other.

The vocational stage is a compulsory year's course at the Inns of Court School of Law and, for student barristers intending to practise, a series of practical exercises covering matters such as advocacy. The Bar Final examination contains certain compulsory elements (General Papers covering tort, contract, equity and trusts and papers on civil and criminal procedure and evidence) and a number of options with a new emphasis on advocacy, negotiation and practical skills. Students' choice of optional subjects is restricted because they cannot elect to study certain options they have already chosen to pursue in their law degree.

Students who wish to take the Bar examination but do not wish to practise at the Bar in this country cannot study at the Inns of Court School of Law. Such students will include those intending to work in industry, to become academics or to practise as lawyers overseas. Courses for such students are run at a number of polytechnics and other institutions.

Students who pass the Bar examination are "called to the Bar." They are barristers. In contrast to the solicitor's qualification, the Bar qualification does not entail the successful completion of a period of apprentiship training. However, barristers intending to practise, rather than teach law or to go on to some other career, must complete a period of apprenticeship ("a pupillage") which is normally for a period of one year, during the last six months of which the pupil barrister can undertake work for a fee.

Pupillage

In selecting pupillage a student must have regard not only to the range of training on offer but also to the future prospects in the set of chambers which offers a pupillage. Regard must also be had to the number and amount of pupillage awards given by the chambers to help off-set living expenses for pupils. Many sets of chambers, particularly those in the provinces, do a mixture of litigation work covering crime, personal injury litigation and other common law areas. Students wishing to obtain pupillage and to earn a reasonable living at an early stage at the Bar will often choose such chambers. In London, particularly, there is a large number of specialist chambers covering such fields as commercial law, chancery, patents, tax, libel, planning and so on. Competition is very fierce for places in such sets of chambers. A very good academic record is required and even those students who are offered places are not assured of making a career at the specialist Bar. Even if offered a place for pupillage there is no guarantee that the student will subsequently be offered a position in the chambers ("a tenancy") after its completion.

PRACTICAL POINTS: SOLICITORS AND BARRISTERS

The following points may be of assistance to those considering entering the legal profession:—

—places for the solicitors' final examination course tend to get booked up so that an early booking should be made.

—places for the Bar final course should be booked early in a law student's final year, after the student has gained admission to one of the Inns of Court.

—intending solicitors should give thought to the various advantages and disadavantages of choosing either the College of Law or a polytechnic solicitors' final course. Some local education authorities are willing to give discretionary grants, to cover the costs of such courses, only when a student chooses the institution nearest to the home address. Some firms of solicitors will help their propsective trainee solicitors with both the course fees and living expenses.

—intending entrants to the legal profession should assess the total costs of entry, (*e.g.* tuition and subsistance costs, membership fees and other expenses), the possibility or not of obtaining a discretionary local authority grant, a bank loan or, in the case of the Bar, the availability of scholarships or other forms of assistance from the various Inns and the conditions attached to such awards, (*e.g.* age limitations).

—the desirability of obtaining work experience in a solicitor's office or attached to a barrister's set of chambers during student vacations. Many firms of solicitors and barristers' chambers now organise student placement schemes.

—advice should be sought to ensure that you obtain a satisfactory apprentice training which reflects your career and subject interests either as a trainee solicitor or as a pupil barrister and that the articles or pupillage is arranged at the appropriate time.

—an assessment should be made of prospects in either branch of the profession and the overall treatment of trainees and new recruits.

APPENDIX I

Careers directory

This alphabetical list of career opportunities is an attempt to summarise a selection of those careers which have some legal content or contact with the legal profession. The materials contained in this book are designed to be of assistance to trainees for the vast majority of these occupations. None of the careers requires a student to have a degree in law. Some of the careers require entrants to be graduates. Students who have studied law will sometimes find that they can negotiate exemptions from law examinations in professional courses. In some cases they will automatically have such exemption. (Some professions and occupations have not yet caught up with GCSE examinations. Where appropriate below, substitute GCSE for "O" level.)

ACCOUNTANCY

Accountants are usually thought of in association with companies. Working both as the employees of the company and as independent advisers they are involved in the day-to-day financial control of businesses as well as larger-scale matters such as the creation of new businesses and the restructuring of established ones. All companies must appoint independent accountants to audit (check) their accounts. In recent years their work as liquidators and receivers, dealing with the closing down of businesses, has expanded. The accountancy profession has shown itself to be very adaptable and enterprising. Its work has blossomed over the past decades. They have also expanded their activities into the more general area of management consultants. They are also heavily involved in tax planning both for individuals and companies. They often have to work closely with solicitors and, in recent years, have expanded their business into areas traditionally the prerogative of solicitors. Many accountants work in industry or local authorities. Some firms of accountants employ lawyers. Many firms of accountants take on law graduates as trainees. There are a number of different kinds of accountant, *e.g.* Chartered, Certified, Management, etc.

Minimum entry standards:	2 'A' levels, 3 'O' levels (including Maths and English at grade C or above.) (provision for graduate entry).
Training period:	One year per stage of training.

Further information:

Institute of Chartered Accountants in England and Wales, P.O. Box 433, Chartered Accountants' Hall, Moorgate Place, London. EC2R 6EQ.
The Chartered Association of Certified Accountants, 29, Lincoln's Inn, London WC2A 3EE.
The Chartered Institute of Management Accountants, 63, Portland Place, London. W1M 4AB.
The Chartered Institute of Public Finance and Accountancy, 3, Robert Street, London. WC2N 6BH.

ACTUARY

Most actuaries work for insurance and pension fund companies. They calculate matters such as the life expectancies of certain occupational groups and assess a wide range of insurance risks.

Minimum entry standards:	2 'A' levels (one being at B in Maths or C in Further Maths) and 3 'O' levels. (Mostly a Maths graduate profession.)
Training period:	5–6 years for graduates.

Further information:

Institute of Actuaries, Staple Inn Hall, High Holborn, London. WC1V 7QJ.

BANKING

The High Street Banks have expanded the range of services they offer to their corporate and personal customers. Advice is given on a wide range of services including investments, taxation, securities, foreign securities, loans and leasing schemes. The Banks have substantial trust and probate departments. Merchant banks give specialist advice, manage clients' investments, and advise on company acquisitions, flotations and mergers. In both of the banking sectors there has been a growth in the number of qualified lawyers that are employed.

Minimum entry standards:	Normally 4 GCSE passes A–C (including English and a Maths). (Special provision for graduate entry.)
Training period:	Depends on qualifications.

Further information:

Banking Information Service, 6th Floor, 10, Lombard Street, London. EC3V 9AT
British Merchant Banking and Securities Houses Association, 6, Frederick's Place, London. EC2 R8BT.
Chartered Institute of Bankers, First Floor, 10, Lombard Street, London. EC3V 9AT.

BARRISTER

See Chapter 8.

BUILDING SOCIETY MANAGEMENT

At present Building Societies have to deal with solicitors over the granting and drawing up of mortgages. They employ a small number of lawyers themselves. It is likely that the scope of Building Societies operations will grow in the future to include more commercial initiatives and the provision of a wider range of legal services for their clients.

No mandatory qualification exists but there is provision to obtain a "building society" qualification from the Chartered Building Societies' Institute.

Training period:	Variable

Further information:

Chartered Building Societies Institute, 19, Baldock Street, Ware, Hertfordshire.

Building Societies Association, 34, Park Street, London. W1Y 3PF.

CHARTERED SECRETARY

Chartered Secretaries are professional administrators who know about finance, law, personnel and information systems. The work will vary depending on the size and function of the organisation. It may include looking after pension schemes, insurance, premises management, liaison between directors and shareholders, company law, committee management and office management, amongst other things.

No academic qualifications are needed for entry but exemptions from professional examinations may be granted for degrees, Higher National Awards and some professional qualifications.

Training period: Variable.

Further information:

Careers Department, Institute of Chartered Secretaries and Administrators, 16, Park Crescent, London. W1N 4AH.

CIVIL SERVICE

The range of jobs in the civil service is enormous; from prison warder to Permanent Secretary. Many have legal content. The civil service employ a large number of solicitors and barristers. For details of the various openings in the civil service write to:

Civil Service Commission, Civil Service Department, Alencon Link, Basingstoke, Hampshire. RG21 1JB.

ENGINEERING

Most professional engineers study aspects of law during some part of their training; generally this will relate to matters such as contract, employment and building law.

Further information:

Engineering Careers Information Service, 54, Clarendon Street, Watford. WD1 1LB.
Engineering Council, Canberra House, 10–16, Maltravers Street, London. WC2R 3ER.

ENVIRONMENTAL HEALTH OFFICERS

Environmental Health Officers are local authority employees. The work includes responsibility for ensuring that certain food, hygiene, housing and other regulatory provisions are complied with. The job includes some involvement with lawyers and the courts and requires detailed knowledge of a number of Acts of Parliament and related statutory instruments.

Minimum entry standards:	2 'A' levels and 5 'O' levels (including English, Maths and 2 science subjects). (Provision for graduate entry.)
Training period:	3 year sandwich course or 4 year day release course or 4 year sandwich course.

Further information:

The Institution of Enviromental Health Officers, Chadwick House, Rushworth Street, London. SE1 0RB.

FACTORY INSPECTOR

Much of a factory inspector's time is spent visiting appropriate premises advising on safety requirements and ensuring that a variety of statutes are complied with. The job involves some contact with courts and lawyers.

Minimum entry standards:	Graduate entry plus further experience normally required.
Training period:	2 years.

Further information:

The Health and Safety Executive, 25, Chapel Street, London. W2 4TF.
Civil Service Commission, Alencon Link, Basingstoke, Hampshire. RG21 1JB.

HEALTH SERVICES MANAGEMENT

Health service managers play a key role in the organisation, staffing, equipping and functioning of hospitals. Moves towards privatising some services, (*e.g.* catering and laundering), industrial relations problems, and intricate commercial decisions which have to be taken by health authorities have all increased the legal content of the work done.

Minimum entry standards:	No set pattern.
Training Period:	Variable. It is possible to take the Institute of Health Service Managers courses but other qualifications such as those in law, accountancy or personnel management may be adequate.

Further information:

National Staff Committee, D.H.S.S., Hannibal House, Elephant and Castle, London. SE1 6TE.
Institute of Health Service Managers, 75, Portland Place, London. W1N 4AN.

HOUSING MANAGEMENT

Housing managers are local authority employees with a wide range of responsibilities for council houses and housing policy. Because of the statutory framework for local authority powers much of their work has a legal content.

Minimum entry standards:	2 'A' levels (including English) and 3 'O' levels. (Graduate entry provision.)
Training period:	3 years. (Less for graduates.)

Further information:

Institute of Housing, 12, Upper Belgrave Street, London. SW1.

INSURANCE

The insurance field offers a wide range of different employment opportunities. The precise nature of insurance contracts and the wide range of specialist legal rules means there are many openings for lawyers in this area.

Further information:

Careers Information Officer, The Chartered Insurance Institute, The Hall, 20, Aldermanbury, London. EC2.

JOURNALISM AND BROADCASTING

This is a wide field offering opportunities not just as a broadcaster or journalist but also behind the scenes in the administration and management of businesses.

Further information:

National Council for the Training of Journalists, Carlton House, Hemnall Street, Epping, Essex. CM16 4NL.
Newspaper Society, Bloomsbury House, Bloomsbury Square, London. WC1B 3DA.
B.B.C. Appointments Officer, Broadcasting House, London. W1A 1AA.
I.B.A., 70, Brompton Road, London. SW3 1EY.

LEGAL EXECUTIVES

Legal Executives work as assistants to solicitors, predominantly in the area of private practice. They must take the Fellowship examinations of the Institute of Legal Executives. They do a wide range of legal work and often develop their own individual specialisations (particularly in the field of conveyancing, accounts, trusts, wills and litigation). It is possible to move from being a legal executive to qualifying as a solicitor. Some people are employed by solicitors to do the same work as legal executives although they are not qualified as such.

Entry qualifications; 4 GCSE levels in approved subjects.

Further information:

The Institute of Legal Executives, Kempston Manor, Kempston, Bedford. MK42 7AB.

LOCAL GOVERNMENT

Specific careers in local government are listed here under the appropriate heading. There are also a wide range of general careers in local government. For information about them you should consult the appropriate department of the Town Hall or Council Office in the area in which you wish to work.

PATENT AGENT

Patent agents advise on all aspects of the protection of ideas through patents, copyright and trade marks. Registration of a patent or industrial design is a way of preventing anyone copying your invention without them first paying an appropriate fee. The job involves a knowledge of both science and law and is particularly suitable for a science or engineering student with an interest in law.

Minimum entry standard:	Science or engineering degree.
Training Period:	3–4 years.

Further information:

Chartered Institute of Patent Agents, Staple Inn Buildings, London. WC1V 7PV.

PERSONNEL MANAGEMENT

The continual development of employment law and health and safety legislation over the past decades has resulted in an increased need for some personnel managers to have a specialist knowledge of law so that they can advise their companies on such matters and, if necessary, represent them in Industrial Tribunals.

Minimum entry standards:	Varies. (provision for graduate entry)
Training period:	Variable.

Further information:

Institute of Personnel Management, 35, Camp Road, London. SW19 4UX.

POLICE

For details of entry schemes write to your local police force or to:

The Police Recruiting Department, The Home Office, Queen Anne's Gate. London. SW1H 9AT.

PUBLISHING

Some publishers are interested in employing law graduates and newly qualified lawyers in their editorial and marketing departments. If you are interested in working for a particular publisher you should contact them directly. Your law tutor should be able to advise you about which publishers you should approach.

SOCIAL WORK AND PROBATION

Social work

The majority of social workers are employed by local authorities. They provide a social work service to families, children, the elderly, the sick, the handicapped and the community at large. They are employed in a variety of settings; hospitals, residential homes and in the community. Some are specialists working in such areas as mental health or child care where a good knowledge of the relevant areas of law is particularly important. Other elements of social work include providing advice and support where a general awareness of the law is frequently required.

Probation

Probation officers are social workers with special responsibility for offenders. They prepare social inquiry reports to assist the courts in determining sentences, supervise probation orders and community service orders and provide an after-care service for former prisoners. Through the Divorce Court Welfare Service probation officers also provide services for families involved in marriage breakdown. They assist with conciliation of parties and prepare welfare reports for use in resolving custody disputes. A legal background in this work is helpful though not essential.

Minimum entry standards:	A Certificate of Qualification in Social Work is needed to practice as a qualified social worker. The entry standard for this varies.
Training period:	For a graduate 2 years.

Further information:

C.C.E.T.S.W., Derbyshire House, St. Chad's Street, London. WC1H 8AD.
Probation Service, Home Office, Queen Anne's Gate, London. SW1H 9AT.

For Graduates:

> Clearing House for CQSW Courses, 4th Floor, Myson House, Railway Terrace, Rugby, Warwicks. CV21 3HT.

SOLICITORS

See Chapter 8.

STOCK EXCHANGE

Graduates with either law or law-related degrees may find jobs in firms of stockbrokers working in their research and investment analysis departments. There is no formal training for these positions. Those who wish to become members of the Exchange must take the Stock Exchange examination.

Further information:

> Public Relations Department, Stock Exchange, London. EC2N 1HP.

SURVEYING AND AUCTIONEERING

Membership of the Royal Institution of Chartered Surveyors (12, Great George Street, London. SW1P 3AD) and the Incorporated Society of Valuers and Auctioneers (3, Cadogan Gate, London. SW1X 0AS) requires either full or part-time study and the passing of a number of examinations some of which have a legal content covering such topics as contract, agency and land law.

TAX INSPECTOR

Those who are interested in tax law or the tax system and who have a good degree or an accountancy qualification may be interested in this career option. Progress in the tax inspectorate depends on both the ability to pass internal Revenue examinations and the willingness to be mobile. Some tax inspectors later leave the service in order to start work as tax consultants with firms of accountants.

Minimum entry standards:	First or second class honours degree or equivalent.
Training period:	3 years.

Further information:

Civil Service Commission, Alencon Link, Basingstoke, Hampshire. RG21 1JB.

TEACHING AND POST-GRADUATE OPPORTUNITIES

If you are interested in either of the above options you should consult your law tutor or your careers tutor. The majority of university law faculties and some polytechnic law schools have facilities for post-graduate research and/or run taught post-graduate courses. You normally need a second class honours degree to obtain a place on such a course. Most of these courses can either be studied full-time or part-time. It is very difficult to obtain state funding for such courses. Some universities are able to offer scholarships or other forms of assistance. A post-graduate degree is of some assistance to anyone wishing to teach law. The majority of university or polytechnic law lecturers have an upper second class honours degree or better. Many also have a professional qualification or further degree or both. Law is also taught at college level and qualifications required there are somewhat lower. Although opportunities to lecture in law are limited there are more openings than in many other disciplines.

It is possible to pursue post-graduate research in foreign countries, particularly the United States and Canada, where funding is sometimes easier to obtain. Career opportunities for non-nationals in these countries are limited.

Further information:

For particular courses write direct to the appropriate institution.

Study in the United Kingdom:

Grants Information: The Department of Education and Science, Room 1/27, Elizabeth House, York Road, London. SE1 7PH.
The Economic and Social Science Research Council, 1, Temple Avenue, London. EC4Y 0BD.
Registry of Post-Graduate Research Topics in Law: The Institute of Advanced Legal Studies, 17, Russell Square, London. WC1B 5DR.

Overseas Opportunities:

> Association of Commonwealth Universities, 36, Gordon Square, London. WC1H 0IF.
> British Council, 65, Davies Street, London. W1Y 2AA.

For the U.S.A.:

> The United Kingdom Educational Commission, 6, Porter Street, London. W1M 2HR.

TRADING STANDARDS OFFICER

Trading standards officers are responsible for the enforcement of a wide range of legislation including the Trade Description Act 1968, the Consumer Credit Act 1974, the Consumer Protection Act 1987 and other regulatory provisions covering food and drugs and weights and measures. They are also often involved in the provision of advice and assistance to traders and to consumers. They are employed by local authorities.

Minimum entry standards:	2 'A' levels and 3 'O' levels (including English, Maths and a science subject). (Provision for graduate entry.)
Training period:	3 years.

Further information:

> Institute of Trading Standards Administration, Estate House, 319D, London Road, Hadleigh, Benfleet, Essex. SS7 2BN.

APPENDIX II

Abbreviations

The short list below contains some of the standard abbreviations that you will find most frequently referred to in books and case reports. It is not exhaustive. It will help you whilst you are beginning your study of law but, if you intend to acquire a more detailed knowledge of law, you will need to consult one of the detailed lists found in the books mentioned in the section, "General Reference," in Appendix III.

A.C.	Appeal Cases (Law Reports).
All E.R.	All England Law Reports.
C.L.J.	Cambridge Law Journal.
Ch. D.	Chancery Division (Law Reports).
C.M.L.R.	Common Market Law Reports
Conv. (n.s.)	Conveyancer and Property Lawyer (New Series).
Crim. L.R.	Criminal Law Review.
D.L.R.	Dominion Law Reports.
E.L.R.	European Law Reports.
E.L. Rev.	European Law Review.
E.R.	English Reports.
Fam.	Family Division (Law Reports).
Fam. Law	Family Law (A journal which also contains notes about cases).
H. of C. or H.C.	House of Commons.
H. of L. or H.L.	House of Lords.
I.L.J.	Industrial Law Journal.
K.B.	Kings Bench (Law Reports).
L.Q.R.	Law Quarterly Review.

L.S. Gaz.	Law Society Gazette.
M.L.R.	Modern Law Review.
N.I.L.Q.	Northern Ireland Legal Quarterly.
N.L.J.	New Law Journal.
P.L.	Public Law.
O.J.	Official Journal of the European Communities
Q.B.D.	Queen's Bench Division.
R.T.R.	Road Traffic Reports.
S.I.	Statutory Instrument.
S.J. or Sol. Jo.	Solicitors' Journal.
W.L.R.	Weekly Law Reports.

APPENDIX III

Further reading

The number of books about law and legal rules increases each day. They range from simple guides, written for the GCSE student, to thousand-page, closely argued texts, written for the academic. Some are encyclopedias; others are exhaustive surveys of a very small area of law. This short list of further reading is intended to be of use to those readers who want to to take further specific themes raised in this book. The list is not a guide to legal literature as a whole. Readers who have specific interests should consult their library catalogues for books in their area.

INTRODUCTORY BOOKS

Atiyah, P. *Law and Modern Society* (1983) Oxford University Press.
Intended for the lay reader, rather than the student already studying for a law degree, this is an introduction both to the legal system and ideas about law. It is written in an accessible style and is suitable for those contemplating studying law at degree level as well as anyone with a general interest in law.

Waldron, J. *The Law* (1990) Routledge.
Another general introduction to law. The author is a political scientist and philosopher. The book is particularly concerned with questions about the relationship of politics and law in the United Kingdom.

BOOKS ON THE ENGLISH LEGAL SYSTEM

White, R. *The Administration of Justice* (1985) Basil Blackwell.
This is primarily a textbook for law degree students studying an English Legal System course. It gives the reader a basic background in the institutions and rules of the system but concentrates

on how the system actually works in practice. The book is written in a more accessible style than many other similar books. It presumes no previous knowledge of law.

Cross, R. *Precedent in English Law* (3rd ed., 1977) Oxford University Press.
Cross, R. *Statutory Interpretation* (2nd ed., 1987) Butterworths.
These are standard textbooks on traditional doctrinal theory (the theory of the way in which judges use previous judgments and statutory material) for students and practitioners.

Farrar, J. H. and Dugdale, A. M. *Introduction to Legal Method* (3rd ed., 1990) Sweet and Maxwell.
This is both concerned with the nature of law and the way in which it functions within the English legal system. The book draws on sociological literature as well as traditional doctrinal and legal theory.

Goodrich, P. *Reading the Law* (1986) Basil Blackwell.
Like Farrar and Dugdale, above, this book is concerned with the nature of law and legal reasoning. However, it takes its inspiration from studies of literature and theology. It is the best introduction to the newest and most innovative analyses of legal reasoning.

BIBLIOGRAPHICAL TECHNIQUES AND DICTIONARIES

Dane, J. and Thomas, P. *How to Use a Law Library* (2nd ed., 1985) Sweet and Maxwell.
A very detailed account of the different techniques used in finding and updating legal material. The title is somewhat misleading since the book also gives guidance in how to find material outside the confines of the law section of a library. Useful for those interested in advanced study.

Osborn's Concise Law Dictionary (7th ed., 1983) Sweet and Maxwell.
A good pocket guide.

APPENDIX IV

Exercise answers

The answers in this section are intended to help you understand the material contained in the exercises. Some questions can be answered in a precise way. However, law is not like arithmetic. In many cases, there is room for a number of different views. In cases such as these, the important thing is not, "does your answer agree with the one below," but, "do you have evidence to support your answer," and, "do you understand the evidence for our answer?" Remember we have provided answers only for Section A in each exercise.

EXERCISE 1

1. The Act creates criminal liability. Note that section 1(1) of the Act says, "[a] person is guilty of an offence if . . ." This phrase is repeated elsewhere in the Act. Note also that section 1(5) of the Act specifies the various punishments which the court may use in respect of offences under the Act.

2. Section 1(1) of the Act says that, "[a] person is guilty of an offence if in Great Britain. . . . " "Great Britain" means England, Wales and Scotland although it is commonly but inaccurately used to include Northern Ireland. Section 7(4) clarifies the matter by saying that, except for section 6, the Act does not apply to Northern Ireland.

3. The normal rule is that an Act comes into force on the date that it receives the Royal Assent unless that Act itself says otherwise (see page 74). In this case section 7(3) of the Act says that section 1 does not come into force until, "the day after that on which this Act is passed," (*i.e.* the day after the Royal Assent) and that section 2(1), "shall not come into force until such day as the Secretary of State may appoint by an order made by

statutory instrument." With these two exceptions the rest of the Act came into force on the date that it received its Royal Assent.

4. Section 1(1)(*a*) of the Act prohibits payment for the supply of "organs." Section 7(2) of the Act defines "organ" as "any part of the body consisting of a structured arrangement of tissues which, if wholly removed, cannot be wholly replicated by the body." Blood is not "a structured arrangement of tissues" and it can be replicated by the body. Therefore, Jane does not commit an offence under the Act.

5. The Current Law Statute Citator will list any such cases.

6. Section 5 of the Act proscribes prosecutions unless they are either by or with the consent of the Director of Public Prosecutions. Thus, unless the Director of Public Prosecutions consents to Usha's action, Usha will not succeed in her prosecution even if Rachael has committed an offence under the Act (as it does appear she has).

7. Section 1(2) of the Act makes it an offence to publish an advertisement which invites people to supply organs, intended for transplants, for payment. Normally the word "publish" is used in ordinary conversation to refer to people such as the publishers of this book. However, if you look at either a legal dictionary or an ordinary dictionary you will see that "publish" means no more than "make generally known." Putting a card in a shop window is an act of publication. Therefore, Susan has committed an offence under the Act.

EXERCISE 2

1. Section 6(2) of the Act says that statutes referred to in Schedule 2 to the Act are repealed to the extent mentioned in the third column of that Schedule. Schedule 2 tells us that sections 1–6 of the Mobile Homes Act 1975, all definitions in s.9(1) (except those of "the Act of 1960," "the Act of 1968" and "mobile home") and section 9(2) of the 1975 Act are repealed.

2. "An Act to make new provision in place of sections 1 to 6 of the Mobile Homes Act 1975."

3. Section 5(3) of the Act defines the term family for the purposes of the Act. A person is a member of another's family if, amongst other things, they are living with the

other "as husband and wife." Thus the question is, are lovers who live together but have no intention of marrying living together as husband and wife? This would be for the court to determine. The Act gives no further assistance.

4. Paragraph 8(3) says that the Secretary of State has to exercise the power given under the Act by making a statutory instrument. In order to find out if such a statutory instrument has been made it is necessary to look at the Statute Citator. The Statute Citator for 1972–1988 tells us that an order under Schedule 1 was made. It gives the reference 83/748. This tells us that the order was Statutory Instrument number 748 in 1983. If we look up this statutory instrument we find that the maximum rate of commission set is 10 per cent.

5. Section 1(2)(*b*) of the Act says that, within three months of making an agreement to which the Act applies, the owner of a site must supply the occupier of a mobile home with a written statement. This statement must detail, amongst other things, "particulars of the land on which the occupier is entitled to situate the mobile home sufficient to identify it." Ronald does not appear to have done this. Barbara can apply to the court under section 1(5) of the Act for an order requiring Ronald to comply with the Act. However, under section 1(1)(*b*) of the Act this will only apply if Barbara is entitled, under her agreement with Ronald, to occupy the mobile home as her "only or main residence."

6. Under paragraph 9 of Part 1 of Schedule 1 to the Act, an occupier is entitled to give their mobile home to a member of their family approved by the owner. "Family" is defined by section 5(3)(*b*) of the Act in such a way as to include illegitimate children. Under paragraph 9 of the Act the owner of the site cannot unreasonably withhold their approval to an occupier's wish to give their home to a member of their family. The only question then remaining is, has Ronald unreasonably withheld his consent? The Act gives no criteria which the court must use in deciding this question.

EXERCISE 3

1. The Council (see p. 65 g).
2. None were reported at the time of writing. You should

have consulted the Case Citators in order to answer this question.

3. The Council sought possession of a caravan site plot which they owned and had been occupied by the Powells (see pp. 65 j, 66 a–b).

4. (i) Civil. (Note the nature of the remedy and the court where proceedings began.)
   (ii) Woolwich County Court; Court of Appeal; House of Lords (see p. 65 a, g).
   (iii) The judge ordered the Powells to give up possession (see p. 65 g–h).
   (iv) Yes, by the Court of Appeal (see pp. 65 g, 66 c).
   (v) No. (Note county court cases are not reported.)

5. Whether the site in issue was a "protected site" as defined by section 5(1) of the 1983 Act.

6. Yes (see p. 71 f–h).

7. In order to discover the "intention of the legislature" (see pp. 70 a–b, 71 a–b).

EXERCISE 4

Cases II (i)

1. (i) 25th–29th April, 3rd May (see p. 798 d).
   (ii) 29th July 1988 (see pp. 798 d, 801 g).

2. (i) Christopher Bathurst Q.C. and Michael Brindle (see p. 801 f)
   (ii) Berwin Leighton (see p. 830 j)

3. [1989] 1 All E.R. 798

4. Queen's Bench Division of the High Court (see p. 801 e).

5. (i) A brief statement, written by an editor, about the details of the case.
   (ii) No.
   (iii) A definitive record of the case.

6. Civil.

7. No. Only the auditors, (*i.e.* the third defendants, Touche Ross & Co.) (see p. 801 f).

8. Damages (for fraud against the defendant directors and for negligence against the auditors) (see p. 800 j).

9. The issue has been isolated and a decision on it would be made by the court in a hearing taking place before the full trial of the main action.

EXERCISE 4

Cases II (ii)

1. Viscount Bledisloe QC, Michael Brindle and Craig Orr. This information is to be found immediately before the opinions of the judges are reported.

2. 38. All the cases referred to in the opinions are listed in the editorial notes at the beginning of the report at pages 569f to 570g. The actual number of cases referred to in an opinion is unlikely to be of any interest to you at any stage. However, which cases were used (and which were not) may be of assistance.

3. At the beginning of his judgment, at page 581e–f, Lord Roskill says that he is giving judgment "out of respect for the two Lord Justices from whom your Lordships are differing and because of the importance of the case".

4. At page 585g–h Lord Oliver says that " '[p]roximity is, no doubt, a convenient expression so long as it is realised that it is no more than a label which embraces not a definable concept but merely a description of circumstances from which, pragmatically, the court conclude that a duty of care exists." If Lord Oliver is correct how do the courts decide "pragmatically" when a duty of care exists? Lord Oliver goes on later, at page 587a–b, to discuss the possibility of "argument by analogy" as a way of deciding whether or not a duty of care exists. However, if argument by analogy offers some form of objective reasoning which will guide the courts in deciding whether there is or is not a duty of care then it should be possible to outline that reasoning in the kind of formula Lord Oliver has said cannot be written. If for some reason that is not possible must we then conclude that judges decide whether or not a duty of care exists on the basis of their own subjective attitudes? Would not the outcome of a case rest entirely on who was doing the judging? Would this be just? How would one advise somebody about their legal liablility if the law depends not just on "rules" but who judges? Although there are clear problems inherent in the line of reasoning used by Lord Oliver it is worth noting that

similar arguments are used elsewhere in the case. Thus, for example, Lord Bridge in his opinion refers, at page 573i, to the "inability of any single general principle to provide a practical test which can be applied to every situation".

5. Lord Oliver explores this point at pages 598c onwards in his judgment. He has two main objectives. First, that the majority view in the Court of Appeal will produce, as he says at page 599a, "capricious results" of which he gives one example. Secondly, at page 599e–g, Lord Oliver argues that the majority of the Court of Appeal have misunderstood the test of proximity seeing it as a more precise term than it actually is.

EXERCISE 5

1. This question can be answered after reading the first paragraph of the article. Morgan suggests that, despite a large prison building programme, there is a continuing problem of prison overcrowding. He also asserts that this is largely due to an increase in the number of custodial remands. Finally, he says that this has occurred regardless of the fact that the Government has adopted most of the measures that critics have suggested will arrest the increase in remands. He asks two questions. Does the continued increase in remands indicate a failure to understand the reasons for the increase? Alternatively, does the continued increase indicate that the measures intended to stop it, adopted by the Government, have been improperly implemented.

2. Two different kinds of question should have been raised in your mind when reading the first paragraph of the article. First, why does Morgan consider this issue important?

Implicit within the article is the view that if we know more about what is currently happening we will be able to reform the system and thus improve it. Such reform might produce benefits to individuals who, for example, would no longer suffer the loss of freedom inherent in being held in custody. Reform might also benefit society as a whole in that, for example, if fewer people are held in custody less money needs to be spent on prison buildings, extra prison staff and so forth. One criticism of this kind of approach is that it involves making many assumptions about basic ideas that are being used. For example, why is freedom assumed to be a benefit? Why is it better to be out of prison rather than in prison? Are we indeed freer in any significant sense if we are out of prison rather than in it? What do we mean by freedom? On a common-sense, everyday approach answers to these questions may seem obvious. However, as we all know, common sense may be no more than common ignorance or prejudice. Common sense has told people that the world is flat and witches should be burnt. Thus, what does it really mean to say that I am free. Why I behave in particular ways, the choices that I make, can be explained by reference to such things as my social background, my culture, my education and the advertisements I have seen. If these had been different so would the choices that I make. If what I do is determined by my background in what sense am I free? Do I really choose to do anything or am I no more than the creature of my background? And if I am not free then why does it matter whether or not I am in prison?

A second kind of question that should have occurred to you when reading the first paragraph is, if we accept the validity of the approach taken by the author, how far does he prove or even provide evidence for what he is saying? For example, when he says that the Government has adopted most of the measures that critics have suggested for stopping the increase in custodial remands how do you know that this is true? In the article it is a mere assertion. There must be empirical evidence for the assertion but, at least at this point in the article, the author has not provided it. When Morgan suggests that the continued increase in custodial remands must either be due to a failure in analysing the reasons for the increase or in failure to implement reforms, are these really the only two possible explanations? For example, Morgan suggests that the Government has adopted "most" of the measures that critics have suggested for preventing a further increase in custodial remands. Most means not all. Another alternative explanation not suggested in the first paragraph is that a measure already suggested but not adopted by the Government might solve the problem.

Thinking in this way can seem unduly critical. You will soon find that everything you read contains weaknesses and flaws. You might feel an author is doing as much as can reasonably be expected within the space they have. This may indeed be so, but it is important to remember that in reading something the judgment that you are making is about what it tells you, not the character of the author. If the thing that you are reading contains unanswered questions or assertions without evidence then you know less than you would do if this were not so. It is vital that you realise this. If you do not know something you do not know it and the fact that the author is trying their best or that no one knows any more than the author is telling you is wholly irrelevant.

3. The article is concerned with prison overcrowding. One question which arises in this context is, is the increase in prison overcrowding due to an increased number of people being sent to prison or to those people who are being sent to prison being kept there for a longer time? Table 1 tells us about prison reception (by legal category of prisoner) whilst Table 2 tells us about how many people there are in prison (again by legal category of prisoner). The most important point to be derived from comparison of the two tables is that the proportionate increase in the number of untried prisoners being sent to prison is less than the proportionate increase in the number of such prisoners in prison. This means that this category of prisoners must be spending longer in prison. Morgan supports this conclusion by providing figures for the length of time for both male and female prisoners in 1975 and 1987 respectively, showing that in both cases the number of days spent in prison has gone up (see page 210).

4. Morgan looks at two different kinds of trial. First, he considers cases where magistrates decide whether the defendant is guilty or not (cases tried *summarily*). He says that there has both been a drop in the number of such cases and a drop in the number of defendants in such cases who are remanded on bail. Secondly, he considers cases where the magistrates are not deciding the guilt or innocence of the defendant but simply deciding whether the prosecution can prove that there is a possible case to answer. If the magistrates think there is such a case they send the defendant to be tried by the Crown Court. Cases like these are known as *committal proceedings*. In this second category of case, Morgan says that between 1975 and 1987 there has been an increase both in the number of such cases and in the proportion of defendants in such cases who are remanded to the Crown Court without bail. Finally, Morgan says that there has been an increase in the number of cases where the defendant can be tried either by the magistrates' court or by the Crown Court, being tried by the Crown Court. (For all of this see page 211.) On the basis of all of this Morgan concludes that the upward trend in untried prisoners being held in prison results from more cases being heard in the Crown Court and more of these prisoners being held without bail. "It is principally because of this shift in their mode of trial that prisoners are waiting longer for their cases to be heard." (page 211)

Morgan's conclusion is not the only one which could logically be derived from the data he has provided. For example, even if there are less people being tried by magistrates and even if fewer of them are being held on remand without bail, if the time they are being held has grown by, say, 500 per cent. this would have a significant effect on the figure for the daily average prison population. A growth in court waiting lists would then be an important factor in the rise of the number of such prisoners. Nothing in the information that Morgan presents us with prevents us reaching this conclusion. It is, however, less likely to be correct than the conclusion which Morgan reaches. Unless there has been a sudden decrease in the number of magistrates, a sudden increase in their other workload or a sudden decrease in their productivity, why should court waiting lists increase so dramatically?

The important point to observe here is that in reading research materials the conclusions which can be drawn never have the certainty of mathematical proofs. In mathematics or symbolic logic once axioms have been accepted conclusions necessarily follow. Research in law, as in every other area, merely provides conclusions which are more likely. Something which is less likely may, nevertheless, be true.

5. The principles that Morgan uses are to be found on page 213.

6. Two points should occur to you here. First, Morgan "submits," these are the principles to use in analysis; that is to say he asserts that they are to be used. The reader is left to think why these principles should be used and cannot know what reasons Morgan has for thinking they are important. Secondly, as Morgan notes, the first two principles can contradict each other. How, in such a case, do we know which principle to follow? It is, perhaps, worth observing that the answer to this cannot be, as is commonly said, that one principle should be weighed against another. To say one should weigh a principle is a metaphor. However, on closer thought, we realise that this is a metaphor that obscures rather than explains. I know an elephant weighs more than a pencil because I have in my mind some scale of weight. Even if that scale of weight is unstated it is still there; it is the measure of the balance. If one weighs one principle against another what is the measure of the balance?

EXERCISE 6

Some comments

The objective of this exercise is to help you to develop powers of criticism and assessment for use in relation to your own work. Many students do not read their own work through after it has been completed and leave all evaluation up to their teacher. By putting yourself in the teacher's place, you are forced to think about the criteria for judging an essay and about ways to improve the essay. You will find that the criteria with which you come up are likely to be very similar to those used by your teachers.

Not all things on your list will necessarily be appropriate. Many students are over-impressed by technical jargon and "originality" and do not give enough credit for a well-structured, simply-expressed piece of writing. Students are often harder in their marking than teachers, finding it easier to spot and condemn faults than to notice the good points. The exercise is best done with a friend or, better still, by a small group of students. This is because idiosyncratic or misconceived criteria will tend to be dropped as you try to reach a consensus.

Here are some further comments on the two "essay" answers and the two "problem" answers which you were asked to evaluate.

Each pair of answers shows different merits and deficiencies and, in our view, justify roughly the same mark range, though for entirely different reasons. The answers are briefer than the average student essay, but not much shorter than an examination answer. They are below average, compared with what most first-year law undergraduates achieve in examination conditions, and therefore most law degree students reading them should feel confident that they can do better.

Notice that the two students in each pair are doing different things, and, presumably, differ in their own understanding of the criteria for a "good" answer. For both sets of answers, one student has placed greater emphasis on giving facts and the other has concentrated on arguments and concepts. Neither, of course, is adequate on its own. An argument needs to be supported by evidence and a catalogue of facts does not amount to an argument and rarely answers a question. You may find that you tend towards one approach rather than the other in your own writing. Think about improving your own skills in the other respect.

We have not given you our own list of criteria for evaluation, nor detailed criticisms of the answers, because the idea of the exercise is to get you thinking about the *process* of evaluation rather than to achieve a "right" answer. The student essays are not so much "wrong" in the sense of being legally or factually inaccurate but poor in quality of work.

If you would like to know more about the subject-matter of the two titles, try the following:

Essay (Are MPs representative?) see:

Michael Rush, "The members of Parliament," in S. A. Walkland and Michael Ryle, *The Commons Today* (Fontana, 1981).

A. H. Birch, *Representative and Responsible Government* (Allen & Unwin, 1964).

J. A. G. Griffith and Michael Ryle, *Parliament: Functions, Practice and Procedures* (Sweet and Maxwell, 1989).

Problem (False Imprisonment). Look up false imprisonment in any standard Tort textbook and read the three cases.

Use this technique in the future

When you write your next essay, try marking it yourself as if you were the tutor. Alternatively, exchange essays with other students in your group. You will probably find that you can think of a lot of ways of improving your work without waiting for your tutor to help you.

INDEX

This index is meant to be used in conjunction with the detailed list of contents at the beginning of the book. Those interested in looking at the range of careers with a legal content should also refer to the Careers Directory at pages 247–258.

Law as a degree course—*cont.*
Universities Central Council for
Admissions—*cont.*
address for further information,
234
Law as a profession,
barrister,
Council of Legal Education
address, 244
Inns of Court address, 244
education and training, 244–245
pupillage, 245
careers with some legal content. *See*
Appendix I, 247–258
core subjects, 235
legal executives, 253
professional examinations,
relationship to degree courses, 239,
244
solicitors,
College of Law address, 240
education and training, 239–242
Law Society address, 239
types of articles, 242–244
Law in action,
definition of, 27
Guide to Official Statistics, purpose
of, 32–33
samples, purposes of,
difficulties of, 80–81
socio-legal research,
bar charts, example of, 82
bar charts, explained, 81
defined, 27
examples of, 208–223
graph, example of, 83
graphs explained, 81
methods of, 78–81
pie charts, example of, 82
pie charts explained, 81
statistical tests, purpose of, 32–34
Law in books,
definition of, 27. *See also* Black-letter
law; Casebooks; Law Reports;
Statutes.
Law Reports,
abbreviations, 259–260
All England Law Reports,
described, 39
examples of, 58–62
Appeal cases, 39
approval of a case, importance of, 43
Case Citator, 41
Chancery Division, 39
Current law, 43–44

Law Reports—*cont.*
English Reports, 38
Family Division, 39
headnote,
meaning of, 63
editor's opinion of *ratio*, 65
how to cite, 40–41
how to find them, 41–42
how to use them, 40–42
Incorporated Council of Law
Reporting, 38–39
Obiter dictum,
discussed, 8, 66
Probate, Divorce and Admiralty
Division, 39
Queen's Bench, 39
New Law Journal, 39, 45
Ratio decidendi,
discussed, 64–66
Solicitor's Journal, 39, 45
The Times, 39
up-dating case law, 42–44
Weekly Law Reports,
described, 39
Legal rules, definition and binding
nature of, 4
Legislation. *See* Statutes.
LEXIS, 46

Morality and law,
obedience to law as a matter of ethics,
26
minimum moral content of law, 30

National law,
defined, 16

Post-graduate study in law, 257–258
Precedent,
defined and described, 8–10
table of, 9
Primary legislation,
defined, 4. *See also* Statutes.
Public international law,
changes in, 17–19
defined, 16
disputes resolved under, 17
effect on national law, 18–19
sources, 17
Public law,
definition of, 21
judicial review, definition of, 24
origins of, 23

Obiter. See Law Reports.